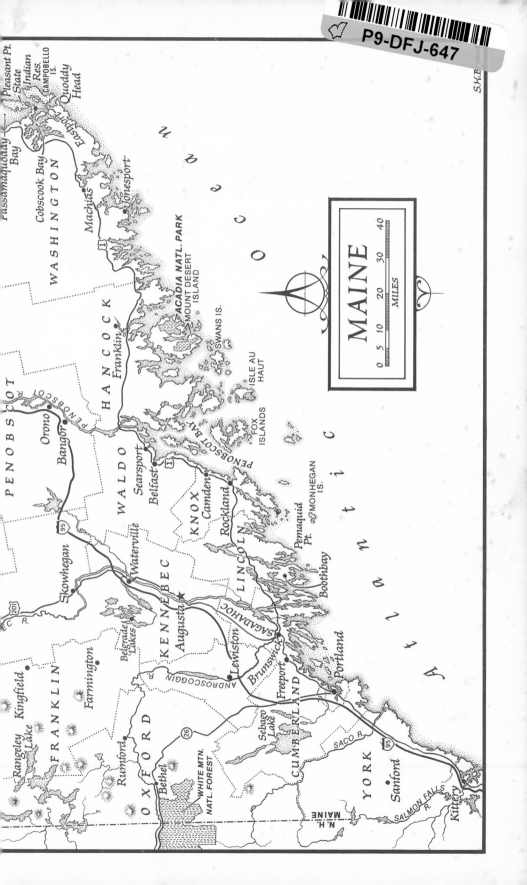

BOOKS BY RICHARD SALTONSTALL, JR.

YOUR ENVIRONMENT AND WHAT YOU CAN DO ABOUT IT

BROWNOUT AND SLOWDOWN
   (with James K. Page)

MAINE PILGRIMAGE:
   The Search for an American Way of Life

MAINE PILGRIMAGE

RICHARD SALTONSTALL, JR.

MAINE PILGRIMAGE

The Search for an American Way of Life

Drawings by Polly Warren

LITTLE, BROWN AND COMPANY — BOSTON – TORONTO

FIRST EDITION

T 02/74

Library of Congress Cataloging in Publication Data

Saltonstall, Richard, 1937–
  Maine pilgrimage.

  Bibliography: p.
  1. Maine—Economic conditions. 2. Environmental
policy—Maine. 3. Maine—Description and travel.
I. Title.
HC107.M2S24   330.9'741'04   73-14738
ISBN 0-316-76967-3

Published simultaneously in Canada by Little, Brown & Company (Canada) Limited

PRINTED IN THE UNITED STATES OF AMERICA

For Emmy

CONTENTS

As Maine Goes

I AM DRIVING DUE SOUTH on Route 11, ten miles below the Canadian border, where the town of Clair, New Brunswick, looks across the St. John River at Fort Kent. According to legend, it was just upstream that the natives fooled Daniel Webster and Lord Ashburton when they met in 1842 to decide upon the location of the United States–Canada border. Webster's reputation as a hard drinker has given rise to different versions of what happened. His apologists say that the hollow-legged New Hampshireman plied the English negotiator with Old Crow, then convinced him that the St. Francis River, which comes down from the north to meet the St. John, was in fact the St. John, which they agreed should be the border. The other version has both Webster and Ashburton, made tipsy by the local patriots, being taken by boat up the St. Francis, which they are told is the St. John.

Either way, Maine and the United States ended up with an enormous patch of forest, well over a thousand square miles — bigger than Rhode Island. Look at the map and you will spot this "accidental" addition easily. It looks like a crouching bobcat with a thick neck and beaked snout. His haunches merge with the headwaters of the St. John, and the river as it flows northeastward for some seventy-five miles is the cat's belly line. The top of his head is marked by Estcourt Station, a place where U.S. roads don't go.

Maine history is full of such tidbits, and I have just driven through a region that has more than its share. It is the section that was settled by French-speaking Acadians from Nova Scotia, some of them perhaps descendants of colonists who came to the St. Croix River with the Sieur de Monts in 1604. They are a different breed from the

Franco-Americans who migrated to southern Maine from Quebec to work for low wages in the mills. The Acadians were exiled in the 1780s when they refused to take an oath of allegiance to the English king. Many of them went no farther than Aroostook County, where their descendants are abundant and influential today.

I have read, too, that others among the first white men in this territory around Fort Kent were successful lumbermen who came up from southern Maine roundabout through New Brunswick, Englishmen with names like Hunnewell, Savage and Wheeler. They chopped down the woods and put up regular estates with fine large houses, enormous barns, and mills that turned saws, made flour and grist, and pumped water. As I drive along I strain to either side, looking across the deep valleys. Where I see tidy-looking farms, I wonder if these were once those estates that I have read about and whether they were built high up on the hillsides for the view or for protection.

What I am thinking about most, though, is how surprised I am by the diverse beauty of this part of Maine. I had expected mostly two kinds of landscape: dense stretches of blue-green spruce forest and the undulating earth-toned potato fields. Instead I am lurching up and down in a sea of steep ridges. The valleys are troughs between the crests of the waves. Down them I see potato fields flecked with wilderness, to be sure. But up on the hills are those civilized-looking farms, with their hayfields sloping beneath them and clusters of oak and elm trees that were allowed to grow up after the wilderness was cleared a long time ago.

A cold front is moving in fast from the northwest, dispersing the morning's drizzle. Cumulus clouds stretch away to the horizon, casting deep shadows over the hills and valleys where the sun does not shine through. I look around but cannot find a rainbow.

So many people think of Maine as an endless coastline, with rock promontories and ledges, and islands without number; or as the wooded lake country that you find around Baxter Park or in the Rangeley Lakes region. These are people like me who have gotten to know Maine in the summer. They should be here right now in the final days of September on Route 11, a stretch of over a hundred miles along which there are only thirteen towns, some consisting of no more than a few houses and a gas station grouped together, and one of them no more than a graveyard beside the road. I stop here to read the epitaphs on elegant granite monuments that have been tilted in every direction by the winter frosts.

Route 11 is about as far west as the larger productive potato fields go. As I look to the right, after coming up a long hill just before the town of Patten, I see where the spruce forests begin. At first there are lowlands and swamps with some small ponds possibly created by beaver dams. The land rises up slowly to the massive range of Baxter Park. On this clearing afternoon I am compelled to pull off the road to gaze for a few minutes at these mountains. The centerpiece is Katahdin, 5,267 feet, the highest in Maine. On a good day its summit is the first point of land in the United States to be warmed by the rising sun. But at this hour of the day the sun has passed the southern angle; Katahdin and its neighbors are silhouetted in dark blue against the lighter sky. Such vistas make me think of the time our family moved to San Francisco from Seattle, when we drove through the rich, rolling farmland of Oregon's Willamette Valley. Only then it was early morning, and we never stopped on ridges with views like this.

Now I am passing through Patten and I am struck by the certitude and good taste of this country center. It does not advertise its presence. There is no modern shopping "mall" flung up on its outskirts. Like the houses, the stores seem well established. Patten is fortunate. Too many Maine towns the same size have given up their village identity and now have that indiscriminate, impermanent look that always comes when people are unsure of themselves and the future.

On the right, less than a mile from the stores and churches that identify the center of Patten, there is a potato farm teeming with activity. The land rises up behind it and the roof of a big old barn is etched against the sky. A school bus and half a dozen cars are parked off the field and their occupants, almost all young people, are stooped over in a long line picking up potatoes and dropping them into barrels that a truck will pick up. The scene is solemn in the dying light and I am envious.

By their very actions these people appear attached to their land, knowing what they must do to keep an old relationship going and their personal roots secure. Earlier this day I have been among potato harvesters in Caribou, but this time, for reasons I can't describe,

I am awed and feel like an interloper, especially in my car. I drive on.

Patten has over 1,300 residents and is the biggest town I have seen since Fort Kent. It is a commercial center for a big region; it is a lumber town with a productive and clean plywood mill, and, as far as I know, it has the best logging museum anywhere. Yet at this precise moment, Patten is a world by itself, set apart from the towns not much farther along Route 11 and a deep chasm away from busy Sherman Mills ten miles distant where I can see rising a plume of smoke.

The Patten restaurant and the inn look empty. The people on the street are conspicuously schoolchildren. As I stop for the traffic light and open my window, it is disturbingly still.

I am thinking that all of Maine, like Patten, is remote at this time of year. The summer tourists who take this route to Baxter Park have gone. It is a season when you sense Maine's apartness. During the summer, contrasts in the weather and the harsh and poignant details of life are muted, or obscured entirely, for an outsider. You are lulled by your enjoyment of the land into thinking that Maine is especially blessed. The air is balmy, the ground is green, the sea is blue, and it is easy to become caught up in the folklore and the myths.

Yet even in fall and winter, for reasons not so apparent, Maine is an opportune place, particularly if you are worried about life in America today, if you think that the people who are running things have lost touch with the truth that is taught by the land; and that is what I am trying to find out about as I drive down Route Eleven.

It all began one day in February 1969. I sat in my cubicle in the Washington offices of *Time* magazine, where I worked as a correspondent, and I spotted in the *Washington Post* a story about Machiasport, Maine. The state had come up with a plan that would place a large oil refinery there. It would refine 300,000 barrels of oil a day and not only provide significant relief during New England's chronic winter fuel shortages but greatly enhance the material prospects of Maine and Washington County. The *Washington Post* described the region as being poverty-stricken, and statistics were cited to show that Washington County was even more destitute than Appalachia. Some 43 percent of the youths between ages 20 and 24 were leaving, unemployment then averaged 11.2 percent, and 57.7 percent of the county's families brought home less than $4,000 a year in income. According to the *Post* story an oil refinery would provide needed tax revenues and create at least 350 jobs directly, not counting an equal number of jobs in construction and in various services growing out of the boom. Moreover, the state had visions of an industrial complex growing around the oil refinery. There would be cheap fuel for a power plant, and both power and oil would be handy for petrochemical plants and even an aluminum reduction facility.

At this time only the briefest mention was made of the possibilities of environmental damage or of how the way of life in this part of Maine would be changed. Even Maine Senator Edmund Muskie, known to his friends as "Mr. Clean" because of his role in combating air and water pollution, favored the Machiasport project. What seemed most important was the issue of Maine's being a poor state in an economic and social backwater, where its citizens could not join in the conspicuous consumption of the nation as a whole.

Less than a week later I went to Machias to see for myself what the people of Washington County were thinking and what I, from my all-presuming vantage, thought was needed.

I found right away that you couldn't put much stock in the statistics. True, the county was poor by official standards. Young people, it is also true, were moving out, placing a heavy burden on the aging. Income levels were comparatively low. Many households suffered health problems and lack of nourishment. But there were a lot more things that you couldn't measure, and many of the people I talked to were distressed that their traditions, their security, and the peace and quiet of their surroundings were threatened by the refinery proposal.

Still, most people went along with the state at that time. There was humility beneath their proud reserve, the feeling that perhaps they should give change a chance and catch up with the rest of the world. There were real grounds for worrying about the future, too. Fishing had died. The once lucrative sardine industry was virtually dead. Lobsters and clams were scarcer and less economical to obtain. The Georgia Pacific pulp mill, the largest employer in the area with a payroll of 600, gave no promises against future cutbacks, and the forest industry in general was not doing well in Washington County.

7

So people were getting desperate. They saw their traditional opportunities breaking down and they began to wonder. Any promise looked better than none at all, even an oil refinery.

Yet there was no panic among the people I met, and to the last one they were upset that their county had been referred to in the press as a "depressed area." Wesley Vose, a former municipal judge, was the first man I interviewed. "The people are kind of resentful about some of the reports," he said. "I don't think you'll find too many here who feel they're hellishly abused 'cause they live in Washington County. The banks don't own the homes here. The people do." Then he gave a look of resignation. "But we *do* lack industry."

The Machiasport proposal had become a full-blown controversy. From the outset it aroused the furious opposition of the big oil companies, the so-called "majors." The firm that had announced plans for Machiasport was Occidental Petroleum, something of a maverick company, whose colorful president, Armand Hammer, had asked for a special import quota of 100,000 barrels of oil a day. Hammer counted on the state to obtain a free trade zone so that the rest of the oil would be free from tariffs. The "majors" thought that such an arrangement would undermine the cozy and lucrative system that presently helped them control their markets, and they were alarmed that the special quota, if granted, would create a bad precedent. They fought tooth and nail through their lobbyists and politician friends in Washington. The Johnson administration conveniently passed the whole matter along to Richard Nixon, who gained time by assigning a task force to review the entire oil import quota system.

Almost a year passed, after my visit to Machias, before the presidential panel made recommendations that dealt entirely with national oil policy. By then, opposition to the Machiasport plan had come on strong from another quarter. Now the issue was drawn mainly in environmental terms. Whatever happened concerning oil development in this corner of Maine was viewed as being pivotal in terms of coastal conservation and public enjoyment of the scenic qualities of the northeastern seaboard. Actually, these second thoughts about the oil refinery had always existed. Yet, since they were openly voiced by only a *few* local residents and a minority of outsiders who enjoyed the area during the summer, such considerations had not swayed high public officials. And it was not until there were disastrous oil spills off the California coast and in the Gulf of Mexico during 1969 that the conservationist position on the coastline gained widespread public support.

But when I made my first visit, I felt that environmental concerns were perhaps the most important ones lying ahead, as surely the Machias proposal would not be the only refinery planned along the Maine coast. After talking with Judge Vose, I visited Charles Dorchester, a thirty-five-year-old Methodist minister who had brought his wife, Mary, and their two children from Connecticut three years before. From the very beginning, Dorchester was depressed about the physical impoverishment he found in his parish, but he also knew instinctively that a refinery, along with an industrial park, would wipe out vital spiritual assets, the stable surroundings and the routine these people were used to and counted on. And Dorchester confessed that he liked to walk along the shore and spot birds. "The thought keeps plaguing me that if one of these oil spills we read about takes place here, our wonderful wildlife will suffer," he said.

Virginia Cheney was another thoughtful opponent. She was the descendant of a Hessian soldier who in 1824 had built the farm where she and her husband had returned to live. Bernard Cheney had quit his job as a state patrolman and become an insurance adjuster. The farm was not far from where the refinery was planned, and Mrs. Cheney stressed that her feelings were deeply tinged by the vision of how their property would be affected.

I met Mrs. Cheney at the Washington State Teachers College where she is teaching principal. She is a pretty, auburn-haired lady with a gentle, convincing way of presenting her thoughts. It didn't matter, I felt, that she had an ax to grind. "Since I'm involved landwise, what can I say," she said. "It seems very selfish. But an oil refinery could take away the things we cherish. You love the freedom here. You love to walk to the shore and see it the way it has always been. I hope people in this area think very carefully and look ahead. It seems to me that there is great promise here for recreation, but if it's an industrial area they want, then that's fine. I personally will be very sad."

I drove away from Machias that night during a blizzard that by morning had covered Washington County and the rest of Maine with nearly a foot of snow. I had become as depressed as Mrs. Cheney. Just before leaving, I had chatted with a boy in a gas station where I fueled up, and he too had been against the refinery, even though he wasn't sure how much longer he could maintain his pride — much less how he could get married and raise a family — on paychecks coming from odd jobs. Nearly all the way to Milbridge I put my gloomy thoughts into a tape recorder that I usually carry next to me on the front seat.

In Augusta, Maine's capital, I was reassured by no less a person than the governor, Kenneth Curtis. He said he was well aware of the environmental problems posed by an oil refinery in Machiasport and that his people were developing laws that would give the state the leverage to cope with different kinds of industrial development entirely in the public interest and not mainly on industry's terms, in spite of Maine's economic needs. "We're going to make sure that industry cranks in conservation at the very start," he said. "It isn't too costly. They're going to have to get a license from our environmental improvement people. As badly as we want the industry, we know there are tremendous profits for them and we know they can afford to do it."

To me, it still seemed that heavy industry would never be compatible with the unspoiled coastal beauty found in places like Machiasport, despite all the latest pollution controls that Curtis talked about. But I took some solace in the thought that if the governor found that fighting pollution was good politics maybe he'd take the next step and consider the social and economic payoffs of different sorts of development or no development at all, regardless of what laws were passed to keep the air and water clean.

Early in 1970, under increasing pressure from groups concerned about the consequences of rapid change in Maine, the state legislature passed two unusual laws. One, known as the Site Location Act, gave the state's Environmental Improvement Commission the power to review all proposed developments that required nineteen acres or more of land. The other was a stiff provision to deal with pollution from oil spills. (This became known as the Conveyance Act, because it also placed a charge of one cent per barrel on any oil delivered in Maine from a tanker.) The state anticipated that this levy would produce $3.5 million annually that would be put into a Coastal Protection Fund to be used for cleanups as well as for the acquisition of scenic rights on shore property.

It was clear that events of national significance were happening in Maine. As I covered environmental developments from my office in Washington, I saw Edmund Muskie reverse his position on Machiasport. Plans for an oil depot in Casco Bay were denied by the Environmental Improvement Commission. By the time that decision was overruled by the state supreme court on the grounds that facilities for the depot were in place before the state had its new siting authority, the developer, King Resources Company of Denver, was running out of money for the project.

But it was not just oil that was the issue anymore. The talk about refineries and industrial parks had launched a broad discussion among conservationists, the politicians in Augusta, and town officials throughout the state about Maine's natural assets and traditional advantages. There were few who didn't know that Maine was poor by conventional measurements, but a lot of people began to question the costs and adverse side effects that certain kinds of development would bring to Maine. What is more, they also took a new attitude toward the traditional polluters, the industries who for years had avoided censure by warning that payrolls were more important than pickerel.

So throughout Maine there were new misgivings. Maybe the Kennebec and Penobscot rivers would be more valuable for fishing, boating and swimming. Certainly the water was worth more without the millions of tons of pulp wastes that were dumped in it daily. Maybe the shorefront was worth more kept wild instead of being gobbled up by land speculators who would sell off small lots at outrageous prices. Maybe the vast forestlands and lakes of the interior should be opened to controlled development or reserved for fishermen, canoeists and backpackers instead of being stripped of their timber. Which would do more for the famous coastal bays — industrial development or encouragement of summer homes?

There were these questions and there were these new issues before the legislators: changing the property tax structure to relieve farmers and those who keep their land open; coastal and shorefront zoning; protection of estuaries and wetlands; management of the unorganized half of the state that is owned by a handful of big corporations;

banning log drives on the rivers; controlling snowmobiles; controlling tourist numbers; a wildlife and game management policy; a transportation policy to encourage rail travel and ferries; air and water codes; and solid waste disposal.

John Cole, editor and co-founder of the *Maine Times*, a weekly that consistently advocates environmental quality, went so far as to suggest quite seriously that Maine close off its border and go its own way. Since Maine is bordered by only one state (New Hampshire) and already contained the seeds of a counterculture, the idea had practical merit even if it was politically impossible. Many of Cole's readers wanted it. Cole saw Maine as being much more than a place where a balance might be struck between conservation and development. He was thinking about reviving traditional ways of American life based on strong family units and neighborly cooperation. This could still happen where the small rural towns have not yet turned into shapeless suburbs and where the land still retains much of its primitive character.

"What better place can be found," Cole asked, "to build the models of a new America?"

The United States remained a rural society long after Thomas Jefferson declaimed, "Those who labor in the earth are the chosen people of God." It was not until the 1920 census that city people outnumbered the "chosen" ones in this country. But by 1970, 149.3 million Americans lived within metropolitan limits while only 53.9 million, 25 percent, lived in rural places, towns no larger than 2,500 people. Demographers predicted that by the year 2000 only 10 percent of the population would be left in the country. Demoralized by urbanization, it is small wonder that a lot of people began to yearn for the simpler, slower ways.

It is not entirely the fault of city life, although the big centers like New York, Chicago and Los Angeles have become virtually ungovernable. It is far more the failure of science and technology to stay within human bounds. Since the modern world is summed up in the workings of a city, this is where people first feel, and feel most painfully, the breakdown of life: so much wasted motion, so much wasted time, so little to show for it. On top of this there is the physical decay of the cities. The streets are unsafe. Garbage reeks in the alleys. Lead particles, carbon monoxide and hydrocarbon poisons drift above traffic congestion and seriously endanger human health, actually taking lives during periods when weather conditions will not allow the polluted air to escape.

Machines have taken over, dehumanizing every endeavor, just as Stephen Vincent Benét predicted in his poem "Nightmare Number Nine," nearly fifty years ago. Gadgets and gimmicks are no longer such a delight when you realize that it takes fantastic amounts of energy both to make and to use them and that they give very little in return. No sooner do we become used to an automatic oven cleaner than there is a plastic "browning" bag to keep our roasts from spattering.

People in the suburbs will not admit that the city is their problem, even though they work there. Commuting is a disaster. Many a healthy male finds himself hunched over the wheel of his automobile for more than twenty hours every week.

As I sat in Washington, doing my best to keep in touch with events in Maine, it seemed clear that not only were more and more Americans questioning the dominance of technology but that they were anguished about the emptiness of their lives.

Just as the edifices and creations of our science and technology were intended to become obsolete, so were people programmed to be on the move. I could feel this as a correspondent for *Time,* which believed that you would stagnate in your work or, just as bad, become involved in your temporary community if you stayed in one place more than two years. And this was the rule throughout America's corporate establishment. A man was told *not* to plant roots anywhere if he wanted to get ahead with the company. It did not matter that the most ambitious, the most energetic and the most creative of America's men and women were short-timers in their communities. They were supposed to have far more important things to worry about than school systems and town meetings or the way a place would be and look in future decades. In short, it was the company, not the community, that counted.

The concept of a family place, a house where you grew up and where you understood what your parents did and what was expected of you — all this died. And it was inevitable that the new generation, the young people, should rebel against the established culture and way of doing business. They had grown up mobile and rootless in the roar of the machinery changing the face of the land and transporting them from place to place. There was no philosophic legacy for them to support. Sound value systems cannot germinate and thrive when people are concerned mainly with their material survival and when the ground is always moving out from under them.

Of course this frenetic materialism was understandable to some extent. The older generation had fought a depression, then a war, then another war, then another war. But to understand is not wholly to excuse.

And this is why Maine and other rural states and regions became important points of refuge in the late sixties and early seventies. They were the second frontiers where American values could, perhaps, be revived.

The hippies were the first to take to the hills, setting up communes in the open spaces. Many other young people termed themselves modern homesteaders, searching throughout the American countryside for an abandoned or neglected farm that they could resurrect. However, too many of these new farmers lacked discipline and patience. Having never sensed the importance of having a plan, they were mainly concerned with devising a means of escape from the cities and the oppression of technology and the contradictions of established policies. They wanted to make peace with themselves. But in seeking to do so, it is questionable that they knew how to make peace with the land they settled.

Not everyone who went back to the land wanted only to find himself. Some people looked outside and ahead of their small worlds and saw that they might be able to prove something, that maybe if they could succeed, the whole American civilization would be the gainer. As this happened, there was yet another exodus.

I simplify, of course. It was not as neat as this. There were overlaps. History is never tidy. But in any case, men and women who had made it in the established circles decided to join the movement to the country. I found them throughout Maine, and their feelings are typified by the wife of a successful electronics consultant, who told me, "We are here for our sanity and because we wanted our children to grow up in a village."

Maine's 1970 population of 993,700 ranks 38th among the 50 states. Its population density (the average number of people per mile) is 32.1, the lowest of any state east of the Mississippi River. (Vermont is next in New England, with 48 people per square mile.) Nearly 50 percent of Maine lives in rural small towns. Maine is vast, equal to the other five New England states lumped together. Aroostook County is larger than Connecticut and Rhode Island combined. The state's 3,478 miles of tidal waterfront are the longest stretch of any state on the eastern seaboard, although as the gull flies from Kittery to Quoddy Head on the New Brunswick border, the distance is only 228 miles.

There are more lakes and more miles of river in Maine than in any other New England state and a higher percentage of forest than in any state in the nation. Of its 19.8 million acres, 1.5 million are on inland fresh water, and 17.4 million, an astonishing 88 percent, are forest. Much of this land lies in the dense wilderness of northern Maine, though some of it consists of forests near the coast and in the southern and central portions. Maine's entire wooded area is larger than the state of West Virginia and is three times as big as Massachusetts or New Hampshire. Between 50 and 60 percent of the state — no one seems to be certain — consists of unorganized territory called "wild lands" (which means that there is no form of municipal government within it).

The inland counties have most of the wild lands — Aroostook, Piscataquis, Penobscot, Franklin, Somerset and Oxford. They comprise 14.6 million acres but contain only 326,400 people, less than a third of the population. Maine has thirteen lakes of over ten thousand acres in size, the biggest being Moosehead, with 74,906 acres.

The state's most precious resource, for industry, commerce and recreation, has been its multitude of rivers: the St. John, Penobscot, Piscataquis, Kennebec, Androscoggin, Aroostook, Saco, Machias and St. Croix, to name the most important ones. Look at a map and you will see that these water systems, with thousands of miles of headwater tributaries and branches, interlace the entire state. The jagged, meandering character of tidal river estuaries has contributed to the isolation of coastal communities, but Maine's rivers have had the opposite effect inland. They have opened up the wilderness and been vital arteries for the forest industries. They enabled towns like Bath and Bangor to become major shipbuilding and trading centers. They floated logs down to the mills. They gave Maine power.

As the glacier retreated north, 12,000 years ago, it scoured Maine's topsoil and then littered the landscape with boulders and gravel. But this did not deter rural settlers. At one time nearly a third of the state was cleared for small family farms that men worked for subsistence. Now most of the farmland has gone back to the woods and only 14.1 percent of the state, or 2.8 million acres, is classified as fair or better farmland. The growing season is less than half a year, an additional handicap for agriculture. Even so, along the river floodplains, in fertile lowland valleys and in the rolling north, there are real opportunities for agriculture. Potatoes grow well, even though the season starts late, and those sunny fall days and cold nights make the MacIntosh apples turn bright red and fetch a premium price in the market for the grower. Dairy cattle and beef do well too, since the raw climate is healthy for livestock.

The statistical picture of Maine shows, in sum, that it is a comparatively rural state, that it has not been devastated by excessive applications of industry and new technology. In many ways, indeed, Maine is like an underdeveloped nation. Where development occurs, more often than not there is exploitation *within* Maine and the profits are enjoyed *without*. That has been the case from the very beginning. Whereas the settlers of Massachusetts put down roots, and their way of life and their government were based on strong religious and philosophic ideals, just the opposite happened in Maine.

Treating it as a region, and forgetting for the moment that until 1820 it was governed by Massachusetts, consider Maine's first explorers. They were adventurers, fishermen and traders. They took cod, hake and herring, traded for beaver, and hewed at the forests for ship timber and masts.

When the men of the Plymouth Colony ventured "downeast," they too were only interested in what they could take away. The Pilgrims were hungry and in debt to England. They turned to fishermen in Damariscove for relief supplies in the summer of 1622, when provisions from the previous harvest had run out. And in 1625, after a bumper harvest of their own, the Pilgrims opened a trading route to the Kennebec: the white man's surplus corn for the Indian's beaver. From the proceeds of this exchange it was not long before the colonists were able to reestablish their credit for clothing and other goods supplied from England. And trading posts were built on both the Kennebec and Penobscot rivers.

Even during settlement a century later, the predominant interests in Maine were exploitive. The king's men carved "broad arrows" into every pine tree they found of two-foot thickness or more as a mark that this wood was reserved for the Crown's use as ship timber or spars. Smuggling was big business during colonial days and later. Eastport flourished as a flagrant contraband center during the period of the Embargo acts and the War of 1812.

During the nineteenth century, Maine prospered and permanent settlements took shape where ships were built, lime and granite were quarried, lumber was processed, and mills were located to take advantage of the rivers. Economic growth and the cash economy were not the dominant features of American life in these days. Then a man was content to run a farm just to take care of his family's needs. But today, as in the beginning, Maine's resources provide by far the most benefit to out-of-state interests.

None of the five major forest products companies operating in Maine is headquartered there, and thirteen of the largest firms doing business in the state have absentee ownership. The heads of major corporations all over the country, titans of the U.S. economic and political establishment, have summer places along the Maine coast. But before the fall frosts strike, these men and their households are gone. Their investment in Maine has been on the line only during the short, superlative summer.

Thus Maine has not prospered in the twentieth century. Indeed, the state has hardly participated at all in the staggering rise of the Gross National Product. Looking again for a moment at statistics, it is safe to say that Maine is poor. Per capita income in 1969 averaged only $2,625, compared to the New England average of $3,366. (The next lowest New England state, Vermont, averaged $2,852.) In 1968 some 46,000 families, including 218,000 people or a fifth of Maine, had incomes below the federal poverty level at that time, $3,500 a year. And yet primarily because of high transportation costs for essential goods, the cost of living was not noticeably less in Maine. Moreover, the exploitation syndrome was particularly cruel as it applied to land values. Outsiders vied to obtain choice property, particularly along the coast and around inland recreation areas, so that real estate prices soared beyond the means of most Maine citizens. A Maine man could be excused for thinking with some bitterness that his state had never ceased to be a colony.

For two years, beginning on the fourth of July, 1845, Concord's Walden Pond was for Henry Thoreau the spot where he could reduce life to its lowest terms, to borrow his words. Thoreau found a vantage from which he could make his famous observation about the world at large: "The mass of men lead lives of quiet desperation." The universal truths, the truths about ourselves and the subtle rhythms of the natural world, always show up most clearly in the most under-developed places or within confines where the lines of demarcation are plainly visible.

For a great many people, myself among them, Maine was such a Walden as the decade of the 1970s began. Richard Goodwin, the brilliant speechwriter for both Presidents Kennedy and Johnson, found privacy on a farm in Kingfield, on Freeman's Ridge looking toward Sugarloaf Mountain. There he wrote a book about the need for drastic institutional and political changes in our system. And one day, speaking to Bowdoin College students, he described the conditions of life in America today that had driven him to Maine. "It is almost impossible for the individual to escape the vast and frenzied throng of the stranger, stripping him at once of isolation and a place in the community," Goodwin said. "The dissolution of family and neighborhood and community deprive him of those worlds within a world where he once could find a liberating sense of importance and shared enterprise as well as the security of friends."

As I traveled more than ten thousand miles through Maine in 1971 and 1972, interviewing people, spending time with them to become familiar with their way of life, exploring the wilderness on foot and by canoe, sailing down the coast, I heard Goodwin's observation made many times in different ways. The words were not always as articulate but they were often more poignant — and came from the depths of bitter experience, from men and women and their sons and daughters who had strong feelings about Maine. Some despaired of being able to make a living there and were sad that they might have to give up and leave. Some made great material sacrifices in order to pursue a career there. Others were well set in their ways and outlook and held contempt for the affluent life. Still others had just arrived and were full of optimism about being able to find a place where they could establish themselves and their family on their own terms.

Maine's forests, lakes, rivers, tidal inlets and islands, the mountains and farms, presented infinite challenges to those who were trying hard to work out solutions to environmental problems. And thus, even though the state resembled an exploited colony, Maine was a fortunate place, too. In this book I mean to tell you why.

For, having suffered less than other states from industrialization and urbanization, Maine presents opportunities to those who would attempt to establish prototypes for living in harmony with industrial and technological progress. And as I will try to show, the search for solutions to basic environmental problems is only the first challenge. The recapturing of an essential American way of life, where the family is paramount, where a person has control over his own destiny, is the inevitable next step.

ONE

The Coastal Dilemma

DEEPWATER

ON JULY 22, 1972, IN CLEAR DAYLIGHT, the M.V. *Tamano*, a large tanker carrying No. 2 oil for Texaco, tore a gash in her bottom on Soldier Ledge as she came into Hussey Sound, off Portland Harbor. About 100,000 gallons of oil spilled, making an awful mess throughout Casco Bay. The oil remained evident well into August, depending on where the currents carried it.

Members of the U.S. Coast Guard Atlantic Strike Team, specially equipped to deal with such emergencies, took charge of the cleanup. There were booms to contain the oil, vacuum devices to suck it up, skimmers to clean the intertidal surfaces, straw to absorb it on the beach, and a variety of cleaners, from kitchen Comet to kerosene. Yet according to local observers (myself included), all the latest techniques could not stop the oil from coating boats and beaches and causing untold damage to lobsters, clams, sea birds and countless other creatures.

Unlike the *Torrey Canyon*, the *Tamano* was not a total loss. In fact, the ship's damage was only minor. It galled the people of Casco Bay considerably that, before the cleanup was concluded, before even an official inquiry was begun, the tanker departed, as unconcernedly as she came.

This accident — which could have been a lot worse — was not Maine's first oil spill. Nor would it be its last. But the incident occurred at a moment when the state's most famous asset — the entire coastline and its deepwater anchorages — was the object of unprecedented concern. The debate that had become so intense over Machiasport still was no nearer a conclusion. More than ever, in fact, the Maine coast had become a pawn in the national energy crisis.

Different federal officials were saying that as early as 1980, well over half the U.S. oil supply would come from foreign countries. In the most dramatic terms this would mean the arrival of a super-tanker at a U.S. port *at least once every hour of the day.* Yet in 1972, there was not even one active port on the East Coast that could take a ship over 60,000 deadweight tons, *one-fifth* the size of supertank-ers, and the only region that possessed any good natural anchorages was Maine. (New York and Baltimore, for example, have channels 50 feet deep, whereas the supertankers now being built draw up to 80 feet.)

Throughout the summer of 1972, the U.S. Army Corps of Engi-neers conducted an intensive search for potential deepwater port sites on the East Coast. While many high officials, for environmental reasons, favored the concept of an offshore port, for example, off the mouth of the Delaware estuary, connected by underwater pipeline to land-based refineries, there was plenty of pressure for land har-bors too. President Nixon committed the nation to subsidizing six new supertankers, ranging from 225,000 to 265,000 tons, and Com-merce Secretary Peter G. Peterson said, "Those who raise environ-mental objections to . . . the construction of deepwater ports that will accommodate supertankers must realize that they are asking us to flip a coin and make it land on its edge."

Much of that oil brought to deepwater ports would be used by utility plants to produce electricity. That is, unless the nation suc-ceeded in turning to alternative methods of power generation like nuclear reactors. And if this happened, again the Maine coast would be critical, because both regional and federal projections counted on Maine's coastal bays and estuaries for the millions of gallons of cooling water demanded each hour by nuclear power plants. The very moment that the M.V. *Tamano* glanced Soldier Ledge, setting off new alarm about oil port development, the Central Maine Power Company was undergoing a severe cross-examination in its attempt to begin operations at the Maine Yankee nuclear power plant at Wiscasset.

So deepwater ports for oil transport and great volumes of cold water to cool nuclear reactors were two of the Maine coast's most

24

desperately sought-after assets and both were tied to future solutions to the energy crisis. More will be said on this matter later in this chapter.

Another important reminder must be interjected quickly. There is a third threat to the coastal environment that may yet prove to be the most dire and difficult of all, if it is not already: *too many people.* The threat of overcrowding is almost impossible to bring under complete control in a democratic society, because it means we must first determine which of our very own collective impulses are good, which ones are bad, and then set up a system of workable restraints.

As I was finishing this book, the Governor's Task Force on Energy, Heavy Industry and the Maine Coast delivered its report. The members of this group, it turned out, were as worried as I about the consequences of the coast's extraordinary and unique appeal to millions of Americans. Joseph L. Fisher, chairman of the task force, is a patient and thoughtful person whom I have interviewed several times in his capacity as head of Resources for the Future, a Washington-based nonprofit study group. Fisher has a summer place in Cherryfield, and his wife paints excellent watercolors of their favorite coastal spots that hang in his office. In his submittal letter to Governor Curtis, Fisher wrote this caveat: "It was brought repeatedly to the attention of the Task Force that the deleterious environmental effects of continued unplanned, helter-skelter development of land uses along the coast would probably be more damaging than any likely heavy industrial development."

If people alone or people's most pressing needs, such as energy, constituted the main peril to the coast, then an understanding of what people have been doing from the very beginning might provide clues toward solutions. Certainly some uses of the coast are compatible. Maybe such occupations can be revived or modified and brought up to date.

The Indians used the coast for centuries before the white men came. From the analysis of bone and shell remains found in the diggings of Indian encampments and graveyards, it is presumed that ancient tribes not only fished and foraged along the shores in summer months, but that some also sent boats well out to sea. In excavations, archaeologists have found remains of swordfish, big tuna

25

and other creatures of the deep. One thing is crystal clear about the Indians. They did not abuse the coastal environment. To the contrary, they kept it in perfect condition. This is obvious from reading the glowing reports of the first French and English explorers about the vegetation, wildlife and the marine harvest.

Captain John Smith, the same man who led in the settlement of Jamestown and was saved by Pocahontas, sailed to Maine in 1614. As an old hand in the New World, Smith was expected to reduce the hyperbole of earlier explorers to the realm of truth while appraising the potential of different coastal ventures. Yet Smith turned out to be just as enthusiastic as his predecessors. While he wasted valuable time chasing whales, missing the best month of both the fishing and fur seasons, his small expedition took enough of both these resources to make a profit. His famous account is worth excerpting, for the sheer excitement it conveys.

> I have seen at least forty habitations upon the seacoast and sounded about twenty-five excellent good harbors. . . . From Penobscot to Sagadahoc [the Kennebec River] this coast is all mountainous, and isles of huge rocks, but overgrown with all sorts of excellent good woods for building houses, boats, barks, and ships, with an incredible abundance of most sorts of fish, much fowl and sundry sorts of good fruit for man's use. . . . I made a garden upon the top of a rocky isle [Monhegan] in 43½ degrees, four leagues from the mainland in May, that grew so well that it served us for salads in June and July. . . . All sorts of cattle may here be bred and fed in the islands or peninsulas securely for nothing. . . . You will scarce find any bay, shallow shore, or cove of sand where you may not take many clams or lobsters, or both at your pleasure, and in many places load your boat if you please; nor isles where you find not fruits, birds, crabs, and mussels, or all of them for taking at low water. . . . Worthy is that person to starve that here cannot live, if he have sense, strength, and health, for there is no such penury of these blessings in any place but that a hundred men may in an hour or two make their provisions for a day.

To read the journals of other discoverers, as they came upon other regions of primitive America, is to savor their exuberance over a land unspoiled — a country we've never seen. Giovanni da Verrazzano mistaking Pimlico Sound for the Pacific Ocean, missing the mouth of the Chesapeake, but finding New York Harbor. Jacques Cartier maneuvering through ice floes off Newfoundland, leaving us his amazed description of the new extinct great auk. Cabeza de Vaca, sweating in armor all the way from Florida to Mexico, burning fires to drive off mosquitoes, keeping a wary eye on the stalking Indians. Cabrillo, Drake and Unamuno excited over the rugged beauty of the California coast. Arthur Barlowe, one of Sir Walter Raleigh's captains, landing in the Carolina Banks and finding "the highest, and reddest Cedars of the world." Samuel de Champlain, the Frenchman who charted the Maine coast, coming out of the forest to discover the lake now named for him, but, to his extreme dismay, never seeing the Niagara Falls he had heard about from a young Indian. Father Jacques Marquette getting past the feared Iroquois to explore the Mississippi River as far south as Arkansas, and the Mississippi valley, "fertile land, diversified with woods, prairies, and hills."

Yet none of these other regions of the continent combined so well the natural diversity, seasonal flavor, and maritime potential that Captain Smith found on the Maine coast. Maine's deepwater anchorages, in particular, set her apart from all the rest.

The wave of settlers that followed Smith and Champlain took a long while to implant communities. Although the fishing was unsurpassed, the tall timber, standing within sight of the sea, invaluable, and the pelts of beaver, otter, and muskrat obtained much-needed credit from suppliers back in England, the territory was tough. Very tough. Yet without such rigor the coast would long ago have been overwhelmed and destroyed by the same rapaciousness and stupidity that has accompanied the development of every other stretch of U.S. shoreline, except those few strips that share some of Maine's defenses. A map will show you the most obvious deterrent to orderly colonization: the coast is deeply indented by inlets and estuaries. There are 3,478 miles of tidal shoreline within an arc of 228 miles, from Kittery Point to Eastport. Seemingly easy distances of 25 miles turn into 75-mile jaunts around bays far inland in order to cross a river or get around an arm of the sea. Even today, by car, the distances are considerable.

In the early period of settlement, the main mode of travel was boat, even though the hazards were numerous. Maine is blessed with tricky tidal currents, an abundance of reefs and hidden shoals and, best of all, dense fogs that come rolling in out of nowhere during the mildest and best months of the year. (I say "blessed" because again such obstacles have also impeded reckless growth.) In the winter months the coast is wracked by storms and often the coves are covered with ice. Yet these adversities, as Charles W. Eliot wrote in *John Gilley*, "develop in successive generations some of the best human qualities."

Those who settled the Maine coast were hard-hewn, self-reliant individuals, who operated beyond the bounds of traditional laws and manners, creating traditions unto themselves. At first theirs was a life of subsistence. For nearly a century, beginning with King Philip's War, they never knew when an Indian attack might come from the woods, and they often took flight offshore to distant islands such as Monhegan and Matinicus. Later they turned to shipbuilding — and to fishing, trading and smuggling in the boats and large vessels that they built. Gradually, Maine coast people became rich in worldly connections. In their ships they carried the flag far and wide. The dissolution of these times was captured poignantly by Sarah Orne Jewett in *The Country of the Pointed Firs*. As Miss Jewett's Captain Littlepage put it, "When folks left home in the old days they left it to some purpose, and when they got home they stayed there and had some pride in it. There's no large-minded way of thinking now: the worst have got to be the best and rule everything; we're all turned upside down and going back year by year."

Perhaps some more statistics about the coastal strip — the so-called coastal zone — are in order. Its land boundary runs in and out, from Portland to Augusta, for example, back to Muscongus and Penobscot bays, and then inland again to Bangor, as far as the tides go on the Penobscot River. The zone contains 139 towns, a permanent population of 443,717 (as of 1966), which is swelled during the summer to 614,627. Forty-five percent of the state live in the coastal zone, which amounts to eleven percent of Maine's land area. Moreover, when you consider the river basin characteristics that have a profound influence on the coast, the coastal zone's environmental impact extends throughout almost the entire state. And vice versa. The sickness of a river spreads rapidly to a coastal estuary where it may destroy a shellfish area that has supported many of the people in a coastal town.

The coastal density, or the population per square mile, was 129 people in 1970. It is expected to be near 140 by 1980, 170 by 2000, and 200 by 2020, unless some extraordinary and imaginative planning is done soon. The main impetus for this growth is summer colonization, recreational development, and the growing attraction of small towns both to young people wanting out of urban and suburban America and to older people who want to retire in peace and who can afford to vacation south for a month or more during the winter. Of nearly 180,000 homes in the coastal zone, 33,000 or more are seasonal. In 1969, some three million tourists inundated coastal areas, and at the rate things are going, according to a study by the New England River Basins Commission, the tourist volume on the coast alone could well multiply ten times by the turn of the twenty-first century.

Joseph Fisher, whom I cited earlier, has also studied recreation land trends. He had this to say at a conference sponsored by Bowdoin College's Center for Resource Studies, back in 1966:

> The Maine coast of course, is a matchless scenic and recreation resource ... It is within a day's drive or two hours' flight of what I estimate to be some forty million persons. Even if there are no improvements in transportation, by the year 2000 there will probably be seventy million people within this same region; with the transportation improvements that will certainly take place, the entire North American continent and all of Europe will be within a couple of hours of the Maine coast.

This is disturbing enough. Worse, only 27 percent of the coast is subject to any kind of land use controls and only 32 out of the 139 towns have even the most primitive zoning laws. Of all this coast, only 2 percent is included in a public park or recreation area, and there are a mere 25 miles of public beaches in the entire state.

If shipbuilding, ship trade and fishing had continued to prosper at their peak levels, there would at least be some economic base on which to build when Maine considers coastal alternatives and future plans. But these activities have so atrophied that for the past decade the state has felt entirely secure in arguing for heavy industrial development. We will listen to the views of the industrial advocates, but at the outset I must confess to being bitterly skeptical of their claims. The maritime occupations have far greater potential if they are adjusted, changed, or revived to accommodate new needs and new conditions that the state doesn't appear to grasp yet.

Among heavy industrialists the oilmen come first, identified as they are with the nationwide energy and fuel crisis. At first, proponents of oil development pointed out that New England was placed in a weak position by the oil industry; there was no refinery, no ready source of fuel, and because of the maze of protective policies created for the oil industry, the cost of oil in New England was too high. The state published a brochure advocating *A Core Refinery and Deep Draft Anchorage Project for Machias, Maine,* and just about every elected representative in New England spoke loudly of the need for drastic changes in the oil import quota system coupled with a refinery on the Maine coast. In talking about oil politics, at least, they were right. But in claiming that a refinery would get rid of the price gap and do wonders for the Maine economy, they were wrong. The oil industry has never passed along its economies to its customers. The classic example is the Hawaiian refinery of Standard Oil of California, where gasoline is refined from crude oil that comes from Arabia and Iran. It is shipped to the West Coast, where gasoline is sold three cents a gallon cheaper in Seattle and three and a half cents cheaper in Los Angeles than in Honolulu, home of the refinery. This results from the oilmen keeping a close watch over market conditions, regulating supply in accordance with demand, and taking full advantage of depletion allowances, tax benefits, and an import quota system that makes no sense at all since its sole expressed justification is national security. On these grounds, oil coming from Alaska or from Texas via the sea is far more vulnerable than oil coming from Canada, even though the Canadians are victims of the quota system.

In New England, oil is not only used for electricity and transportation, but is the heating fuel for about a third of the region's homes. The oil industry has managed, however, to keep New England's supply so short that fuel prices have remained at the top, and in recent years there has been a fuel crisis almost every winter. Thus, in the contention that the Maine coast needed an oil refinery, environmental considerations at first seemed lesser — though not for long, as I have noted earlier.

As different parts of the coastline faced immediate development threats, environmental battle lines were quickly formed. Yet, by then, what had been a regional oil and energy crisis had turned into a nationwide problem. More and more cities were threatened with "blackouts" and "brownouts." Various attempts to build massive new electric power plants — in the Southwest, using fossil fuel; on the coasts, with nuclear power; and on the rivers, with both nuclear and hydro power — stirred intense opposition, and the spotlight was focused as never before on the question of how to cope with America's soaring energy demands.

A few hard facts are sufficient to show the gravity of the situation.

By the most conservative estimates contained in a 1969 study for the National Academy of Sciences, world oil reserves will be depleted by the middle of the coming century. Natural gas is already being rationed across the country. Although coal reserves are counted on to serve our needs for maybe another three centuries, they will do so *only* if the use of coal as a fuel for energy is minimal. In other words, this estimate does not allow for gasification of coal to produce a new fuel or desulfurization to produce a clean-burning coal.

Turn from the fossil fuels to nuclear power and a whole new box of troubles is opened. Uranium 235, the fuel for the present generation of lightwater reactors, is in critically short supply. This makes development of the fast-breeder reactor an urgent matter — at least in the opinion of the energy planners. Called the fast-breeder because it makes more nuclear fuel than it consumes, this reactor poses all kinds of hazards, according to a large body of scientific knowledge. Radiation exposure, radiation wastes storage, and keeping this reactor cool are among the troubling considerations. Even if a prototype is developed soon, and even if it is deemed safe, fast-breeder electricity will not be meeting our exorbitant energy demands until 1990.

Nevertheless, the solution to the terrible problems raised by the energy crisis appear quite obvious to objective students. First we must penalize heavy consumption, particularly by new technologies which have magnified industrial-manufacturing energy loads from 200 to 2,000 percent during the past two decades. Second, we must achieve immediate energy savings (that is, cut the current rate of growth in half) by a combination of taxes, rate changes and new building codes. Third, we must commence a crash program to develop the only natural, environmentally sane means of producing power: the sun, the tides, the winds. All of these forces have been harnessed by man on a select basis since the beginning of time. They can be harnessed again for mass consumption.

You may scoff, but you shouldn't. Outside of Washington, D.C., lives a man named Harry E. Thomason, who more than a decade ago built his first solar-heated, solar-cooled house. In the first winter, a severe one with many cold snaps and lots of snow, Thomason's supplemental oil bill (for a backup furnace) came to $4.65. His solar operation cost $2,500 to install (of course it was a custom job), which was only $1,000 more than a conventional furnace-cooling system and without any of the fuel and maintenance costs to come.

Federal government energy experts are enthusiastic about a solar energy installation proposed by Aden Meinel and his wife, Marjorie, who have devised an efficient large-scale means of sun collection at the University of Arizona. It is scientifically sound and has great economic potential, say the experts who have studied the plan. The Meinels hope to build a huge solar station in the southwestern desert that in twenty years would provide power costing 5 mills per kilowatt hour, competitive by today's projections. So large-scale solar installations can be working well before the end of this century.

Why aren't more people talking this way? It must be because so much is at stake, politically and economically, for the oil establishment. And now the oilmen want to use the Maine coast, even while imaginative, dynamic efforts to develop a new energy ethic are entirely within reason — which of course would not depend on the Maine coast for anything but its magnificent tides. With varying degrees of success, Maine coast settlements have held on to their present way of life and dependencies for three centuries. It makes no sense to change things in favor of an industry that is doomed and will be obsolete, like everything else in technology, during the lives of our grandchildren. What do you do with a defunct refinery, an outmoded industrial center?

Regardless of what makes sense, however, the Maine coast will be subject to enormous pressures because of its deepwater development potential. According to a report by state geologist Robert G. Doyle, who analyzed the harbor potential of nine locations in eastern Maine between Penobscot Bay and Perry Basin (at the mouth of the St. Croix River), all nine locations are deep enough and sufficiently protected to accommodate the supertankers that are expected to be carrying all that oil needed for energy in the coming decade. Already, the

Canadians are building a $60 million port, to be called Saint John Deep, in the town of that name at the head of the Bay of Fundy. Continental Oil Company of the United States is a joint backer. Docking facilities will serve supertankers ranging up to 300,000 deadweight tons and drawing eighty feet or more. The Canadians have a head start. If U.S. oil interests are to challenge Canada, their challenge will be issued from Maine.

What is the opposition? Since the Machiasport battle, the established conservationist bodies have gathered evidence and mustered witnesses against heavy industry and new groups have sprung up. There are the Natural Resources Council of Maine, Maine Audubon, The Sierra Club, Audubon Naturalist Council, the State Biologists Association, the Coastal Resources Action Committee, Maine Coast Heritage Trust, the Penobscot Bay Plan, Inc., Citizens Who Care, Landguard Trust, and The Allagash Group — to mention the most prominent of those who are concerned about mismanagement and environmental disaster along the coast.

They are all worried about the possibility of an oil spill. They read about accidents in other places that have terrible effects on shore birds, marine life and small bottom organisms: spills in Santa Barbara, the Gulf of Mexico off Louisiana, San Francisco Bay, Long Island Sound, the *Arrow* grounding in Chedabucto Bay, and at least a dozen reported "minor" spills during oil transfer operations right on the Maine coast, at Searsport and in Casco Bay. Maine coastal beaches are not smooth strips of sand. Strewn with rocks and boulders, they are creviced and cobbled. They are full of tide pools where barnacles, limpets, periwinkles and snails rule over a world of a million smaller life units, the microcosm of the ocean sphere. The Labrador Current spins counterclockwise, east to west, so that tidal waters that wash over the beaches of Machiasport and farther east in the Bay of Fundy eventually strike the shores of Casco Bay and as far south as Provincetown before they spin westward again, around the northern hump of the Georges Bank. If oil is spilled, it is going to be well distributed along the coast. And it will be impossible to clean up effectively because of the nature of the shoreline.

Yet, as I have said, oil is only one of several threats to the Maine coast. The pressures for industrial development will not wane, of course, but the public debate over oil port possibilities has generated

33

constructive thinking on both sides, and there is a good chance, as I will point out later on, that industry will be accommodated in a manner that will minimize damage to the environment.

The danger that receives far less consideration — the threat outlined by Joseph Fisher — is ill-considered, ill-planned recreational development. Small lots, saltwater farms, coastal cottages, and waterfront recreation communities are advertised and sold at an alarming rate. Coastal land transactions run into the hundreds of millions of dollars annually. And the situation is aggravated by private landowners who have enjoyed the coast for years and yet won't deign to enhance public enjoyment and understanding of the coast until it is way too late.

As I read the land and house advertisements, I was convinced that the realtors and the oilmen had much in common. Their intentions were honorable enough, in theory: the oilmen were going to solve Maine's unemployment problem, the realtors were going to put more people in a position to enjoy that lovely coast. Yet both forms of development are irrevocable and will leave the coast scarred forever — at least until some ultimate disaster, when nature resumes control. Real estate advertisements were bringing the Maine coast to nationwide attention. And the asking prices seemed unbelievable compared to values in the postwar years, and even in the sixties, when it was not difficult to find an old saltwater farm in a price range that a great many people could afford. By 1972, saltwater farms seldom appeared on the market, and that description had been expanded to include rundown houses on hopelessly overgrown land that *just* touched a tidal marsh quite some distance from the sea.

Skimming through magazine and newspaper ads in one sitting, I found ten acres of undeveloped saltwater land in the Penobscot Bay area selling for $3,000 an acre. Down in Corea, "Louise Dickinson Rich's beloved peninsula," said the ad, lots under five acres started at $9,995. On Mount Desert, there was a sixteen-room house on two acres, asking price $215,000. Down on Roque Bluffs, practically in Canada, you could get 300 feet of "pink granite shoreline" on four acres of woods for $25,500. Compared to coastal values close to large port cities like San Francisco, Seattle, Boston and New York, these prices for recreational living may not seem way out of line. But for Maine, and for two months of summer occupancy, they are very high indeed — particularly when you consider that a decade ago they were two to five times less for houses, and five or more times less for land.

George Jennings, a retired merchant marine captain turned realtor, can't find enough saltwater farms or islands for the people who write and call him, almost all of them from out of state. He counts heavily on natives who will jump at the chance to make a fat profit on a cut-over woodlot or an old place that has fallen into disrepair. "Fishermen have trouble making money," Jennings told a *Maine Times* reporter. "Then someone offers them a high price for their shack on a point of land. The fishermen don't care for the view: they take it for granted. So they sell and move into a trailer."

My own contact on the coastal land scene is Goodwin Wiseman, a very shrewd and energetic broker who holds forth in a wood Victorian house in Bangor where the walls are filled with maps and charts marked with recent sales, going businesses and future possibilities. Wiseman and I have an understanding, developed over several meetings. He sympathizes with my strong views about open space on the coast, about the islands that I have always enjoyed as if they were my own on some warm summer midday. And I can't *blame* him for selling coastal and island property for the highest price he can get, even though I am disheartened at the prospect of a coast whose wild stretches are invaded by vacation homes, where the islands are all posted "no trespassing."

My family has a vacation place in a summer colony established many decades ago. If many other colonies were to continue to spring up farther east, where the coast is less settled, it would be too bad for everyone who enjoys the remote beauty of that environment. But where do you draw the line and say, in effect, "No more summer colonies; you who got there first are home free"? Is that fair? Of course not.

I once told Wiseman that, not only was I fortunate in having a family summer place to sail from, but that if he could ever find that quiet old farm or raw land on a back cove, at the right price, to let me know. I thought I had the best of notions about coastal development. Wiseman agreed with me that no more construction should be allowed right on the shoreline, destroying the view of the land from the sea and certainly sealing an important strip of open space from everyone but the fortunate propertyowner. He also agreed with the principle of cluster development, the challenge to imaginative architects and planners to locate house units close together, preserving a sense of place and privacy, while gaining common open space in the scenic areas of a development property. Yet as our discussions ended, I asked Wiseman not to forget about that secret place I wanted. And so I was left to face the fact that I was the enemy, too.

The prize real estate is an island, at least for the man who wants that summer escape and isolation where he can be at peace with himself and his family and feel for a moment in control of his destiny, his world. This feeling is beautifully expressed by Clinton Trowbridge, a New York City English professor, who wrote a book about his seven acres called *The Crow Island Journal*. "Because it has been here," he says, "essentially unchanged, since the plutonic action that formed this granite coast subsided, one feels immeasurably young in the presence of this island." Trowbridge, his wife, Lucy, and their children rest and play together or go their own ways on Crow Island. They pick raspberries, study passing boat traffic, swim bare, muse in the fog (it "nourishes our sense of timelessness"), weather the storms, engage in all kinds of adventures and projects in this very small place, and enjoy the melancholy of the clear, brisk days of September before Crow Island must be abandoned until next year.

Like Captain Jennings, Wiseman can't find enough islands. Americans have this urge to be able to have their property well ringed, the boundaries uncontested or unencroached upon, he tells me. Then there are the intimate challenges, adversities and inconveniences. "It's something to talk about," is the way Wiseman puts it. An island barely over five acres sold for $22,000. A two-acre rock dumpling with a cottage and a few trees was going for $10,500. A fifteen-acre island way down in Jonesport with two "rough" fishing cottages would fetch $35,000. "You cannot fight the market," Wiseman says. That I could see. Waterfront-foot prices on the shore have jumped in a few years up to over $100 from $10 to $15. They will double within the next ten years.

Wiseman is piqued by conservationist attempts to protect the coast from further cottage development. To him, the coast is still undeveloped. There are relentless pressures to develop it and the existing approaches are damaging, he agrees. But instead of trying to freeze the development rights of coastal landholders, Wiseman argues, conservation groups like Nature Conservancy should use their capital leverage to take part in the real estate business themselves. Not only could such organizations provide counseling services to land agents, subdividers and landowners in a position to develop, says Wiseman, but they could actually build or contract model developments. Of course, if conservation groups did contract to have open space developed imaginatively and in a model manner, they would have to do so on a nonprofit basis or put their profits into funds dedicated to nonprofit, worthy causes in order to preserve their tax-exempt status.

Wiseman and I never have arrived at solutions to these questions. Certainly the participation of nonprofit groups in the land business would help to check the incredible rate of land inflation that results in undeserved windfalls for land speculators. Would Wiseman accept this? I hope so.

His position in general is typical of all the real estate people I talked with. Just as foresters argue that cutting bans condemn a stand of timber to eventual death (because without proper management it will become choked and rotten), so do realtors feel that development bans foreclose enlightened free enterprise initiative in land use. "When you take a piece of land and say you can't build on it, you sterilize it," Wiseman has said. "It's only good to look at. I've never butchered a piece of property. I don't want to see it murdered."

He describes the coastal domain as a jeweler talks about gems in intricate settings. "I like the pink granite, some spruce and fir, sand between the ledges and some open fields sweeping toward the water: a pastoral quality."

Yet Wiseman realizes full well that enlightened land use approaches would result in the highest real estate prices in his market. He is a strong advocate of coastal zoning and building controls. "What pleases you keeps land values up," he says. "And what keeps land values up is a monetary advantage to me."

Holding up land values is a lot different from land speculation and the windfall profit that result from an unforeseen trend or twist in the market. If Maine is to be preserved, the profit motive must be tempered considerably in *land* transactions, perhaps done away with entirely. A landowner or a real estate broker should retain incentive based on the way he manages or develops property, but not on the speculative investment potential of the *land* as a separate commodity. If he builds a summer house or puts up a farm, he is entitled to make money on the facility, plus inflation and original investment on the land. If he builds a condominium or lease housing, he deserves to make a reasonable profit while managing and selling these developments, no more. This of course can never happen until tax-collection authorities make drastic adjustments in property assessments and taxes based on speculative potential, so-called "fair-market value."

Of course I've never gotten into this with Wiseman. Where we openly disagree is on how much of the Maine coast should be developed. Privately. Publically. To me, open land is not sterile at all. It has a multiple worth. Its value is equal to the number of people who enjoy its wildness times its appraisal as undevelopable land. On a certain afternoon, arriving by sailboat with my family, I have owned a score of Maine islands. To be denied this "ownership" in the future will be not only my loss, but yours as well.

LONG ISLAND AND SEARSPORT

MAINE'S NEW SITE LOCATION ACT was first tested by the King Resources Company within the city limits of Portland, at Long Island on Casco Bay, where the U.S. Navy built underground fuel tanks to service the North Atlantic fleet during the troubled years of the Second World War. King very cagily opened the Maine door by signing a contract with the state to explore the offshore bottom. The state was most anxious to validate its claim, under an old grant by King James to the Massachusetts Bay Colony, to the waters as far out as 120 miles. If King Resources found any oil out there, sure as anything the federal government would raise a ruckus over the jurisdiction, and then, the hope went, Maine could validate its right to cash in. Anyway, a year after the contract was signed, King surfaced not with a mineral strike but with the revelation that the company had acquired over 350 acres of the 912-acre Long Island, was already storing oil in the navy fuel depot, and had plans to construct a tank farm with a capacity of eight million barrels of oil.

King Resources' sudden disclosures precipitated a battle. Summer people and year-round residents of the Casco Bay islands — Cushing, Peaks, Great and Little Diamond, Chebeague and Cliff — mobilized under a new banner: Citizens Who Care. Their cause was led by Harold E. Hackett, a Bates College marine biologist whose specialty is seaweed. Their case was represented by a bright young Portland lawyer named Harold Pachios, who also happened to be one of two legislative lobbyists for the statewide conservation movement. Pachios had also been an influential figure in the passage of the Siting Act.

The city council of Portland favored the King plan since it would provide substantial tax revenues. The firm's manager, John J. McNamara, Jr., made quite a few promises — the litany of the oilmen when they're wearing their pinstripe suits, anticipating the resistance of the environmentalists. Water service, fire protection, road improvements, junk and litter cleanup, new dock facilities — nothing short of a total renaissance and restoration in this Maine community where the local economy needed shoring up, the people needed jobs, the town needed taxes, and so on.

I am told that it might have worked, but for McNamara's manner and the natural inclination of the people to be skeptical toward the proposals of outsiders. Quick-witted, imaginative and thoroughly versed in all of the possibilities of oil development, McNamara was certainly the man best suited to draw up King's plans. But not to argue them at public hearings. Maine people found him abrasive or too smooth — or both. And it didn't help when it was reported that he had conjured up the entire scheme as his yacht lay becalmed off Long Island during the annual Monhegan Race.

As if technology could cope with any obstacle, he explained that Soldier Ledge, a forty-foot spot in the middle of Hussey Sound, the approach to Long Island, would have to be blasted out to make a channel for supertankers. (I must confess, this would at least prevent a repeat of the *Tamano* accident.) King was going to build a long dock that would handle two supertankers at once, transferring up to two and a half million barrels of oil, pumping the oil to the mainland through a pipe laid seven feet beneath the bottom of the bay. At this point King's plans became fuzzy, and the people, angered by one fait accompli, began to have visions of others: a huge oil station in the middle of the bay; a big spill or lots of little ones, the beaches sticky with the stuff; lobsters and other shellfish contaminated; a refinery to process the oil maybe even in South Portland at the end of the underwater pipeline from Long Island — or who knows, maybe eventually a refinery on the island, processing crude oil brought around from Alaska. There was more emotion than fact, but that's usually the way it is in the beginning of such confrontations, and it seems necessary, in order to offset the obfuscations and machinations of the oilmen.

The battle took the classic shape. First a few staying actions to muster support and to gather funds to pay for court action and the compilation of data and expertise to present during hearings. Then, hoping that the big menace would grow impatient and become even more arrogant and stumble, Citizens Who Care tried to take to the voters, by a referendum, the issue of Portland having to rezone Long Island. But they didn't get enough signatures to put the zoning question on the ballot. "We never would have won it anyway," Hackett told me. "We simply had to have something to do."

By the time these delaying rounds were over, the state's Environmental Improvement Commission had decided to hold hearings to judge whether King's plan was environmentally suitable under the conditions of the Siting Act. The EIC decided it wasn't — that the marine environment of Casco Bay, that recreation, that summer residency, that the year-round livelihood of fishermen all would be threatened by the Long Island project.

King took the decision to the state supreme court, which overruled the EIC. The project was not subject to consideration under the new site law, the court said, because the navy fuel depot had existed on Long Island long before the law's enactment. Attorney Pachios presented a strong brief. Although King had purchased the old facility from the government, he argued, none of the facilities were as yet installed that would make the fuel depot a modern oil terminal; and King had hardly begun to invest in the development. But these arguments had no effect in obtaining a legal solution. By then, something else had happened. King Resources Company was in deep financial trouble and could no longer afford to go ahead with its plan.

But I remain apprehensive. A bad precedent was set by a court citing an archaic eighteenth-century statute (favoring the property-owner) as well as the so-called "grandfather clause." The Long Island oil base still *could* become the nucleus for oil development.

The next battle was over Searsport, at the head of Penobscot Bay, more than a hundred miles east of Portland. It had all the makings of a jarring confrontation. By that time the EIC was better prepared to conduct orderly hearings, to elicit economic and scientific testimony through witnesses and written submissions. In the wake of the Casco Bay controversy, the EIC had made good progress in developing guidelines that could be applied consistently to various kinds of coastal industrial development, but particularly to oil sites. The donnybrook atmosphere and emotionalism of the previous hearings was to be avoided at all cost. The conservationists also realized that their case would have to be set forth in a much more substantive manner, with their own witnesses and data to rebut the economic and technical presentations of the oilmen. To this end, the Coastal Resources Action Committee undertook to represent a spectrum of coastal conservationist groups and hired attorneys to prepare the case. One of these lawyers was Harold Pachios. Finally, to round out the battle order, the state government became deeply involved — albeit in a most confusing way. State agencies seemed to be pitted against each other. The Department of Economic Development, under its director James Keefe, openly advocated the Searsport oil refinery. Air, water and fisheries specialists had deep misgivings. The governor termed the hearing "the first clear-cut test of Maine's ability to analyze and regulate heavy industry under the Site Approval Law."

Governor Curtis was under considerable pressure to make a pronouncement flatly favoring or opposing the oilmen. Wisely, he pointed out in a statement read at the opening of the hearings that the EIC was the panel created to bring fair judgment and due process to bear on the oil question, "to reconcile the incalculable recreational and fishery value of Searsport and the Penobscot Bay area with the undeniable economic and energy benefits" of the refinery.

What promised to be an epochal moment, however, perhaps a turning point in the coastal dilemma, proved to be no more than an inconclusive skirmish. For it turned out that Maine Clean Fuels (the oilmen) was merely a bush league operation. Its plan was from the very beginning shot full of holes, and was miserably presented, even though the hearings consumed over sixty hours and cost Maine taxpayers a shameful amount of money. I attended most of these sessions. I came away from each one with my perspective dimmed, my senses numbed, sometimes even having forgotten entirely what was at stake.

Briefly, Maine Clean Fuels was a hastily put together group of speculators who hoped to take advantage of an oil import allocation granted to David Scoll, MCF president, during the waning days of the Johnson administration. An admiralty lawyer, Scoll was a political appointee to the maritime administration under President Kennedy.

He proposed a refinery on Sears Island just east of the town that would process 202,000 barrels of oil a day (making it the twelfth largest in the United States), producing mostly low-sulfur fuel oils to meet stringent new air pollution standards and lowering fuel prices in Maine by as much as 20 percent. Scoll claimed to have a "loose arrangement" with Ashland Petroleum Company under which the big oil company would share development costs and take over operation of the refinery once EIC approval was obtained. Scoll's case was badly eroded when these initial contentions were either qualified or revealed to be entirely unsubstantiated in the course of the hearings.

The proceedings were not without excitement, colorful language, some truly delightful exchanges that revealed the con artistry and condescension of the dark-suited proponents and the deep-rooted native sagacity of some of the opponents. It's hard to fool a man like Ossie Beal, head of the Maine Lobstermen's Association. Ossie spoke in an emotionless, matter-of-fact manner about the importance of lobstering on Penobscot Bay and how it would be gravely threatened by oil traffic and oil spills. Oil barges and tankers could well sweep away the pot buoys put out over lobster traps by fishermen from Matinicus, Vinalhaven, Rockland, Owls Head, Port Clyde, Tenants Harbor, Spruce Head and, offshore, Monhegan Island. In the bay and its immediate approaches, Ossie pointed out, there were set some 186,000 traps, representing a $2.2 million investment and a way of life for over a thousand families. Figuring that each trap meant about $60 in income, an industry worth $11,160,000 would be placed in danger from oil development. "We have spent all our lives on the coast of Maine," Ossie said, pausing before his final understatement. "We know the winds and the currents. They're tricky. Spills are inevitable."

Nothwithstanding these moments, the hearings only established three things: that by denying the Scoll application the EIC showed it will refuse any industry proposal if it is not supported by substantial and specific details, in effect amounting to a presentation costing up to a million dollars; that environmental groups can hold their own when they too muster expert witnesses and produce specific rebuttal material; and that in the future the EIC will have to limit drastically the extent of its public hearings on a given proposal, to a day at the very most, or else this body will be prevented, by time and a strained budget, from considering other matters that might be equally significant, if not so controversial.

The Searsport exercises *were* costly. Transcribing the testimony alone consumed a lot of time and money. Although I'm not suggesting that the EIC should forgo such hearings entirely, after going through the Searsport business I feel certain that the EIC can probably get most of the information it needs by studying written submissions, pro and con, and by assigning staff experts to probe into the most complex scientific aspects of a proposal. This data should be *easily* available to the public and a *full opportunity* be given to opposition experts to present rebuttal material. Then let the public be heard, let human nature shine, let the EIC consider the emotional aspects of the concerned citizenry and perhaps some local factors overlooked in closed-session deliberations.

The EIC ruling on the Searsport proposal was summed up in five findings.

— Maine Clean Fuels showed neither the financial nor technical ability to comply with Maine standards against air and water pollution.
— The proposal did not provide for adequate water supplies.
— It did not have a plan to interconnect with public roads.
— It failed adequately to provide "for fitting itself harmoniously into the existing natural environment" and thus was a threat to the present scenic character and ways of life in the Penobscot region.
— It did not "adequately protect the public health, safety and general welfare."

I have quoted phrases of these findings because they can mean different things to different people. Yet it is clear how they were interpreted by the EIC, which found Maine Clean Fuels specifically without an answer or a contingency on twenty-five counts. Then there were the EIC's own caveats: "The quantity of marine resources harvested in the three-county area which includes Penobscot Bay and Sears Island approximates $50 million annually and comprises a significant portion of the total marine resources harvested annually in the state of Maine." Stacked up against such a statement, could any oil development win a place in Penobscot Bay?

It is doubtful. But this does not exclude other forms of heavy industry or even an oil transfer station receiving smaller tankers. The Searsport hearings made it clear that Penobscot Bay will *never* accommodate supertankers, but already fuel oil is shipped to a Shell tank farm in Searsport, so it is only logical that the oilmen will keep up some pressure. Moreover, the state has plugged for industrial centers in both Bangor and Searsport, thirty miles apart by way of the Penobscot River, that would make efficient use of convenient air, rail, sea and highway connections. In 1969, the federal government gave to Bangor the Dow Air Force Base, a $100 million bonanza. Now in business as Bangor International Airport, it is a real economic hub. Light industry and commercial development is sprouting around it. It has the longest runway in New England (11,400 feet), can easily handle 747 jumbo jets, and is 400 miles closer to Europe via the Great Circle Route than New York. Interstate Highway 95 runs right between the city and the airport. Rail links between Searsport, Bangor and cities in all landward directions — both American and Canadian — are provided by the Bangor and Aroostook and the Maine Central. It will be hard to stop the push for this segment of the coastal zone to become an industrial center of some kind. But if it must come, it ought to be based more on rail and air service, less on highway and sea transportation. And it should be based in Bangor. If a big plant is to be located in Searsport, if Penobscot Bay must have a new industry, it should be a shipyard where Mainers' traditional inclinations and skills will fit naturally. If the bay has to take on supertankers, let them be *built* there and sent away empty.

The hearings over Searsport gained time, time to think about a gaping weakness in the strategy so far of both the state and the environmentalists. *Each was without a coastal policy.* James Keefe was hung up on a jury rig approach to solving Maine's economic difficulties. The conservationists were hung up on the same old platform of opposition to anything that impinged on their view of the natural world, the peace and privacy that *they* could afford.

First of all, one had to concede that sooner or later a big league corporation would present a concrete plan, authenticated by heavy outlays in research and development, supported by reams of data to answer every conceivable question, and advanced by the sort of smoothly blended public relations cum lobbying campaign that the environmentalists are ill equipped to put down. Maine Clean Fuels' plan was full of technical flaws and lacked the most basic environmental safeguards. A major oil company would certainly be prepared to avoid these shortcomings. In short, the anti-oil forces now would have to come up with a truly sophisticated formula: meaningful measurements for aesthetic and environmental qualifications; hard figures concerning social and economic impact; and an assessment of both the probable and possible alternatives. Once you have this equation in hand, you can rise to poetic heights in discussing the probable influence of industrial development on the community's spirit and soul, on the way of life that people count on and feel comfortable with.

An old hand in the economic development field, who had spent much of his life working for the federal government in Maine, once told me, "You've got to remember that in these coastal and rural towns you love so much, the smell of unemployment is just as bad as the smell of pollution." My response is that once it is understood that heavy industry more often than not is *counterproductive*, the rural assets — open spaces, proximity with nature, close personal relationships and ties with the whole community — seem as good as gold.

I can't emphasize this point enough. Let's look at the statement of intent by the Maine legislature, when it passed both the Site Location and Coastal Conveyance acts.

> The legislature finds and declares that the highest and best uses of the seacoast of the State are as a source of public and private recreation and solace from the pressures of an industrialized society, and as a source of public use and private commerce in fishing, lobstering, and gathering other marine life used and useful in food production and other commercial activities.

Yet this is not as straightforward a declaration as it seems. It will be plenty tough just defining and quantifying the sources of public and private recreation. But in order to do battle with the oilmen, if the environment is to be won, there has to be a persuasive method of evaluating "solace from the pressures of an industrialized society." Because these boys in their pin-stripe suits, who commute from Connecticut, Long Island and Beverly Hills, have no end of ways to show how the "industrialized society" is *good* for you.

46

Actually, as the Searsport hearings droned on, some progress was made toward the formulation of coastal policy. At the suggestion of their professor, Richard Barringer, three students at the John F. Kennedy School of Government at Harvard analyzed the "Employment Impact of Constructing a Refinery on Sears Island." These men, José A. Gomez-Ibanez, Ronald T. Luke and Gregory Treverton, attended EIC hearings, interviewed 27 persons, and poured through 25 papers and publications dealing with Maine economic problems, the oil industry, recreation and coastal planning. Their report came to a hundred pages. It is tough reading — formal, analytic, and not for the home bookshelf. But its overall verdict is clear. The impact of the refinery would be negative on all counts.

The Harvard investigators weighed three basic factors to arrive at one set of conclusions, and then they inserted these values in three different equations. The factors were:

— Economic benefits, jobs and taxes, etc., that would result from a refinery.
— Negative effects upon fishing, recreation, etc., if a refinery were built.
— Economic alternatives that could be pursued if a refinery were unacceptable.

The three equations arrived at an economic impact if the following three alternatives were pursued, once a refinery was denied:

— The state expended no effort at all to improve the existing economic plight of the Penobscot Bay region.
— Present industries, particularly poultry processing, were expanded through state support.
— New industries — electronics, metal fabricating, prefabricated housing, broiler (chicken) production, etc. — were attracted to the region.

Part One of the study evaluated the positive employment effects of a refinery. The second part assessed the impact of oil spills that inevitably occur from tanker traffic and the transferring and refining of oil. The team devised a scale of accident probabilities, then balanced the gains cited in Part One with the losses figured in Part Two. The

47

conclusion was an employment deficit amounting to a net loss in the regional payroll of $948,000 a year. Part Three analyzed alternatives and arrived at these payoffs:

— If new industry were attracted, $3,241,911.
— If existing industry were strengthened, $2,513,110.
— And by "muddling through," doing nothing to change economic conditions, a payoff of $540,926.

A University of Maine team looked at a single aspect of oil development — native employment and the probable economic spillover — and concluded that the benefits from a refinery alone would be extremely limited. The Maine team consisted of two professors, Roderick Forsgren and James Wilson, and two business school students, Kevin Daily and Harold Price. Their study was not nearly as analytical or thorough as the Harvard report, but it did benefit from a sympathetic understanding of the Maine worker and Maine employment characteristics. They concluded that a large refinery would employ at the most 25 Maine men, and that the boost to the local economy would result in no more than 50 additional jobs for natives. This so-called multiplier effect (or spillover) was probably optimistic for a coastal town, the team said, because it was based on an old study of Bangor, a self-reliant city producing a large portion of its own goods. By corresponding with oil company executives, the Maine team learned that 77.3 percent of a refinery's work force consists of experienced men and that presently unemployed Maine laborers were not suited to fill many of the remaining unskilled jobs. To be sure, the construction of the refinery would require additional help, but even then the oilmen invariably rely on specialized contractors, not local tradesmen.

Both the Harvard and University of Maine reports, particularly the wide-ranging Harvard study, represent a kind of analysis long overdue. They avoid abstractions and worn-out assumptions and avoid the extremes of conservationists and developers alike. Carried a few steps further or expanded to represent a diverse collection of Maine coastal communities, such studies should establish the framework for a coastal policy. Indeed, after the Searsport hearings, the governor created a Task Force on Energy, Heavy Industry and the Maine Coast.

The Machiasport controversy, then the Long Island and Searsport hearings, for the moment had put Maine in the position of being what the economists like to call a hinterland. Basically, the term is applied to a region whose destiny lies in the hands of outside forces.

Hinterland is defined by *Webster's* as "1: a region behind a coast 2: a region that provides supplies 3: a region remote from cities and towns." To a greater or lesser degree, all three definitions apply to Maine. The inland wilderness, the region farthest behind the coast, supplies the wood and paper markets. Its economic future was determined more than a century ago. Fortunately, the desirability of forests for other purposes, notably recreation, does not have to be compromised greatly by present practices in the forest industry.

Unfortunately the coastal zone is quite a different sort of hinterland because its present greatest economic value, measured in conventional terms, may well turn out to be a far greater liability than benefit to Maine's future. This will happen if the coast receives *new* industrial development that is incompatible with present industries such as shipbuilding and fish processing. The confusion and indecision on the part of both environmentalists and state development officials as to how to cope with the coast is a further cause for concern.

One day Governor Curtis told me how a very well known summer resident had written and suggested that the state was ignorant of its power of eminent domain, and that this power should be applied in order to control the future development *and* protection of the coast. "Thank you for your advice," Curtis told me he wrote back. "We know how to take land. We just don't have the money to pay for it." To me he put it this way. "You summer people have got to look around — beyond the fight over an oil refinery. We used to say, 'Come buy our land and pay our taxes.' But now the summer propertyowners do us no favor. Industry stands in line to have that coast, offering jobs and economic benefits."

Curtis didn't exactly say it, but he agreed when I did, that summer people have failed to apply themselves to the solution of Maine's hinterland troubles because they have not helped the state to develop environmentally beneficial payoffs along the coast. The summer people are tied to exploitive interests. For the most part, they have made their money in or off industry. Typically, *they* complain about the ill effects of exploitation long before these repercussions are felt by the exploited. Their fall, winter and spring habitats have become unbearably foul and now they're worried about the summer nest.

Maine's hinterland also compares to the plight of undeveloped nations. To these countries, smoke in the air, filth in the rivers, and the cutting up of the landscape are indexes of power, progress, prosperity. This was, in fact, the greatest obstacle encountered during the 1972 United Nations Conference on the Human Environment: how to tell backward people, poor by our standards, that they really are lucky because they've never had to pay the price of progress. In a paper prepared for that gathering in Stockholm, Anthony Wolff wrote, "For the developed countries to insist on environmental good manners after enriching themselves under the old no-holds-barred rules is tantamount, in the eyes of poorer nations, to slamming the door of the rich man's club in their faces."

Which takes us right back to Maine and Governor Curtis saying, "We've got 31,000 unemployed and in selected areas we need major economic stimulants."

HEARING EASTPORT

SINCE AN OIL REFINERY was viewed by the state as being the fore-
runner of — the catalyst for — the kind of industrial development
that would solve Maine's unemployment rate and general economic
deficiency — it was inevitable that the oil debate should spread to
Eastport. No deepwater town on the entire Atlantic coast has suffered
more ups and downs. Once busy and prosperous, by 1972 Eastport
was a graying, ghostly place whose people admitted they were just
hanging on. The situation didn't bode well for anyone, except those
prepared to exploit it. What I found in Eastport, admittedly on a
brief visit, clouded many of my preconceptions. For I had assumed
that coastal townspeople were as tolerant as they were narrow-minded,
were as gentle as they were proud; that young people escaping urban
society, their families, and the war would assume the burden of
proving themselves worthwhile in their flight to the land — that above
all they were anxious to pull their own weight within the traditional
rural framework. Wrongly, I had assumed that wherever both sets of
values were blended there was hope for the happiest form of American life, an existence based on the union of family, of community
and of place.

But just as Eastport is obscured in fog more than sixty days a year
(a statistic based on U.S. Coast Guard fog signal data), so did I become confused in my bearings in that place, rendered uncertain and
truly troubled. I left with only one thing as well established in my
mind as when I came: the environment (land and sea both) dictates
the terms by which people can prosper in or suffer a falling out with
a place. The land weaves an ethic all of its own, and where our beliefs

51

and customs are not in accord with the ethic, there is bound to be tragedy. And what deepens the sense of disaster is the awful realization that immediate solutions may well be impossible unless the ethic is abandoned (and then there will still be tragedy in the long run), or unless we admit to ourselves that society at large *does not* have an obligation to carry communities that have run out of reasons to exist.

The question was nicely phrased by Bob Monks, the young man who unsuccessfully challenged Senator Margaret Chase Smith in the 1972 primary. We were talking about the deepwater towns that no longer prospered from fishing, shipbuilding or maritime commerce, the three economic activities that once made places like Eastport hum. "Must we do all that is in our power," Monks asked, "through social, economic and political initiatives, to keep people where historical accident put them a hundred years ago?" At that moment neither he nor I dared answer. His reluctance stemmed from his aspiration to represent the people. Mine was based on my despair over the rootlessness in American living patterns, my feeling that our civilization had suffered from our prevalent nomadic ways, our economic and technological transience, and thus our failure to develop a true sense of place . . .

But back to Eastport. Here the coastal dilemma was to be captured in its most basic terms: an exciting, glorious section of shoreline, replete with bays, islands, twisting coves, scenic thoroughfares and river estuaries, yet a region whose human resources were abused, whose people were plunged into an economic depression, hoping desperately for a major uplift. The occasion of my going there was a public hearing held by a state legislative panel, created just to look into the "feasibility" of an oil refinery in Eastport. Inasmuch as Maine already had an Environmental Improvement Commission to study such matters, it was never clear to me why a special panel was necessary, except on political grounds. The hearing was initiated by David Kennedy, Speaker of the Maine House of Representatives and a drugstore owner from Milbridge, some fifty-five miles westward up the coast and also in Washington County. Though it was unannounced at the time, Kennedy was preparing to cap his political career with a proposal for a Maine Industrial Port Authority, whereby a single industrial complex would be developed around an oil refinery on deepwater. It was clear that Kennedy thought Eastport would be the ideal place.

In development terms, there were compelling arguments for his position. The Irving Oil Company of Canada was already bringing supertankers into a new refinery in St. John, forty miles eastward down the Bay of Fundy. Eastport has the depth, maneuvering room and protection for ships drawing over eighty feet. So if there were heavy oil traffic passing just offshore to and from St. John, why not divert some of it to the United States, particularly since the Irving complex apparently had proven acceptable by Canadian environmental standards? Yet in a revealing comment — unintentionally an argument against, as much as for, oil development on the Maine coast — Kennedy told me, "Because of the natural beauty of our coastline, we have to confine it to either one end of the state or the other. I would be appalled if it went into an area like Boothbay. Why I would go on the soapbox all over the state of Maine."

This remark implies a political reason favoring Eastport, even if Kennedy concedes that oil development is at best unattractive. Eastport was the path of least resistance. Unlike Boothbay, it had an insignificant summer colony and up until then had been too remote to attract many vacationers. People with money and influence from Massachusetts, Connecticut, New York and Pennsylvania would not be likely to pay close attention, much less participate in, an Eastport confrontation, nor would the money from these summer colonists pour into the preparation of a case against oil here as it had in Casco Bay and Searsport.

Finally, Eastport was considered the poorest of the poor, the most depressed spot in a county already ranked with the most destitute in the nation, and referred to in a *Wall Street Journal* article as "A Downeast Appalachia." According to the Maine Department of Economic Development — which spends too much of its time fooling with such statistics — in 1970, 24.5 percent of the households in Washington County had total incomes under $3,000 (the federal poverty line for a family of three) and another 19.1 percent had incomes below $5,000. The unemployment rate had never been less than 10 percent in a decade, while the work force had dwindled by nearly 20 percent between 1960 and 1970.

Yet until the 1950s, Eastport enjoyed a succession of heydays. No

coastal town boasted a more colorful history, even if the place is probably most familiar to New England because it is the outer limit in the
Eastport to Block Island weather reports.

Actually, whether Eastport was even a part of the United States was
not clarified until Maine became a state in 1820. The inside cover
map of Doris Isaacson's first-rate *Maine Guide* makes Eastport a part
of New Brunswick. The town's uncertain territorial status was in fact
fundamental to its growth and early importance. The seaport always
played by the rules of the nation (the United States or England)
whose momentary policies (and sympathies) favored its economic
interests. Out in the harbor on Treat Island, Benedict Arnold ran a
fishing business. Indian Island, three quarters of a mile across Western Passage, the entrance to Passamaquoddy Bay, was a busy trading
post. Out on Campobello Island, a mile southeast across Friar Roads,
the Canadian fishermen depended on Eastport for supplies. Much
later, Campobello was the site of Franklin Delano Roosevelt's summer home, now an international monument. Fishermen from Marble-
head, Cape Ann and Portsmouth turned Eastport into a thriving outpost immediately after the Revolutionary War. Then, when the 1807
Embargo Act forbade trading with England (i.e., Canada), the place
boomed as a smuggling center. British warships cruised back and
forth to receive and protect transactions of contraband goods. The
price of flour jumped to 12.5 cents a barrel and local entrepreneurs
took it up to an astronomical $3 a barrel on the border market. The
English seized Eastport in 1814, during the so-called War of 1812.
They also occupied Castine, on Penobscot Bay. Eastport prospered
as the trading center of the entire region — Canada and United States
— for the three years of British occupation.

Then trading gave way entirely to shipbuilding and fishing. The
first U.S. sardines (what they call herring packed in a tin) were
canned in Eastport in 1875. By the turn of the century there were
close to twenty sardine plants, and the town population was at a peak
of 5,311 persons. The depression dealt the fishing business a blow
from which it has never fully recovered, except for a short time during the Second World War, when sardines went into war rations and
people were not so fussy about how they got their protein. (To be
sure, in the thirties the Passamaquoddy tidal project created a brief
boom, and during the war, air and Seabee installations bolstered economic conditions.)

As I drove into Eastport on a lovely September afternoon, only two sardine plants remained. Gone were thirty or so piers, replaced by a government-financed breakwater and docking refuge. The water-front presented a picture of sad decay and disrepair: buildings abandoned and rotting, stores and houses boarded up, and only a few older people visible on the sidewalk. By this time, in 1971, only two thousand people, more or less, were left in Eastport, not enough to qualify it as a city (and thus giving Lubec full claim to being the easternmost "town" in the United States). Yet for me, anchored as I was to my car seat, the dominant feature of Eastport was not visible at all. Rather, it existed as a smell — a terrible stink of rotten fish, coming with the prevailing southwest wind from the Mearl Company, a mile or so distant, which produced "pearl essence" (fake mother-of-pearl) and fire-fighting foams from the parts of herring (caught mostly by Canadian fishermen).

I parked behind the Shead High School, where the hearing was to be held. The school used to be the site of Fort Sullivan and the view was breathtaking, out over the rooftops of the town below. To the south and east you could see how the islands gave the harbor all the protection it needed, and I thought how, one day back in 1831, over thirty large English trading vessels had come to anchor in this view, with cargoes of plaster and grindstones in exchange for flour, lumber and fish. Now the only boat I could spot was a Canadian herring smack, throwing forth a big bow wave as she ploughed through the incoming tide on her way back to Canada from the Mearl Company.

Early in the hearing, Louis Jalbert, a state representative, expressed his view of what it was all about. "The function of this committee is to find out the feelings of the good people of this area," he said. In these terms, then, the hearings revealed no consensus — only deep polarization — and were unrepresentative as well, because an important segment of the population was missing: the workingman, employed or unemployed, the man who would feel most directly the costs or benefits of oil development. Nor was there a soul present from the oil industry to discuss the various possibilities connected with what one or more companies had in mind at Eastport.

Dana Jacobs, Eastport city manager, announced that the Metropolitan Oil Company of New York, a subsidiary of the Pittson Company, a major East Coast fuel distributor, had definite plans for a refinery in Eastport. Jacobs quoted from a letter written by Herbert Warren, Metropolitan's president, and he also expressed what was probably on the minds of other residents. "Eastport is in serious need of economic development if it is to survive," he said. "The answer may or may not be oil, but oil is the only prospect, the only industry that has even made an approach."

Jacob Cohen, Eastport businessman and president of the Washington County Chamber of Commerce, was typical of other pro-oil spokesmen who counted on a refinery to restore the tax base, plug the unemployment gap, and trigger a sweeping resurgence in the local economy. Cohen, Jacobs and others reported that they had gone as a delegation to the Irving Company refinery in St. John and that they were impressed with the benefits bestowed by that development and by its environmental compatibility.

It was left to Virginia Pottle, a farmer from nearby Perry, to remind the gymnasium crowd that inspection delegations, whether they are chamber of commerce advocates or members of the U.S. Congress being given the official tour of Vietnam, rarely delve very deeply. A short, pleasant-faced woman in work clothes, she held up a plastic bag evidently containing a black, gelatinous mess. "I have brought you a statistic," she said to the men of the legislative panel, "a beach specimen from the refinery at St. John. The committee that went there saw only what they wanted to see."

Other anti-oil witnesses were less eloquent. If anything, they gave native Eastporters a chance to steel their resentment toward all outside intervention. Most of these people would go by the nomenclature of hippies, and it was not at all clear to me which of them were genuinely concerned about the future of the community and which were interested only in preserving a haven for themselves. One of them told of coming from the polluted, noisy metropolis. "We're carpenters and artists and craftsmen," she said. "We work on old houses and we make and sell things." Another identified himself as the son of a Humble Oil Company vice president. "I grew up on money from refineries. But I saw what it did and that's why I came to this part of Maine," he explained. And another was a girl with a cape and an autoharp who asked if she could put her feelings into a song she had composed. "You've given us a beautiful land, Lord," she sang and strummed. Then she lamented the desecration of the land

and how the oilmen had at last come to Eastport. "I don't ever want to have to say,/ It used to be a beautiful land, Lord. / It used to be a beautiful world."

Anywhere else, under different circumstances, these well-meaning protestations might have been effective. But not at that moment in Eastport's Shead High School. An Eastporter came to the front. He was angry. He tore up a leaflet that had been passed out earlier by the students. "I've never read such junk in my life," he said. "I'll come back after the refinery comes in." And he left.

On the other hand, the students from the high school were very effective. Perhaps the best of them was Eileen Dougherty, who stood up straight and spoke in a clear voice. "So far everything has been done in the best interests of Eastport," she said. "So why is it so hard to get facts? We want facts, not promises." Then she upbraided the news media for portraying Eastport as a poverty-stricken town. "Is this auditorium poverty?" she asked. I looked up at the curved, handsome, laminated wood beams, the steel supports and cold cinderblock walls, the smooth, varnished oak floor. I didn't know what to think.

The next morning I dropped in on Jacobs. The City Rooms were in bleak, high-ceilinged quarters with pipes exposed, old-fashioned radiators, the plaster cracking. Here was a place that with a little care and imagination could be restored to something quite fine, I thought. Three chairs and a table were stacked with studies and reports on Eastport's problems. On the wall there was a chart of the sewer district, and then a card saying that "Metropolitan Oil Co. Is on the Move." I found the city manager to be a big, self-assured man with positive views and seemingly no fear of speaking his mind. But he was bitter. His main gripe was the influx of young people over the past two years. As he told it, they contributed little to the town and its future while they alienated the natives by getting on the list for federal government surplus food distribution to the legitimate and hard-pressed poor, by running an arts and crafts store subsidized by federal funds, and by buying an old fish plant and maintaining it as a haven for transients and runaways. "They haven't taken time to wash the dirt off their faces," he said. "They purport to be craftsmen but they want someone else to pay for it."

He was worried about drugs and about the possibility of radical political action being generated by the newcomers. "Under the hippie umbrella, you have dope. I've had them in here that I'm sure are coming off a bad trip. The potential for danger worries me sick. They've got cadres, just like *we* have in the army. That fish plant, where they hang out, it's a cell. There must be a hundred of them out there."

In Jacobs's car we toured the town, really the whole of Moose Island, which is joined to the mainland by a causeway. Near the fish plant where Jacobs believed evil doings were being plotted, and where the young people ran a nursery school is an abandoned building, we were met by a pretty girl, attractively dressed and polite. "Good morning, Mr. Jacobs." She smiled and spoke to me. "Is there anything we can do here to help; can I show you around or answer any questions about our school?"

"No thanks," I said. "Not now. Maybe later."

We drove back and forth on the runway of the abandoned airport on Deep Cove. Metropolitan had acquired an option to this land. All told, the company had put together three hundred acres for which it paid about $90,000. Metropolitan had been looking into Eastport for seven years and would not give up the idea of a big refinery and transfer terminal there without a hard fight, Jacobs was certain.

"Who are the people who are unemployed, who are underpaid, and who really suffer here?" I asked.

He never answered the question, except to cut out on another line of attack. "For the people who really want to work, there's work in this town. There is activity here. There's an opportunity to work and some people just don't want to."

I drove away from Eastport without ever going back to the young people's school. It would have been interesting, but I had to move on to something else and I felt certain I would not learn a great deal more about Eastport, beyond the points of view expressed at the hearings. I realized I still had little feeling for the way Eastporters analyzed themselves and their future. But I was now convinced that Eastport was not the ideal place for a refinery. As the state study of the harbor, done by Robert Doyle, had noted: "The approaches are winding and the currents are extremely difficult to judge and handle. Very effective navigational controls would have to be employed if this harbor were to function as a major development area."

But it wasn't Doyle's assessment or the hearings that influenced my thinking about Eastport as much as the positive possibilities I saw for some far better solution. Conditions in Eastport might get worse, yet if people hung on I felt the area could prosper under controlled development of its recreational assets, even as a summer colony based on arts and crafts. My friend John Cole once suggested that a Washington County Authority should be established to manage a new kind of national park, a patchwork of open space tracts acquired from anybody who wanted to sell his land, decaying town properties and saltwater sections, purchased or protected by easement. Managing and restoring the scattered park holdings might provide several hundred jobs. A time will come when Cole's idea makes belated sense, when Washington County will wish it had indulged in some land banking. The trouble is that money is limited to finance this sort of visionary planning. Probably the best way of going about it is to set up an association of private and public interests, relying heavily on private venture capital with tax breaks, loan guarantees, and subsidy incentives available through the public sector and under government programs.

I too had in mind a Washington County Authority, but it would involve far more than recreational land use. My authority would *also* manage and revive a project that gave Eastport its greatest hope in modern times, the Passamaquoddy Tidal Project, harnessing the tremendous tides (they average over eighteen feet) to provide a significant amount of electrical power as well as becoming a *prototype* for tidal electric power in other select areas of the continent, notably the Pacific Northwest. Some people I talked to traced Eastport's decline and despair to the dashing of expectations that occurred when the U.S. Congress dropped the Passamaquoddy Project in 1937, after some seven million dollars had been expended and Quoddy Village built.

The project had sound roots. On a small scale, tidal dams were used in countless places along the Maine coast in the eighteenth and nineteenth centuries, always to provide power for some kind of a mill, or saws to cut wood and rock (slate and marble). In 1869, one Walter Wells wrote a paper on Maine water power and predicted that large-scale tidal power dams would someday be built. Such thinking was applied to hydroelectric power by a brilliant engineer named Dexter

P. Cooper, who talked about it with Franklin D. Roosevelt when the then assistant secretary of the navy was convalescing at Campobello. During his campaign for vice president in 1920, Roosevelt suggested in a speech at Eastport that a huge tidal power project held all sorts of possibilities. Beginning in 1924, Engineer Cooper conducted surveys for a proposal. There would, he projected, be two pools behind dams: an upper pool in Passamaquoddy Bay, with a low-water surface of roughly 100 square miles, and a lower pool in Cobscook Bay, the saltwater inlet just west of Moose Island (Eastport), with a surface of some 27 square miles. Hydroelectric turbines would turn out electricity in three phases. In the first phase the flooding tide would generate power in the upper pool dam, beginning when the tide level was equal to the level of the upper pool. In the second phase, both ocean dams would be closed and water would flow through a third set of turbines located in the narrow causeway to Moose Island, between Passamaquoddy and Cobscook bays, thus filling Cobscook Bay. In the final phase, when the ebb tide reached the level of the lower pool, the lower dam gates would be opened and power would be generated by water leaving Cobscook Bay.

Cooper figured that this unique facility would produce several billion kilowatt hours of electricity annually and would cost up to $100 million to construct. But the idea was in trouble from the very moment it was disclosed. Maine is dominated by private power. Two companies, Central Maine Power and Bangor Hydro-Electric Company, generate more than 90 percent of the state's electricity. These private interests, which had been getting their way in the state legislature for years, saw the Passamaquoddy Tidal Project as a terrible threat to their sovereignty. It would require public funds and government participation. It would generate enough power to compete for out-of-state markets. While early analysis indicated the Passamaquoddy rates would be very high — actually uneconomical — the concept had tremendous potential, *and in the long term would undoubtedly pay off*. It avoided most of, if not all, the ecological consequences of damming a river, and unlike a freshwater hydroelectric facility, the water supply was constant and uninterrupted. It would mean no pollution from combustion of coal or oil, no adverse thermal effects from steam condenser discharges that occur with both the fossil fuel and nuclear plants of today, no low-level radiation threats, and no problem with waste disposal, one of the most troubling considerations in nuclear power generation.

Roosevelt had great visions about the "Quoddy Project." In a private message to the governor of Maine he said, "It has been my hope that eventually the State of Maine would become not only a great industrial center of the nation but that its agricultural population would be among the first to enjoy manifest advantages of cheap electrical power on the farm as well." One must remember that this was written at a time when industrial growth and the increasing application of technology were the great hopes of America. Under the state, the Quoddy Hydro-Electric Commission planned an industrial complex at Eastport that would include manufacture of nickel alloy and steel, aluminum reduction, ceramic products made from local feldspars and clays, and various electrochemical materials produced from Maine's diverse and plentiful supply of minerals. Of course this industrial complex was conceived to use the vast amount of surplus power that the tidal project would generate. (In 1940, it would have produced 52.7 percent of Maine's power. Today, a two-pool Passamaquoddy project built to Cooper's specifications would generate no more than 10 percent of Maine's total needs.)

Opposition in the U.S. Congress, fear on the part of private power officials that another Tennessee Valley Administration would be born, and general lack of leadership and unity within the state doomed the Passamaquoddy Tidal Project. Because the upper pool depended upon Canadian cooperation, the project was reduced to a single pool facility on Cobscook Bay. Quoddy Village was built, and at one point five thousand men were employed in the construction of the first three exploratory dams, only two of which were completed. But the appropriations stopped in 1937 and Roosevelt never again pushed hard for the project, even though he maintained, "It is a fact that in eastern Maine the economic situation is, today, at its worse — for the forests have been cut off and the fisheries have greatly declined."

One day my wife and I were talking with R. Buckminster Fuller, a humane and visionary scientist, inventor of the geodesic dome. Harness the tides in the Bay of Fundy, Bucky advised. That's the future for Maine coastal development. As I left Eastport, I remembered his plan. It would have to involve Canada, of course, but already the government of Nova Scotia has created a Tidal Power Corporation with initial development funds of $10 million. Although tidal power would not relieve the East Coast energy crisis, it would contribute significantly to the needs of New England. Surely, if the march of technology cannot be slowed down or humanized, projects like this are far more worthy of the engineers' attention than the construction of oil refineries and nuclear plants elsewhere along the coast. Maybe the Passamaquoddy Tidal Project could be the core of clean industrial and port development in Eastport. The power could be used by new plants that would process the aquacultural harvest — from shellfish to seaweeds and mosses — and forest products. (Indeed, having an environmental authority with such direct control over the Eastport region would provide the ideal conditions for the sort of sea farming that has not yet been tried successfully in this country, a subject covered later in this book.) Eastport could be the center of residential development as well, homes restored and new units built for year-round citizens and seasonal colonists. The Washington County Authority could provide the leadership and direction for this development as well as manage the parklands scattered around the county.

Maybe these notions are too utopian. But I hope that somebody will take a long hard look at the prospects for them. I'm sure they would be better than oil in Eastport.

SCENARIOS

LET THE CANADIANS have their supertankers. Already they are dumping their oil cargoes at Point Tupper, Nova Scotia, and St. John, New
Brunswick. And a refinery is on the boards for a port called Come-
by-Chance, Newfoundland. Let the Canadians allow their offshore
fisheries — over 260 million acres, from Newfoundland to the eastern
nose of the Georges Bank — to be leased for oilfields. Sooner or
later, by all the laws of probability, there is going to be a big spill.
Then what? The marine biologists tell us the fishing will be ruined
for· several seasons as a result of a supertanker disaster. And the
accumulation of oil on the bottom from small accidents will take a
heavy toll even over the long stretch. Major General Francis P.
Koisch, as director of civil works for the Army Corps of Engineers,
wrote sobering words in a 1971 paper. "Imagine," he said, "the
damage which could result if a 312,000 DWT [deadweight ton] car-
rier, such as those which are now operating, were to spill its cargo of
2,250,000 barrels of oil. The cargo would have the potential of satu-
rating every foot of a 200-mile reach of shoreline with over two
barrels of crude oil."

Sadly enough, the coast that would be smeared would not necessarily be Nova Scotia's. Those counterclockwise currents I have referred to would most likely spin all the oil right on to the rockbound
coast of Maine. The governor of Maine is well aware of this, and one
of these days maybe he will get together with Canadian authorities
and work out a firm plan establishing procedures for dealing with
oil.

These procedures would cover:

— Regulations governing ship traffic under varying weather conditions.
— Sophisticated navigational and monitoring systems to prevent collisions and groundings and to detect accidents (or deliberate discharges of oil) the minute they happen.
— Ways to deal with accidents, the use of booms and other devices to contain oil, and salvage operations to minimize the extent of the damage.
— Environmental safeguards for offshore exploration and actual drilling. (Remember Santa Barbara and the Chevron fiasco in the Gulf of Mexico?)

In the meantime, Maine officials will keep on telling us that because the Canadians next door already have the oilmen, it makes no sense for Maine not to get a piece of the action.

I suppose that by now you may suspect that I am paranoid about oil coming to Maine. But I hope you will stop to reconsider the facts in the situation. Then maybe you will be just as apprehensive. The oilmen are knocking on the door. And as I see it, there are about three different ways to respond.

— Maine people and Maine leaders can be positively brilliant and solve the coastal dilemma.
— Maine can bend to political and practical realities.
— Maine can do nothing and probably lose the coast in the end.

Let's take them in that order.

The ideal solution would be for Maine to catch the Delaware fever. What's that? Well, actually, the only people who thought it was a bad disease were men like Maurice Stans, then secretary of commerce, who accused Delaware governor Russell W. Peterson of undermining the free enterprise system and damaging national security. Republican Peterson knew something about heavy industry. For twenty-seven years he was a research chemist with du Pont. He saw the debilitating influence on the coastal environment of refineries and a steel mill already located in Delaware. He didn't want it to spread, yet Shell Oil had plans for a refinery on 5,800 acres recently purchased near Smyrna; a thirteen-company consortium had plans for a major oil terminal in the middle of Delaware Bay; and a Texas firm proposed a facility in the bay to transfer coal and iron ore. So Peterson put a task force to work on the subject of coastal land use controls, and as a result of its recommendations he initiated the Delaware Coastal Zone Act of 1971, which barred all heavy industry from the 115 miles of state shoreline. Despite heavy pressure from federal officials, industry lobbyists, local chambers of commerce, and from within his own legislature, Peterson got the bill passed. In an interview for the *Saturday Review*, he said, "I think it's very important that all over America — all over the world, for that matter — people start drawing lines around choice pieces of real estate and say, look, this is off limits for certain kinds of operations." The possibilities of pollution were not all that bothered Peterson. He was moved mainly by the *positive* vision of the incalculable value of the superb reaches of a tidal estuary, its marshes and beaches, preserved in perpetuity for the people.

Applying Delaware to Maine, the legislature, in response to the feelings of Maine people, could pass a sweeping law to zone the entire coast against any *further* development by the oil, chemical and metal industries for purposes of transferring or processing materials. Alas, this will not prevent the federal government from encouraging an offshore terminal, a concept increasingly attractive as states along the entire eastern seaboard have become resistant to heavy industrial development on the coast. Delaware's Peterson fought federal backing of a supertanker facility off the mouth of Delaware Bay, beyond the state's three-mile limit. So did Maryland officials disapprove of plans for a terminal off Ocean City.

The Maine legislature has actually considered a bill that amounted to a weak version of the Delaware law. It was debated heatedly, then David Kennedy, sponsor of the legislation, withdrew it at the close of the 1972 winter legislative session as it seemed headed for defeat. Supporters wanted to preserve the chance for another go-around. Kennedy's bill proposed the creation of a Maine Industrial Port Authority that would confine new oil development to a single port in Maine, involve state backing and control over an industrial port complex, and disburse the benefits of such an activity to all Maine citizens. Moreover, the underlying premise of MIPA was a moratorium on pending oil developments until the single deepwater port was determined.

The bill was hastily put together and, in spite of dogged efforts by some fine people, like Portland lawyer Loyal Sewall, there were loopholes and weaknesses. The proposal posed a constitutional test by extending the power of eminent domain and committing public funds to large-scale private development. It specifically exempted oil transfer or storage facilities such as those already handling huge volumes of oil for overland shipment in South Portland. It was also not specific enough in spelling out enforcement of environmental safeguards by the Environmental Improvement Commission.

However, with the oilmen about to pounce, and with little means to stop them in a place like Eastport, many conservationists wished that MIPA had been passed as a tactical measure, with stronger amendments being attached in later sessions. While the moratorium might not be legally binding, no oil company would dare make a move until MIPA had settled on a port facility, these observers argued. Their spokesman, John Cole, summed up this view in an editorial in his *Maine Times*. "As much as we would like to see oil kept out altogether, we feel it would be irresponsible for the state not to prepare the institutions which can guarantee maximum protection and maximum benefits from any oil installation."

To continue the ideal scenario, the coast would be categorically zoned. Oil would continue to be transferred in small volumes at Searsport and in massive volumes at South Portland.

Certain kinds of deepwater development would be allowed. The town of Perry, at the head of Passamaquoddy Bay, would build a terminal to transfer agricultural products (mainly potatoes) coming from Aroostook County. Eastport would develop a sort of TVA complex combining management of recreation and a tidal power facility. The power might be used by light industries or fish products' processors. Penobscot Bay, Blue Hill and Frenchman's Bay, Boothbay and Casco Bay would develop shipbuilding industries on a scale commensurate with their environmental limitations. An all-encompassing coastal zoning act, enforced by a Maine Coast Authority, would also regulate recreational developments and summer colonies. It would also depend on new enabling legislation, so that tidal waters could be reserved for sea farming. Maine coastal communities thus would prosper in two distinct realms: the modern industrial-technological society, and the world of tradition wherein the occupational skills of the past are carried through the present and into the future.

Now let's explore the scenario of expediency. Just as Bantry Bay has become an oilfield for Europe, so Maine is eyed as an oilfield for northeastern markets. What does this mean? Presently, Gulf Oil Corporation sends 325,000 DWT tankers from the Persian Gulf to the terminal on the west coast of Ireland. Enormous savings result from shipping oil in such great volume. Then, *close to the market*, small tankers take oil from Bantry Bay's storage facilities and deliver it to ports in Europe. The oilmen see Maine in this light. The super-tankers would make great economic savings by getting the oil as far as, say, Eastport. It would be pumped to a tank farm and then either piped to eastern markets or transshipped by coastal barge and tankers.

In this scenario, Maine legislators would finally establish some kind of Maine Industrial Port Authority (instead of a Maine Coast Authority with sweeping power) and eventually authorize the expansion of Maine's *existing oilfield*, Portland, where the Citizens Who Care have girded themselves for a showdown with the oilmen. The point is that Portland is the second biggest oil port on the East Coast, even though most of the oil is pumped through a pipeline to Montreal, Canada. In 1969, some 142 million barrels of crude oil were unloaded by 438 tankers at the South Portland pipeline. Only 22 million barrels were unloaded for domestic use.

Recognizing that Portland already is an advanced industrial center, the Maine legislature would insure that continued oil development in this port was regulated by tight environmental provisions, and that the benefits of expansion were bestowed upon the state as a whole.

Then there are some options within the range of practical alternatives:

— Long Island (the old navy fuel depot) finally would be expanded into a terminal able to receive supertankers. Oil would be piped to South Portland and a refinery built there.
— Long Island would become an oil terminal, but the oil would be refined inland by tapping into the pipelines that run to Montreal. An inland refinery, for example, in a place like Sanford, would be no less of an environmental hazard, only it would not ruin an area that is as extremely fragile and subject to such population pressures as the coast.
— An oil terminal would be built on the outside of Long Island or

just offshore. Thus it would not be necessary to blast a channel and the overall navigational risks would be less. The oil would be piped to refineries in South Portland or inland to Sanford.

The final scenario begins with what might have been an extension or variation of the last, except that it is a truly short-sighted measure of expediency and simply must not be considered as a *practical* alternative. Portland oil operations would be expanded *while Eastport also would become an oil center.*

As I write this, it is quite possible that the expedient alternative will prevail. If Eastport were an important summer colony, if the EIC had not already held off the oilmen in two battles, I would not be so pessimistic. However, the oilmen have had time to overcome the objections raised in previous confrontations and, because of its seeming economic needs, Eastport may be the sacrificial victim. I think David Kennedy will find that his contention that oil could be kept at opposite ends of the state was naive. When you're dealing with supertankers, you're into a whole new order of magnitude — you've taken a quantum jump, as the bureaucrats like to say. *Big development.* Big development triggers a wave of satellite industries and second-rate recreational developments that will converge between Portland and Eastport like two ugly pincers.*

Before the wild parts of the coast are destroyed on land, there will be an accident, or the routine day-to-day spillage will bring about the devastation of Maine's coastal fisheries. Crude oil, distilled products

*As this book was going to press, the governor's Coastal Commission made recommendations that came close to my scenario. They proposed that heavy industry on the coast be planned, developed and regulated by a Maine Industrial Development Corporation, and that such development be limited to two regions — Portland and Machias Bay. Eastport was ruled out for heavy industry — at least an oil refinery — because of its two-nation channel and approaches, tricky currents and tides, and because, I was overjoyed to see, the commission felt that a future version of the Passamaquoddy Tidal Project should not be foreclosed. At the same time, it was held by many of the commission members that, since an oil proposal here was imminent, Eastport's suitability should be left in the hands of the Environmental Improvement Commission. While Machias Bay was designated for heavy industry, Commission Chairman Fisher urged that "oil and related facilities" not be planned until there was "further assurance that such activities will not constitute too great a risk of damage especially to the quality of the water in that presently unindustrialized bay." In recommending that a second industrial zone be created, the commission noted that Washington County needed an economic boost, that land was scarce around Portland, that the Casco Bay channels would have to be blasted and dredged to handle the largest (300,000 DWT) supertankers, and that, in general, a second option provided planning flexibility. As for large power plants — conventional or nuclear — the commission said they should be assessed individually, as they were proposed, in terms of the environmental impact not only of the plants themselves but of their transmission lines.

— it doesn't matter. To one degree or another they all contain acutely toxic hydrocarbons that become dispersed in the ocean or sink to the bottom to become a part of the bottom sediments. Marine plant life, plankton and other small organisms are contaminated. The hydrocarbons move through the food chain of larger fishes and shellfish. And by destroying bottom organisms, the oil reduces the holding capacity of the bottom sediments, and so the contamination is made even easier as these sediments shift and move great distances. Since at least 70 percent of our commercial fishing catch depends on the coastal waters as a spawning area, a nursery, or feeding territory, which is already menaced by the annual accumulation of millions of tons of oil, from deliberate bilge cleaning and from small accidents at transfer sites, the sea fishery that has meant so much to Maine and New England would become past history.

This is the third scenario.

TWO

Coastal Options

BASIS FOR ACTION

MANY DIFFERENT SOLUTIONS to the coastal dilemma have been proposed, ranging from new kinds of boatbuilding and fisheries operations to an industrial port authority. By and large, it seems to me, there are two basic approaches to the overall problem.

Most important, coastal townspeople, vacation colonists, and the growing number of summer-visitors-turned-permanent-residents must independently or all together put into practice various land conservation methods. After a solid land use framework is established in coastal communities, it will be easier to judge or apply different developmental strategies.

At the same time, traditional activities, the underpinnings of coastal life, must be reassessed and modified so that they will continue to be the major contributions to the coastal economy. These activities — three of them — are boatbuilding, fishing, and summer colonies. They are comparatively nonpolluting. And already they have influenced the ways of life of coastal natives to such an extent that quite different forms of industry would create a social upheaval, regardless of their environmental impact, and in the long term I think the economy would benefit little. In any case, if new industry is found to be desirable it ought to be compatible with the existing activities. For example, different forms of food processing require the same skills as the preparation of fisheries' products.

Summer colonies are, of course, an integral part of the Maine "Vacationland," and will be treated again in Chapter 7. They are also inextricably tied to coastal issues, if for no other reason than because the most vociferous opponents of industrial development of the coast include men of industry and the legatees of industrial fortunes who spend moments of leisure in a summer colony.

THE BOATBUILDERS

BOATBUILDING IS THE ULTIMATE WOODCRAFT, the extreme limit of possibilities in the use of woods. Perhaps no other craft demands a wider array of talents. And few other professions compare to boatbuilding as a way of developing the pride of a seaboard town. The people of Maine have carried the art to its supreme height. And boatbuilding still is the native, *nonpolluting* industry of greatest potential to the coast.

On the eve of the Civil War, half the wooden ships then in commission under the U.S. flag had originally slid down Maine ways. Even around 1870, when the age of steel signaled a downturn in the state's economy, Maine shipyards continued to turn out the best wooden vessels that money could buy (as if money was all that counted). In the Casco Bay town of Yarmouth, in the mid-seventies, there was a ship-launching about every six weeks — some big ships, too, like the 1,979-ton *Commodore* and the 2,209-ton *Admiral*.

"Seasonal symphonies" is the way Robert P. Tristram Coffin described the cycles of ship construction in his book, *Kennebec*. "The keel was laid when the grass showed its first green around it," he wrote. "Their planking was finished when the goldenrod blossomed. And they usually went in to the river to meet the rising of the harvest moon. A launching meant the end of two seasons of hard work."

The first vessel built by Englishmen in the New World was the *Virginia*, a 30-ton pinnace built in the fall of 1607 by the men of the short-lived Popham Colony. Later the king's men invaded the forest for masts. By 1691, the Massachusetts Colony Charter reserved all white pine two feet in diameter one foot above ground and standing on land not yet granted as private property. Surveyors set forth into the wilderness to mark such behemoths with three slashes, called the broad arrow. Anyone who felled a broad arrow pine without a license to do so was fined 100 pounds. It wasn't long before the coast corridor was stripped of masts and the surveyors had to search more than twenty miles inland.

Fishing, coastal trade, and commerce with the Old World all depended on ships, and Maine was ideally set up for boatbuilding. The plentitude of native timber was a prime consideration, but its ultimate asset was the abundance of sheltered rivers and coves where the work could be done.

The nineteenth century was Maine's Golden Age, and coastal Maine has never been the same since. "The shipbuilding was like a fever," Coffin wrote, and even inland towns, joined to saltwater by the merest tidal streams, were infected. There are numerous accounts of finished hulls being dragged by oxen down brooks, across mudflats, even through fields. At least once a ship was even built in Lisbon, then dragged by oxen around Androscoggin Falls and launched in Brunswick.

The shipwrights required a steady flow of native woods: white oak for stem and stern pieces, as well as the frames; cedar and yellow pine for planking; white pine for masts; spruce for spars and joists; hackmatack and juniper for the knees; maple for the inside cabinets and joiner work; white ash for oars; elm for the keel. Except for the butt ends of the planks, which were nailed down with bolts and spikes, even the fastenings were wood — pegs called treenails (pronounced trunnels) made from locust.

The aroma and the different shapes and textures of these woods, blended together, were a sensual thing, a solidarity unto itself, an extension of both nature and man, a vital composition. Both the materials and the men crafting them were strong individually. When the finished work was a perfect harmony, when the creators stood in unison, you had the American equivalent of a Chartres or Cologne — the summa of originality, hard work, love and dignity.

The carpenter mastered the broad-ax, handsaw, and pod augur. The shipsmith and his helpers forged virtually every piece of metal that went into the ship. The painters produced their own shellacs and varnishes from local spruce gum. Local shops produced rope, sails, anchors, windlasses, blocks, chains; even the bread and salt pork that would feed the crew was locally made. The Maine coastal towns put body and soul into their ships.

Nowadays, Maine shipbuilders order most of their materials, by phone and by catalogue, from suppliers and manufacturers the world over. These components often are crude and flimsy, the products of men who have no understanding of the ways and demands of a ship. But the men who do the building and launching have changed little. They are hard and proud.

One of them recently built a boat for a friend of mine. His boat shed was a graying ruin above the mudflats. The roof slumped, the sides bowed outward, tarpaper was peeling, and the planks had weathered all they could. But inside was something else. There it was natural to presume that the boatbuilder was the most gifted creator of small fishing and lobstering hulls along the entire coast of Maine, maybe in this whole universe. You'd stand for an hour taking the pulse of the work — the whining of saws, the hammering on chisels and nails, the talk and the smell of wood and wood shavings — and hear the boatbuilder explain the phases of construction, and you'd be taken, swept into a different world, an America that has all but vanished.

I had heard that this man was as canny as the most renowned yacht designer, that he could predict exactly how any of his boats would float on its intended lines. He had designed all but one of the seventy-five or so boats that he'd built since World War II. (The exception was a schooner that he didn't like much but built anyway, after a good deal of pleading on the part of the owners. A woodcarver of great skill, he had done a beautiful figurehead for that schooner.)

He was hard to get to know, much less understand. I visited the shed half a dozen times, alone or with my friend. I asked him questions from time to time, although I didn't press — except once, at the end. But I could never fathom the workings of the mind within. He wasn't deceptive. But he was proud in the best sense, even arrogant. And he hid that pride under a cloak of shyness or barrages of short, pithy statements about his way of life and mankind at large, the sort of sayings that are the basis of downeast anecdotes.

Business was bad. Very bad. But you wouldn't have known it at that moment when I first visited him in January 1971. The boat being built for my friend was really something, patterned after the traditional lobster boat with a sweeping, exaggerated, sheer and simple pilot house. But that was the only similarity. The boat would be inordinately light, eight thousand pounds distributed over 38 feet, and very narrow, 10 feet. Oak frames $1\frac{1}{4}$ by $1\frac{1}{2}$ inches, very light, covered with 1-inch-thick native cedar planking, fastened by galvanized nails. Most workboats carry a skeg — they're easier to build that way. Not this one. Her bilges dropped right down to the keel, so that viewed from her ends she had the classic wineglass shape, not the shallow V so typical of lobster craft. Top controls and a flying bridge, a long pulpit for tuna fishing. And you could slide out the transom, in two sections, so as to launch a dory overboard from out of the cockpit, for duck shooting or getting in close for surf fishing. The engine was an 8V53 Detroit diesel that would produce 238 horsepower and plenty of speed.

Behind this beauty was a nearly finished 55-foot dragger, to be put to work fishing for shrimp and whiting by an ambitious and successful young fisherman from a nearby town. The dragger was built of oak frames and planking twice as thick and heavy as that used on my friend's. This was the kind of vessel that the boatbuilder was famous for.

But business was bad. For the first time in five years the boatbuilder had nothing to follow these two boats. Already his crew had dropped from thirteen to eight men, and without steady jobs to offer them he would certainly lose more. These were men with traditional skills, long trained by experience, who could not be replaced in today's labor market. Yet, as the boatbuilder said, with resignation, "They can get more as house carpenters."

But he was optimistic — at least he pretended to be. He was dead set against advertising and he didn't bother to belong to the state boatbuilders' association. He was sure his reputation would carry him through. "I've been in this long enough so the fishermen know me and I know what they want," he would say. "Yachts? I don't like 'em. The outsiders want to bargain. A boat costs what it costs and that's the best that I can do."

One day we went up to his office and he showed me his drawing table. "This is what I like to do most of all now, design 'em," he said. He darted under a pile of blueprints and got out a half-model he had found in a barn. It was damaged and weathered, but not too badly. During an entire winter's long evenings he had taken the lines off the model and drawn complete plans. He had traced the plans to a local designer who was long since dead. It was a mackerel schooner, circa 1870, similar to six other schooners built from the designer's plans. "Her helm's not balanced right," the boatbuilder said, noting the wide space between the masts, made necessary to provide working space on deck and room for dories. To his knowledge this schooner had never been built. It wasn't his design, but he'd love to see it afloat.

It wasn't until the next December that I returned to the shed. I'd missed the launchings of the dragger, attended by nearly a hundred happy people, and my friend's half-yacht, which had been floated without fanfare. This time I wanted to sit down and take some notes.

Before, when I entered the shed, there was so much business going on that I could stand and watch, unnoticed, until there was an opening for a remark, a question, an observation. And then I would blend back in to the surroundings and not have to say a word for another fifteen minutes or more. This time it was painfully different. A cold, southwest wind buffeted the building and kept right on going, boring through the cracks and openings and cycloning around the inside. There was nothing to stop it. The shed was bare.

I gestured self-consciously. "Kind of empty in here," I said. "Not like it was last time."

The boatbuilder was chiseling on the stem piece of his next boat, a 33-foot lobster boat built on speculation. A young son was planing the oak for the keel. The crew was down to three men, besides the boatbuilder, but they were all away remodeling his sister's house. The spec boat would sell all right and it would serve to keep the men on tap for future business, but it would have to sell cheap to compete with the home-built lobster boats. "If we only lose $500 on this, we'll be happy," he said.

He was festering. As we walked from the shed up a short path to his office, he couldn't conceal his feelings. But it was the only moment he allowed. "There's no money in it. It isn't going to last," he muttered.

Inside, among the clutter of papers, rolls of boat plans, marine paraphernalia that he collects (including an antique outboard propeller converted to a lamp stand, and a huge cylinder head), he became cryptic again. He told about the man who'd recently come to see whether the yard could do a 45-foot offshore lobster boat. "I didn't like his looks and I don't think he liked mine," he said. And that was that.

I commented on his designs — lovely, painstaking drawings, many done on linen. He had spent well over a week, he said, doing plans of a classic model of a 36-foot Friendship sloop. They were based on his experience building maybe ten of these boats. Yet when the lines of the sloop were published, there had been no interest in getting one built. And a man who wanted to purchase just the plans had balked at the price, $125, though it was not much for a week's work and, indeed, a great bargain, considering the quality of the drawings.

I asked whether any young people were coming around, looking for work, and he was skeptical. "If they'd get a haircut and shave," he said, "somebody might hire them."

What had happened to his kind of boatbuilding?

"Fiber glass. Fiber glass. I detest it," the boatbuilder answered. The new material, lacking in beauty, requiring little skill to work with, fit only for mass production, had taken away the occasional pleasure boat that he used to depend upon to keep the business going.

Some Maine builders, larger operations, had taken up fiber glass construction, but there were drawbacks. You have to work with the material at warm temperatures (around seventy degrees), extremely expensive conditions to obtain in a Maine shed during the bitter winter. In California and Florida, fiber glass boatbuilding takes place on a mass scale, in plants, not shops, where the climate is balmy all year. And the environmental cost of fiber glass is high. It is composed of synthetic materials that use up vast amounts of energy to convert to finished products. Nobody can say with certainty whether fiber glass boats will outlast wood ones that are well maintained. The fiber glass continues to cure; it gets brittle and spongy. I know. I own a fiber glass sloop molded in 1964.

But fiber glass requires very little basic maintenance, whereas wood needs love and care. In this day and age, people don't have time for that. Or so it seems. To own a boat is to have it for *use* only, on the weekends of the warm months. You telephone the yard or marina where you keep it and ask them to put it in shape — dewinterize the engine, slap on a coat of deck paint, clean the bottom, and add a coat of antifouling each year. That's it.

With wood, the boatowner comes to know both the material and the capacity of the boat. At sea the wood hull seems to ride better, is more sea-kindly, as they say. But maybe this is an illusion, a prejudice. Then there is the annual scraping or sanding, depending on the condition of the paint and varnish surfaces. The bilges have to be protected and the dead spaces kept well ventilated to avoid rotting. Fastenings need to be checked constantly and sometimes the boat hauled and refastened entirely — a costly job.

If we would only stop to consider our boats an extension of ourselves, to be respected, given the best care and understood. (Maybe this will happen inadvertently, when so many people crowd the waterways that boatowners will escape the mayhem by spending more time in port.) You have to learn a lot about the basic structure of a wood boat, what went into it, where the stress points lie. I keep thinking that the art of wood boatbuilding is not dead, that there will be a revival in the postindustrial age or sooner. That people may get sick and tired of mass-produced hulls that they never get to know. Thank God the Maine fisherman has so far resisted fiber glass, although this barrier has begun to fall, and certainly steel has become an accepted material for larger fishing boats.

Whether there will be changes in time for the boatbuilder is anybody's guess. Certainly the future was preying on his mind. I spotted a hunk of wood, which looked like the butt of a mast, poking out under a sack. "What've you got on this pedestal?" I asked. I should have suspected, because of all the shavings on the floor.

He smiled and lifted the cover. And there it was, a fine likeness, the sculpted head of the boatbuilder himself, with pencil markings on some of the features where he would next work the knife.

"How did you do it?" I asked.

He pointed to a small mirror on the bench and some color snapshots of himself in a checked shirt, looking off in different directions.

I imagined that it must be a work of deep revelation. An excursion of the ego, combined with the urge to find some way to elevate his talent, his residual creativity and strength, to reach above the difficult times, to stare out over the bad seas and bone-chilling southwesters that whistled down the cove, carrying no joy into that boat shed and the lives of the men working in it, or out of work.

The man was decent, humorous, gentle. He was also tough and effective. And a bit mad, as we all should be in good times as well as in bad. "Crazy," his son said, grinning, when his father told me about a horse race he had watched. The horses were turning it on, straining into the backstretch, but, he said, all he could see was one of the boats he was then building, gliding along, taking the seas in stride, a vision of beauty and strength.

Not every Maine boatbuilder carried his individualism this far. Some had realized for a long time, in fact, that the future lay in making adjustments and compromises to stay with the times. On a larger scale — his shop was four times as big — Harvey Gamage was the prime example.

Discounting the period of the Second World War, when, like many other Maine boatbuilders, he was kept busy for Uncle Sam, Harvey hit his peak around 1960. At that time, according to the December 1961 issue of *Fish Boat*, Harvey was master builder over twenty-one other craftsmen. There were ten carpenters, including octogenarian Merton Stapels, a man whose skill with an old-fashioned hand adz was renowned along the entire coast. Bob Woodward was office manager, just as he was a decade later. Rounding out the crew were a joiner, five mechanics, a welder, an electrician and two painters. It was a tightly knit group of men who made the little boatbuilding center of South Bristol rightly proud. It was also in the tradition of the family boatyard. Including the head man, there were four on the payroll named Gamage. "Down east," said the article in *Fish Boat*, "the word 'dragger' has become practically synonymous with one man."

These Gamage draggers were seventy to eighty feet of functional security out in the winter gales of the Georges Banks — oaken beauties like the *Sea Gold, Four Brothers, Grace and Salvatore, Neptune, Antonina, Valiant Lady, Ike and Jens,* and *Angela W.* Their beauty lay not so much in their looks as in the fact that they were put together of the strongest materials and fastenings with extraordinary precision and craftsmanship, and were built quite literally to last half a century. Consider the specifications of the *Angela W.*, a seventy-three-foot dragger launched on October 25, 1961. Keel: 9-inch oak. Frames: 3-inch oak, double sawn. Planking: 2-inch oak. Deck: 2½-inch pine. Fastenings: galvanized bolts (frames) and nails (planks). Engine: 380 hp "Caterpillar" diesel. *Angela W*.'s fo'c's'le held eight bunks that would be secure in a rolling sea. While the finest mahogany was used to trim the joiner work, the emphasis was on durability. There was a huge "Shipmate" galley stove, a big ice-box, a stainless steel sink, and a hot water system. This working boat had what was essential for comfort. No more. She was a real bruiser.

Ten years after the *Angela W*. slid down the ways, in the spring of 1971, a heart attack slowed up Harvey Gamage, then seventy-three years of age and in his sixty-first year of working on boats. Conditions in the business, and in the yard, had changed from the previous decade, but Harvey was still at the top, getting the pick of the few orders that were placed. That very year, the ninety-five-foot topsail schooner *Bill of Rights* was launched, just one of the traditional sailing replicas that the Gamage yard has been called upon to build in recent years. There was the *May Day* in 1962, the *Shenandoah* in 1964, and the celebrated Hudson river sloop *Clearwater* in 1969 — the craft used by folk singer Pete Seeger to dramatize the battle against pollution on the Hudson River and other U.S. waterways.

I stopped by the yard to meet Harvey Gamage in March 1972. It was the first time I had been in South Bristol and I found the boat-builder almost impossible to interview. (Even before I walked into his office, I was badly unnerved by the furious, protective rush of a German shepherd named Lady.) "Are you Mr. Gamage?" I asked the first man I saw, working at a desk.

"I'm Bob Woodward," he replied. We shook hands, and then he gestured to another man who sat directly in the rays of bright sunshine that streamed through a window. His chair was pulled back behind the second desk in the room. He wore the gray bill-cap and the blue denim frockcoat with brass buttons that I had read about. This was Harvey Gamage.

He smiled shyly and said nothing. I had to open and then carry the conversation. He was so laconic that I had no time during his responses to reflect on the direction of the discussion. Nor did he say anything on a particular subject that would keep that line open by provoking further questioning.

"How's the future for wooden boats?" I asked.

"Wood played out, so we went to steel," Harvey answered. "There are no caulkers left. No woodworkers left."

I knew already that there was only one skilled caulker at work along the entire coast. He was Lestyn Thompson of Friendship, and he was on the move constantly, going from yard to yard to fill the seams between the planks of the last wood boats.

At one point, Harvey took from his drawer a carborundum used for knife sharpening and began to file his fingernails with it. Here was an opportunity to lighten the conversation.

"Why, that's a great tool for a manicure," I exclaimed.

He muttered something that I could not follow. Then he offered me the use of the carborundum.

I asked him if he could give me a quick tour of the yard. I should have done so at the outset, because while we inspected half-models of past creations, looked at the patterns on the loft floor, and walked across several empty bays to where two steel boats were being welded together, Harvey was much more at ease. Below the loft, he pointed to a hull of around thirty-five feet, already planked in Philippine mahogany, with a lovely sheer and flared bow. This had to be the boat he was doing himself. I'd read in the *National Fisherman* how he had laid the keel and explained, "I've got to stay close in case some of the boys run into problems — so I might as well be doing something."

The doctors had told him to take it easy, Harvey said to me, but by ordering him to take a. long midday nap they had made it impossible for him to drive to Florida, where he longed to be, far from the bitter cold and on his first vacation in many decades. So instead he was pouring himself into the activity that gave him the greatest pleasure. "I still play at it," he said. "I've done about half the work myself; I'm setting her up as a lobster boat."

Building minesweepers for the navy had brought 135 men into the Gamage works, but now the crew was down to 18, the lowest number in thirty years, said Harvey. The last wooden order was the sixty-three-foot dragger *Acme,* launched the month before. The launch ways had barely stopped smoking when patterns were brought out to cut the steel sides of a thirty-foot self-propelled work barge that would haul supplies to an island near Bremen. Next to the barge, masked welders were finishing a forty-six-foot steel dragger.

The yard was able to adapt to steel easily. Harvey's men had previously worked a lot with this and other heavy metals, forging deck plates, making sheathing and various other fittings to reinforce the wooden draggers. A steel boat took as long to construct as one of wood, Harvey said, and it cost no less either. But once in the water, the annual maintenance expenses were substantially lower. Harvey's son Lynnwood, twenty-eight, was in charge of steel construction. He was optimistic. With steel they had been able to stay in business, said Lynnwood, and there was no reason why they couldn't keep it up.

I walked with Harvey through the two enormous bays, seemingly as big as airplane hangars, where the *Bill of Rights* and the *Clearwater* had stood not long ago. Harvey moved deliberately, looking around him in the cavernous empty space. "At one time we had a 100-footer here and a 120-footer going over there at the same time," he said.

Until the last wooden vessels slid down the ways, Harvey Gamage built a boat just the same way his forebears made the *Jenny Lind* back in 1845. Harvey himself still worked with the wooden planes of his grandfather, Lynnwood A. Gamage, who took up boatbuilding in 1854.

First he would carve a wood model so as to see for himself on a miniature scale exactly what he would obtain when he composed the full-size lines in the loft. If a customer submitted blueprints, Harvey still would carve a half-model. On the floor of the loft, he would lay down the lines, transposed from the model, using compass, straight-edge, chalk line and battens; and trace each frame, the keel lines, stem and stern post.

Then moulds or templates would be cut from light pine to fit the loft patterns. From these, frames, stem, keel and other timbers would be cut. Then the keel and false keel would be laid, stretched out across a row of blocks, high enough so men could work underneath the hull. Then the frames would be fitted, steamed so they could be bent to the proper shape, temporarily held in place by a wood framework and horizontal strips called "ribbands." The best piece of white oak that Harvey could find would be carved into the stem piece. Next the deck beams would be put down and the hull planked, first inside, then outside. Then would come the caulking. In the old days oakum — but later cotton rope — would be forced into the seams, hammered with a mallet and sealed with melted pitch or tar.

Finally, the boat would be finished off inside, the engine bedded down and aligned, the pilot house and all its complicated equipment assembled, and the crew's quarters dressed up. Painted and with stress areas sheathed with copper or steel, the boat was ready for launching. Nearly all of the 253 boats that had been launched under Harvey Gamage's name were built in this manner.

And that explains why, a few years ago, Governor Curtis presented Harvey with an award for his "contribution to the state's cultural life." Bob Woodward showed me this trophy after Harvey had left for lunch and his nap. We both smiled. It was made of gleaming metal and neither of us could determine exactly what it depicted. It was a far cry from the cultural contributions that came from Harvey's yard.

I drove away from South Bristol thinking that the Gamage style of boatbuilding was a lot more than a cultural attraction, even if his half-models were sought after by the Bath Museum and the traditional profession was considered a dying art. I felt certain that Maine's boatbuilders had a place in the future. Some would move into steel and fiber glass and even aluminum. Already, Bob Hinckley's yard in Southwest Harbor had won a reputation for moulding, *and* finishing off in wood and other materials, yachts equal to the highest caliber in the world. Merle Hallett's Handy Boat Works in Falmouth Foreside was doing the interior finishing-off work on fiber glass yachts moulded in parts of the country where manual craftsmanship is nontraditional.

Yet I was hoping most of all that there would still be a demand for custom boats finely crafted from wood — particularly because fiber glass and aluminum are nonrenewable materials that have a high environmental cost in terms of the energy consumed in producing them. Maybe as a final resort, I thought, Maine's coastal woodworkers could turn to the increasingly lucrative market for custombuilt furniture — desks, chairs, tables and cabinets — the sort of articles that one likes to pass along in the family. Maine has the men, the materials and the proximity to the market to exploit this opportunity.

Only on second thought it was hard to imagine men like Harvey Gamage committing themselves to furniture as long as there was the remotest chance of building something that would float.

FARMING THE SEA

OBSCURED OR OVERLOOKED ENTIRELY in public debates and policy discussions concerning coastal land use is a consideration that may well turn out to be the most important of all: the potential of cultivating Maine's marine resources, from seaweed to salmon. The key word is *aquaculture*. It has various definitions going back at least as far as 475 B.C., when a Chinese scholar named Fan Li wrote a treatise on the enormous potential of ponds, streams, bays and estuaries for food production. A federal government report in 1968 defined aquaculture as "the rearing of aquatic organisms under controlled conditions using the techniques of agriculture and animal husbandry." That's good enough for me.

The area where sea farming can take place is larger than the whole of the Maine land mass since it really extends from the head of river tidewaters (as far inland as 40 miles) all the way out to the edge of the Continental Shelf, 200 miles off shore. However, aquaculture should be concentrated mainly near the coast.

This aquatic territory is terribly fragile from an environmental standpoint, as complex and sensitive as any other kind of ecosystem. Already lack of conservation has led to a grave depletion in the renowned Georges Bank and Gulf of Maine fishery. Sewage and other forms of pollution have degraded the richest estuaries. And the lobster, once so plentiful that it was simply gathered up from among the rocks at low tide, is on the brink of being fished out.

The Task Force on Energy, Heavy Industry and the Maine Coast, which I have already mentioned, did not once refer to aquaculture in its conclusions and recommendations, even though it cited the danger of "uncontrolled recreational growth." The group's report evaded the issue, or dismissed it, with the comments that "Aquaculture in Maine is confronted by uncertain economics and legal barriers to ocean floor leasing" and "Whether or not the legal obstacles are removed and pilot projects undertaken in the near future, significant aquaculture impact on the Maine coastal economy in the next five years is unlikely."

The first observation is true and the second may be. However, if options are to be preserevd for the long stretch, it is vital to incorporate aquaculture in all *present* coastal land use planning, and even to integrate it with concepts for a heavy industrial port. "Clearly there is little point in spending great efforts in developing marine resources if the industry is constantly threatened with the possibility of harmful shoreside development," said Spencer Apollonio, the new director of the Maine Department of Sea and Shore Fisheries, at a 1972 conference. While this is all too true, the planning and regulating of coastal development goes right on with little or no attention paid to the way land use patterns determine access to, and use of, estuarine and coastal waters. The prevailing attitude seems to be that the clam flats can be revived once other problems are solved. But what if by then there are no fishermen left and the coastal towns, through inaction or superimposed economies alien to their traditions have abandoned the ways of the sea altogether?

The sea farmers' most vehement spokesman is Robert Dow, director of marine research for Sea and Shore Fisheries, a biologist who as long ago as 1947 asserted in a report for the state that "the natural resources of the coastal waters aggregate the most valuable backlog of natural resources this state enjoys, not excepting the timber resources."

Bob Dow and various associates have conducted successful though small demonstrations for more than two decades. He has given me various papers and reports he has written alone or co-authored, and they rise up in a tower to the edge of my desk. These presentations show very convincingly that there are countless coves, thoroughfares, tidal inlets, river mouths, and tide flats in Maine with conditions suited for the cultivation of such resources as clams, lobsters, mussels, oysters, quahogs, crabs, scallops, shrimp, trout, salmon, bloodworm (for bait), and seaweed (Irish moss). Some will do much better than others. Some will not do well unless environmental adjustments are made, adjustments that are well within reason. Some will be cultivated inshore and harvested offshore. If all of the experiments conducted just up until 1955 had been implemented on a commercial scale, Bob has insisted many times, the annual value of aquacultural production in Maine would have approached $300 million.

There are two ways of achieving his objective, Bob says, through *culture* and through *management*. Culture involves manipulation of different species — for example, breeding, cross-breeding, or improving their diet. Management consists of controlling and even using artificial means to create the environments where culture takes place.

An example of culture was the experiment in rearing lobster larvae at a laboratory in Boothbay as early as 1939. When lobsters hatched before the middle of June did not survive their fourth stage because the water was still too cold, management was introduced: the water was heated to seventy degrees. Survival rates jumped too. Since it takes the lobster five years to reach minimum commercial size, it is not at the top of Dow's agenda for aquaculture, although he thinks that management techniques could help considerably. For example, since lobster feed more actively in warm water periods, an increase in water temperatures of only several degrees would encourage faster growth rates. This most likely can only be done under tightly controlled environmental conditions, e.g., in a bay or harbor where the effects of cold currents can be minimized or negated.

There has been much talk about turning the thermal discharges of power plants, notably nuclear plants, to beneficial use by allowing this hot "cooling water" to warm up coastal fisheries. Dow cautions about this, however. It probably will be possible someday, but at present, power plant discharges contain trace metals such as copper, zinc, aluminum and stainless steel and such harmful chemicals as chlorine, hydrochloric acid, sulfuric acid, sodium hydroxide and detergents. Nor has the cumulative effect of low-level radiation from nuclear plants been clearly defined. But with heat exchangers or improved technology ("thermal enhancement," as the power people call it), it might become a reality. Even then, there still will be many difficult engineering problems in managing and circulating hot water discharges so as to exert the correct degree of influence on colder waters.

Dow is most sanguine, though, about turning promptly to the farming of such resources as oysters, quahogs and blue mussels. The American oyster was a favorite of the coastal Indians, as the incredible shell heaps at Damariscotta attest. Recent experiments with both American and European oysters have been successful beyond all expectations. Under the auspices of the Ira C. Darling Center, the University of Maine's marine research laboratory in Walpole, oysters placed in Casco Bay, the Sheepscot and Damariscotta estuaries, and in Penobscot and Blue Hill bays grew at the astonishing rate of more than a hundred percent in less than three months. The European oysters do better than the Americans in colder water, but that only means that the Maine coast, with its warm estuaries and cold bay and island currents, can accommodate both kinds. If the oysters are suspended underwater on lines hung from rafts during the early growing period, they will escape predation by their natural enemies, drills and starfish.

The Darling Center projects led Dr. David Dean, its director, to predict the production of a marketable half-shell oyster by 1974. Within five years, he said, supporting Bob Dow, Maine could have a multimillion dollar aquaculture industry with select coves set aside as farms for oysters, scallops, mussels, rock crabs and quahogs.

There is abundant evidence, then, that Maine is the place for the sea farmer's wildest dreams to come true. With its indentations, bays and island chains presenting a plentitude of nearly self-contained and extremely diverse marine ecosystems, with a stable and geologically ideal set of bottom characteristics, with wonderful water circulation, currents sweeping in continual new amounts of ocean nutrients, Maine is, as Dow says, "one of the most outstanding places in the world for aquaculture." He also likes to point out that the east-west coastal axis thrusts its many openings southward so that the effect of solar radiation is amplified, making Maine's coastal waters produce far more food than in any other comparable area in the north latitudes.

If the men of Maine went through so much hardship making farmland from forest, then clearing aside both stumps and glacial till, why won't they pursue the same instincts where the harvest potential seems greater and the natural obstacles not as fierce?

It mystifies me, just as it frustrates Bob Dow. To be sure, there are definite answers, complex legal, economic, and even social barriers, but nothing that cannot be overcome in a twinkling with forceful leadership and a unified commitment both in high state political circles and in the coastal localities.

A 1971 document, *Maine Coastal Resources Renewal*, prepared by the state planning office, is critical of fishermen. "Although the independent manner of these traditional citizens enthralls tourists," said the report, "it has also dislodged many attempts to gain a foothold for even minimal aquaculture development on the Maine coast."

While that was true in the past, I'm not so sure that it holds for the present generation of fishermen, particularly those men who do it full time. There is a communications gap, and these men appear desperately anxious to get the word. Bob Dow has suffered his share of setbacks; but usually when he has had a chance to work with the fishermen, there has been an understanding.

The problem really lies deeply rooted in New England laws and traditions. And it poses a curious contradiction. In the beginning, settlers adopted a cooperative attitude toward their land, establishing the doctrine of public trust for purposes of efficiency while driving the Indian trustees away. However, this viewpoint persisted only up until the point at which *private* exploitation was threatened, by which time the farmer had won his security from the Indians anyway. In other words, as with the ancient commons, the territory was open to one and all until individual benefits diminished. So it went with the fisheries, only it has taken another century or more for the diminishing returns to set in.

Under the Colonial Ordinances of 1641 to 1647,

> Every inhabitant that is an howse holder shall have free fishing and fowling in any great ponds, and Bayes, Coves and Rivers, so farre as the sea ebbes and flows within the precincts of the towne where they dwell, unlesse the free men of the same Towne or the General Court have otherwise appropriated them, provided that this shall not be extended to give leave to any man to come upon others propertie without their leave.

Later lawmakers have taken this to heart. The high tide mark has been the limit of private property, and the intertidal areas and all the waters have been free for all. The only exceptions, truly based on the original writ, have been the right of a town to establish a shellfish conservation district on its intertidal areas and the right of the state to set up experimental plots, no larger than two acres, *after* a public hearing and *after* permission is given by waterfront owners.

Ever since the enabling legislation was passed early in this century, however, very few tide flat reservations have been established — and only about half a dozen in the past two decades. In the summer of 1972, the town of North Haven created a much-publicized controversy by setting up a conservation district and levying extra license fees on the out-of-town clam diggers who previously had raided the mudflats unmolested. Challenged on constitutional grounds, the matter still lies in the hands of the courts as I write about it.

"We worry about creeping socialism," Dow told me one day in his office, his puckish features worked into a look of chagrin, "and yet we are far more socialistically inclined, as far as our marine environment is concerned, than probably any other country in the world. In countries such as France, Italy, Portugal and Spain, they have gone ahead and set up institutional provisions for substantial aquacultural investment, although they lag behind us in technical capability."

Before returning to the issues raised by legal or social attitudes, let us look for a moment at what happened to the New England fisheries under the doctrine of catch-as-catch-can. In 1880, New England fishermen landed an all-time high of 294 million pounds of cod, the "sacred cod" that saved the Pilgrims. That catch has fallen to under 40 million pounds, even though more men are fishing and are using the most sophisticated trawling gear and electronic devices. To be sure, some ten nations are out there competing with the New Englanders, because the cod, large and mild-tasting, is considered an important source of protein worldwide. International agreements have been worked out at various times in recent years that purport to establish conservation practices. But these agreements really cannot be enforced, and even if gear restrictions and quotas are set, there will be more and more fishermen scouring the bottom, every inch of it, for ground fish and migrating species. The sardine (herring) and haddock fisheries have been severely depleted, and whiting and yellowtail flounder are now threatened. Not until the fishing nations are willing to enforce aggregate quotas and practice real conservation will the drastic decline come to a stop.

Nearer shore, where Maine fishermen are most prevalent, it's the same story. Whenever I talk with Bob Dow about lobsters, he is pessimistic. Since 1897, the lobsterman has gotten less and less in return for his effort. Now, in places such as Casco Bay, the situation is pathetic. In spite of quadrupling their efforts (some are putting out over a thousand traps), lobstermen over the past decades have watched their *total* catch plummet.

"By 1967 the Maine catch declined 35 percent from ten years before," Dow said. "Ninety percent of the lobsters caught this year were of sublegal size just before their last molt. You can't tell me that this doesn't show very dramatically that the resource is being overfished."

Lobstering has reached such a low that even the Maine Lobstermen's Association has advocated a trap limit, and a 1972 survey of Stonington fishermen elicited near-unanimous support for strict conservation measures, from trap limits to community action in managing all local shell fisheries.

Dow favors not only a limit on traps but a limit on licenses, because the first won't work if the number of fishermen increases. He has even suggested what he calls a *trap-day limit*. It would work like this. Since the average number of days for lobstering is 130, Dow thinks a trap limit of four to six hundred thousand traps could be established without endangering the lobster population. This would mean that one thousand lobstermen could each put out 400 traps. If by June, however, two thousand licenses had been taken out, the traps per man would have to be reduced to 200. At some point, diminishing returns would set the level of fishing activity. Just as important, Dow thinks, such a system would have to include restrictions to discourage the part-time lobstermen who make up a third of the present participants and who fish mainly to pick up a side income.

In 1969 the shrimp industry went into high gear, as 24½ million pounds worth $6 million were landed. Yet now even this activity has suffered, although slight water temperature changes may be as much of a factor as overfishing, since Maine is at the southern edge of the shrimp spawning run. Eventually, though, without conservation, this fishery will also die.

Bob Dow has been attacked for his candor in observing that, even with conservation restrictions, coastal fishing is a form of hunting that is all too often practiced as a means of making *additional* income. And that gets us back to the Colonial Ordinances and subsequent laws that allowed unlimited exploitation of coastal waters and intertidal areas. The situation is particularly applicable to clam digging, which, within the old legal framework, has evolved as a subsistence practice, held to be more of a social right than a commercial asset. To put it bluntly, too many people go clamming in the slack season or when times are hard and they need some small cash. What has resulted, said Dow in a recent study, has been the creation of "a municipal safeguard against pauperism — a sort of low water town poor farm."

Aquaculture is the only solution for ending the hunting regime and for regulating subsistence fishing (because the public must have some clam flats, and surely with conservation management this can be arranged). Maine must amend the old law or replace it entirely, so that a judicious line is drawn between the public trust principle and the right of free enterprise participation in sea farming. For unless an investor is assured that his outlay and effort are legally protected, and that the area he cultivates is free from encroachment, he will not become involved in aquaculture.

On their own, such corporations as Armour, Corn Products Company, Ralston Purina, Monsanto and United Fruit have explored the possibilities of aquaculture. They are ready. Bob Dow and others have built a biological foundation. But it remains a sad reality that under the existing laws, no company has been willing to risk a major investment in aquaculture. If the institutions are provided, I think that even the "independent" traditional fisherman will cooperate, but of course he too must wipe off his hands and do his homework.

What would help tremendously, it seems to me, would be the establishment of a good-sized sea farm cooperative, backed by the state, the public (e.g., the localities of the bay or estuary involved), and interested companies who would process and market the produce. It could be sanctioned by the Coastal Authority that I recommend earlier in this chapter. Or it could be tied to another kind of activity. For example, the oil companies have flooded the air with advertisements telling us how wildlife thrive beside oil activities. They claim that the giant oil depot of Bantry Bay has been improved as a natural habitat. They insist, and even show with pictures, that offshore oil rigs in the Gulf of Mexico and elsewhere have attracted great schools of fish around their footings and that the local fisheries actually appear to have been enhanced. Now, in Maine, there is a prime opportunity, say in Casco Bay, for the oil company that wants a port facility to sponsor an aquacultural operation. (Instead, the oil companies are still in court with their opposition to the Maine Conveyance Act, which would siphon a *minute* percentage of the value of the oil shipments into marine resource research and development.)

Certainly the power companies can do more to match their boast that thermal discharges are a free benefit to coastal fishermen. It may be out of its line of expertise, but a utility like Central Maine Power has the cash assets to back those who do want to find some use for CMP's warm effluent. There is the knowledge and capability, I am sure, for positive aquacultural cooperation at the Maine Yankee nuclear plant, which instead of being a benefit is now a threat to the million-dollar bloodworm industry at Montsweag Bay.

The trouble is that without an economy of scale, an integrated operation involving many different marine species with different seasons and other varied characteristics, and pooling culture and management experts and facilities, sea farming may not be a profitable form of enterprise for a long time, if ever.

But, of course, a sea farm industry of enormous diversity and flexibility is precisely what Bob Dow has in mind. A harvesting division could cultivate live seafoods (oysters, clams, lobsters, sea urchins, etc.) as well as live baits, notably the bloodworm and sandworm, which now rank one and two in per-pound value of all Maine fishing products. This division could also breed selected seed stock for export markets.

A processing division could take these products and can, freeze or sell them fresh. Then a third part of the business, call it the sea compounds division, could prepare the drugs, cosmetics and food additives that already rely on marine resources, from fish parts to seaweeds.

"There is no valid reason why the production of food and pharmacologicals from the sea cannot become Maine's primary industry, employing more personnel at higher salaries than any other industrial activity," Dow has said once, twice, many times.

Yet state support of sea farming, if it really exists, is badly fragmented. Marine research funds from private and government sources add up to around $700,000, less than one percent of the *present annual commercial fishing wholesale volume* of $100 million, and barely a third of the average percentage of revenues routinely spent by other industries on research and development. Coastal towns-people must reassess the way they use (or abuse) their most valuable farmlands, the tide flats and estuaries, so that fishermen or sea farm-ers will, as Dow puts it, "have a vested interest in fishing instead of encouragement to cut out after cleaning out a resource."

At the very least aquaculture *could* be instituted on the seventy thousand acres of shell fisheries that have been closed because of pollution. Not only could these areas be developed into prototype sea farms of experimental value, but their production might be transplanted to clean areas or even sent to market after going through various depuration processes already in use. With the sea farming business launched where other business is befouled and not allowed, and with the sea farm advocates at last given a chance to really show off their capacity, market production from sea farms all along the coast should amount to $500 million by 1980, $2 billion by 1990.

That's what Bob Dow thinks. And there is no reason to doubt this man. Yet even if his estimate were high, and even if the practice of aquaculture is thus limited, it might be the saving of the Maine coast.

SUMMER COLONY

"IT's REMOTE. Away from the rush. It's not a place where tourists drop off unless they make an effort. The sea and the shore here are immeasurably lovely."

Mary Pingree spoke quietly, but with feeling, about a place that really still exists along the Atlantic coast. It is North Haven, where she is a summer colonist. It is not unique, and there is as yet an opportunity to create colonies like it inland, as well as on the coast. But North Haven is the one that I know best, since I too have been a summer resident there much of my life.

Many families hope to spend their next vacation visiting busy cultural centers or places of historic interest. But many hope to be "outdoors" somewhere, and I think that most of these people would like to find a place where they feel secluded amidst scenic natural surroundings. In a sense, I apply this view even to those who join the mobs at Maine's York Beach and places like the southern shore of Long Island and the Atlantic strip of Maryland. I have visited — and enjoyed — the crowded beach, but it was when my time was limited or when I only wanted to swim. Anyway, I think that shorefront speculators, land developers and other hucksters have misdirected the crowds, luring people with the notions that the only way one can enjoy the seacoast is to hold a piece of it, or that a beach's highest appeal is for swimming, and that a marsh is useless — a bug breeder — unless it is filled. Mind you, there are no analyses to bear me out, it is just my strong opinion.

Regardless of myths (or opinions) about coastal recreation, however, I am very certain that the rugged *and* fragile coast of Maine will become an inferior environment if it is overwhelmed by land development. There is room for people, yes; but the conditions must be carefully created or maintained, first and foremost, for the sake of coastal quality.

North Haven has developed its own character and its own constituents over nearly a century of summer "colonization." So it certainly is no exact model for those who would form new summer colonies, except insofar as its essential ingredient is copied. That is the balance between the presence of people and the power of nature: a force that should, and actually still does, prevail.

It is no coincidence, then, that persons in the forefront of the battle to preserve the coastal environment go to summer places like North Haven. But their involvement should not be judged as an expression of self-interest. It is, as I have said, in the interest of the coast, the land itself with its variations in coastal topography, its bays, thoroughfares, and island archipelagos. Thus the best features of the summer colony ought to be considered in the formulation of coastal policy, not only for Maine but for other island and estuarine regions in coastal America, from Quoddy, facing New Brunswick, all the way around to the breakers of Alaska.

North Haven is separated from Vinal Haven, a slightly larger island, by the winding Fox Islands Thoroughfare, and together the two islands are known as the Fox Islands (supposedly after an unusual breed of gray fox that has not been seen since the earliest years of settlement). As the town in Vinal Haven is all the way across the island from the thoroughfare, householders along this scenic passage are considered part of the North Haven summer colony.

Except for my limited purpose, I hasten to say that it would be narrow-minded to refer to these islands, separately or collectively, as a summer colony. They are year-round settlements too, a home base for proud and industrious people whose forebears settled there at a time when the environment possessed many advantages. The islands were attractive for a subsistence way of life secure from the threat of Indian raids. They were heavily wooded for both construction timber and firewood; they were fertile enough for farming, and they were in the midst of one of the most flourishing fisheries in the world. As North Haven chronicler Nellie Brown has written about her ancestors:

"With their flocks and herds, their gardens and forests, and their fisheries, they were self-supporting, and had little use for money."

The most penetrating account of modern Maine island life that I have ever read is Perry D. Westbrook's *Biography of an Island*, a study of the Swans Island community done under a Guggenheim fellowship in 1953. Swans Island has always been more isolated and less busy as a summer colony than North Haven. Yet there are basic similarities between the places and the people. From the late eighteenth century through the early years of the twentieth, both islands were viable fishing and farming colonies. In the spring and fall months, the fishermen caught lobsters. In the summer, when the lobsters were shedding, herring and mackerel were the catch. Throughout the year, there was fishing for cod, pollack, halibut and other bottom species. The local coves were full of flounder. In the winter months the men repaired or replaced boats and gear. Farming also followed seasonal cycles, while winter was the time for cutting both building timber and firewood.

The classic firsthand account of the subsistence way of life of those times is Charles Eliot's *John Gilley: Maine Farmer and Fisherman*, a lovely but sad little book that can be read in an hour. Of the Gilleys Eliot wrote (in 1899), "It is obvious that this family on its island domain was much more self-contained and independent than any ordinary family is to-day, even under similar circumstances. They got their fuel, food and clothing as products of their own skill and labor, their supplies and resources being almost all derived from the sea and from their own fields and woods."

The Gilleys made warm clothing from the wool of their sheep, coarse linen from flax, and flour from their own wheat. Milk and butter came from a few cows, eggs from their own hens. From the sheep there was also mutton, from the hogs pork and bacon, and as winter came they would kill a "beef critter," keeping some salted and some frozen in the natural air. Wild fowl were plentiful. They raised up to three hundred bushels of potatoes to feed themselves and the livestock. They had a vegetable garden.

The situation summed up by Nellie Brown and exemplified in the life of the Gilleys was pretty much intact when Dr. William Weld, Mary Pingree's father, cruised into the thoroughfare on his brother's famous yacht *Gitana* around 1885. Perhaps he had heard from men like Eliot about the extraordinary loveliness of the Maine islands and about the impressive independence and spirit of the islanders. In any event, Dr. Weld was immediately taken with North Haven. Back in Massachusetts, after looking over opportunities for acquiring land on the thoroughfare, Dr. Weld and some of his friends drew lots. With second choice he bought Iron Point, where already there stood a farm that had belonged to the Waterman family. Dr. Weld pulled down the original dwelling and erected an enormous edifice in the manner of the Bar Harbor "cottages," a house, his daughter recalls, in which groups gathered frequently for house parties. Sometimes they would sing to piano accompaniment, and there were games of Sardines or Murder in the Dark, a favorite (with a variation called Vampire) up through the days of my own youth.

Since this new activity occurred as the industrial era was casting a long shadow over the native way of life, the summer trade unquestionably revived North Haven. Dr. Weld supported a new boatyard, and his friends and their friends who gradually formed the summer colony gave the competent island carpenters plenty of commissions for both boats and houses.

The celebrated North Haven dinghy was created by Dr. Weld from the lines of one of the *Gitana*'s small boats. Skilled with his hands, he spent many hours at the boatyard. While he never really had a full-time practice, he made himself available to the islanders when they were sick or injured. On his 150-foot steam yacht, the *Malay*, he was as generous to his summer friends, dropping them off at their docks and keeping the boat at their disposal for shuttles to Rockland, twelve miles across the bay.

While this was an era of uncertainty and even traumatic change for the coastal inhabitants, it was a period of great comfort for the small number of American families who put down stakes in summer resorts. They conducted their lives at a leisurely pace and considered summertime reunions with cousins and old friends to be an important aspect of life.

It was an ironic crossing of paths. Just as the descendants of the frontier settlers were finding that the old frontier was economically exploited, its living conditions poor and primitive compared to urbanizing areas of the East Coast, the descendants of those who had stayed near the cities and led the Industrial Revolution were drawn

99

to what remained of the nation's wilderness and underdeveloped frontier.

North Haven was not, of course, the only summer place centered around nature's setting. At the same time, eastern families journeyed to lake and mountain retreats in Vermont, New Hampshire and up-state New York as well as to the Cape Cod, Rhode Island, Long Island and New Jersey coasts. In these places the vacationers found the feeling of living close to the land (and sea), becoming again a part of the pioneer tradition that had somehow disappeared with all the new conveniences and luxuries of the modern age.

What older generations had found so appealing about North Haven persisted through the summers I spent there while I was growing up. One was reassured by the friendliness of all around him without being pressured into group involvement of any kind. The place itself was the main reason for being there. Yes, it was truly exciting — "immeasurably lovely," as Mrs. Pingree put it. It was only fitting that things should happen cheerfully, almost lazily.

My own happiest memories are of sailing alone among the islands in my father's 17-foot knockabout. I would become lost in thought or I would practice my few seafaring skills, undeveloped as they were. My impression now is that such excursions, as well as explorations afoot, if nothing else, were beneficial for the young ego.

Sometimes we would skinny-dip at high tide into coves where the water was warmed ten degrees from rising over the mudflats and the rocks when they were exposed to the sun. Or we'd find someplace to go to by boat — just as a family or with a few others — and hold a picnic. It was at the picnics and after sailboat races that young people got together. The races were run, then as now, in Herreshoff Twelve-Footers, Crowninshield Knockabouts and the North Haven dinghies. (A truly remarkable boat, the North Haven dinghy is stamped with character and is the oldest of any racing class still active in the entire United States. It was first used as a sort of utility boat, for picking up mail and just getting around. But it is fast and very challenging to make perform well in competition.)

After the races, there were softball games and long sessions of "kick the can," a game played in variations the world over. The Saturday race was followed by an organized (though not formal) tea at the Casino (the name given to the yacht club) where most everyone, young and old, congregated. Different families would put on the teas, at which ice cream cones, rich brownies, and other goodies were also served.

I'd been away from North Haven for nearly a decade when I returned with my wife and children in the summers of 1971 and 1972. I was pleasantly surprised in some ways, confronted with misgivings in others. In absentia I had argued with a journalist friend who has a summer place there that the North Haven summer colony was perhaps built on too narrow a base and that the social atmosphere was stagnant. Usually I was playing the devil's advocate role of one who is momentarily denied a chance to take a certain pleasure. But when I probed seriously, I was reassured by his answers.

You're being far too defensive, he replied in effect. It is true that everyone who comes to North Haven appears to have a common interest — the desire for escape from the frenzy and frustrations of late-twentieth-century life, combined with a deep love of the coastal islands as comparatively undeveloped places. But that is all. Otherwise, the spectrum is wide. He argued convincingly that the price of land in North Haven or Vinal Haven is still less than mainland shorefrontage, and a person who wants to spend most of his future vacations in a peaceful, quiet place can find land or a house here. The people who come now, he noted, include some very dynamic men and women — lawyers, judges, bankers, financiers and corporate executives on the one hand, artists, architects, naturalists and writers on the other. "You can be involved just as much or as little as you want here," he said.

And he is right. North Haven is not a refuge for do-nothings. Yes, the summer colony is unobtrusive and private in the best sense. There is no "organization" except, for example, as families participate in a sailing program for children. Entertainment consists of going out to dinner at a friend's, but maybe the weekends will all pass before this get-together and it may never take place. (Even for retired summer colonists or those who take a whole month there, the time often passes thus.)

Yet there is also a problem, I feel, that characterizes this summer colony and probably others along the coast. *Seasonal North Haven is still more the result of an unconscious, historic evolution than a conscious community state of mind bonded together both by Maine*

citizens and vacationers. The situation might have sufficed a generation or so ago, but not now, while the future of the coast is being
debated so hotly and evaluated so intensively.

To begin with, there is the all-important role of the year-round
resident to consider. Certainly changing postures of the coming generations have created a fresh atmosphere for making social evalua-
tions. Yet as recently as the early fifties, according to Perry Westbrook, the summer people regarded the island citizens very narrowly,
admiring their abilities and their instincts as men and women who
can live on an island all year, but otherwise holding them to be lacking in ambition and perseverence. In other words, the head of the summer family tended, intentionally or not, to rest on his social background and business experience, overlooking the fact that the islander
long ago chose not to compete in the modern industrial and technological world, the taut conditions of which drive the visitor into
refuge each summer. "The ultimate test of mutual acceptance," Westbrook observed, "is intermarriage, which among summer people and
natives of the Maine coast — and the rest of New England as well —
is almost unheard of."

By 1972, I found many of the attitudes of Westbrook's time being
overcome or well tested. Yet there was still a ways to go. It was mostly
a matter of submerging pride on both sides. There are different areas
in which this can happen, but a major priority, and a subject of this
book, is in the complex field of land use.

At least 80 percent of North Haven is owned by summer people.
There is as yet no more evidence that they are willing to commit
themselves to protecting the land than there is evidence that young
island couples have a fair chance to find a place to settle themselves.
The swelling of some summer families has taken on a tribal aspect.
Instead of respecting the capacity of the environment and sharing the
use of existing seasonal development on it, these families have continued to keep apace of the population growth with new construction
while they grouse about the proliferation of summer cottages elsewhere along the coast.

Summer people are in the driver's seat when it comes to a commitment to the Champlain Seaway idea. Their participation in different
methods of open space preservation is long overdue. At the same
time, the summer landowners must search for nonusurping ways to
become engaged in the North Haven town planning process so that

both rusticators and townspeople will be well served by land use controls.

I am on shakier ground discussing the attitudes of year-round citizens, particularly since it appears that they are slightly ahead of the visitors in reevaluating their dependence on summer trade. While the fishing industry has virtually died in North Haven, the town passed a law in 1972 to protect its clam flats. State fisheries' experts I have talked to all say that North Haven waters are ideal for shell-fishing management. Vinal Haven of course remains an important fishing center, probably because it is far less developed as a summer colony.

There should be nothing subservient about the business of providing summer services, although I sense that some islanders feel they are shackled by this trade. As more and more summer people are coming to North Haven in the off-season, finding the place even more splendid in its isolation and solitude when the weather is colder, perhaps such feelings on the part of islanders will subside. Certainly the changing outlook of the sons and daughters of summer people will help. It is they who are questioning the concepts of material prosperity in the context of making peace with mankind and themselves, and it is they who are the most willing to make friendships regardless of the past social context.

By the end of the summer of 1972, I found myself wishing more than ever that both sides would apply themselves to approaches that would make the colony business mutually productive, giving everyone a sense of achievement and pride. At the same time I held out the hope that some of the old ways — fishing and boatbuilding, for example — might be revived or updated with the backing and even participation of those with the capital.

The college girl who helped us with the children in 1972 came from the West Coast and had never seen anything quite like North Haven. An activist in student causes, she exclaimed in annoyance one day, "I just can't see why such a few people should have all this beauty and privacy to themselves."

"Why not," I replied. "Doesn't it depend on whether the 'few' that you talk about fully understand what they have and then make a commitment to maintain its vitality? Certainly this environment will be the loser if it is developed for recreation on a mass scale."

She had a point, in the sense that there ought to be ways in which *more* people can fully savor an island like North Haven without having to own a piece of it or without feeling the urge to develop it. And that should be a priority for the consideration of both islanders and visitors.

The North Haven experience should not be unique. There is as yet some room along the coast and of course unlimited opportunity inland, as I shall say later on, where other "colonies" of Mainers and outsiders can work and plan together for the common goal of protecting natural beauty, privacy and simplicity.

But to use a common expression, the ball is in the court of the summer colonists. If they commit themselves to no more than protecting their own environmental security, the coast will remain up for grabs. And sooner or later, North Haven, as I have known it — and all the North Havens of this land — will be no more.

Summer colonies like North Haven are grand solutions as far as the environment is concerned. But they do perplex open space and wilderness planners, who are under such tremendous pressure to find ways for accommodating the most people. And for someone like me, who has a personal stake in the colony, North Haven's kind of exclusivity poses other questions that lead to the deepest sort of soul-searching. If there are good answers, I must confess I am probably not the man to relay them.

CHAMPLAIN'S SEAWAY

MONHEGAN ISLAND, Captain John Smith's fisheries' base, is some ten miles out to sea on two sides of an equilateral triangle from Pemaquid Point and the harbor of Port Clyde. Here man and nature have formed a perfect union. The place is prepossessingly beautiful and would rank with more famous North American natural wonders even if it had never been settled.

I went out to Monhegan not long ago, in the first week of May when migrating birds make the island a busy junction on the Atlantic flyway. In the top branches of a spruce, I saw a bay-breasted warbler. A duck falcon and a sparrow hawk enlivened the northeastern tip. Red wing blackbirds flocked in the swamp meadow behind the village. I startled flickers along every path and kept finding their yellow wing and tail feathers on the ground. The dense forest of spruce and fir balsam that grows down Monhegan's spine was cool and rich and pungent. Wild flowers were profuse, especially on the bare slopes at the southwestern end. Freshets carrying the winter meltoff raced down to the ocean, cutting trenches in the soft hummocks of new grass that greened the openings above the cliffs on the southeastern, "far" side of the island. (These cliffs are concentrated in three great bluffs — Burnt Head, White Head and Black Head — that plunge from as high as two hundred feet almost straight down into the salt foam where the open Atlantic pounds incessantly.)

Sitting on a grassy shelf on Burnt Head, I became totally immersed in the seaward vastness, assured of privacy because of the thundering of the breakers that appeared even to silence the gulls. Yet back a hundred yards in the woods, the denseness of the trees blocked out the noise of the sea, and it was very quiet, except for the occasional peep of a bird. On this three-day visit, I hiked over all Monhegan's trails. Only once did I meet another soul, a boy who ran along the edge of White Head like a mountain goat, asked if I had seen a friend of his, then raced on. What a place, I thought, for children.

I had heard that Monhegan was a model for other coastal communities in that people had shown enough foresight and imagination to make certain that both the way of life and the environment would be preserved into perpetuity, not as a showcase attraction but as a living, thriving reality. Harry Odom, who met me at the ferry landing in his truck, one of the few vehicles allowed on Monhegan, made this clear right away as we bounced up the hill to the store.

"This is a surprisingly cosmopolitan place," he said. "It has a good outlook on life. In the spring and summer months I get to meet more interesting people than if I lived in Boston or New York. But we've kept our way of life and our land the way we want it. Most of it is undeveloped and no more can be sold for lots. There are twelve fishermen now and room for only a few more."

Harry and his brother Doug own and manage the store, living in quarters above it. Harry is thin, tall and gregarious. He tends the store most of the time, carrying an inventory that is unmatched for its exotic variety anywhere in Maine. When I was there, he was selling Chateau Mouton Rothschild, vintage 1966, at a price only slightly higher than you would pay in downtown Boston. Of course Harry's stock reflects the tastes of his customers, who in the seasonal months include notables of the arts and letters and who are an unusual lot of some forty-five men, women and children even in winter.

Monhegan's good fortune came about not only because of an enlightened attitude on the part of people like Harry and Doug. The initial leadership came from Thomas Edison, a summer resident whose grandfather, the inventor of the light bulb, also came to Monhegan. Edison feared that the island's natural fastness would be ruined by too many summer colonists and that new hotels would be built to turn the present flood of day-tripper tourists into a terrible blight. He personally persuaded the islanders to sell *nearly 80 percent of their land* to an association backed mostly by his own money called Monhegan Associates. It would assure that the land be kept permanently undeveloped. The land was turned over to the town to manage with the stipulation that it remain wild. Edison actually had some summer cottages torn down where they intruded on the wild land that was acquired.

At first Edison ran into resistance, since he was saying in effect that island propertyowners must forsake profitable opportunities in land speculation and development. But after a while, it became quite apparent that equal profits were the result. The island retained its strong appeal to more than a score of artists who have summer studios there, the seasonal colony became stable — much to the joy of both islanders and colonists — and the quality of tourism resulted in far higher returns than would ever have been the case with new hotels and unmanageable numbers of visitors. On good summer days, several hundred day-trippers come over from Port Clyde and Tenants Harbor, but when night falls the public lodgings can only accommodate a small portion of these visitors. And while the number of people on the island at any one moment during the summer does not appear too great, Harry Odom and others in town think even this invasion constitutes a mob scene.

Rest assured, it won't get larger. The Monhegan people have seen to that. A few years ago, the town council even decided to ban camping on the Associates' land. It was a hard decision, because the whole point of the open space preservation was to benefit a public that has been shut off from all but a few miles of the coast and has been almost entirely denied an experience on the islands except by private yacht. However, a horde of young people came to Monhegan and made a mess. Signs of the litter — tin cans, bits of paper, glass and aluminum foil — were still in evidence two years later. I found old tent sites in the most incredible places, in among the thickest clumps of spruce where the mosquitoes must have been devastating.

With a ban on new development, property prices and leases went up terrifically, benefiting both outside and native landholders. The only negative result was felt by some new young fishermen who could not find or afford a permanent residence on Monhegan. On the whole, the fishing colony should benefit by stabilization too, but when the present lobstermen retire or leave, it ought to be possible for replacements to compete with rich outsiders for a place to live. Without the fishermen, Monhegan would lose much of its appeal, even as a summer colony, for these men keep the traditions alive, nourish the sense of history that has been with Monhegan so long, and set an example of living with the environment that is unmatched anywhere. Top priority on the Monhegan Associates' agenda should be the objective to keep the island's dozen or so fishermen in business forever.

By an act of the Maine legislature, the Monhegan lobster fishermen have established a conservation district within their three-mile limit and closed the season between July 1 and January 1. This has worked to their advantage in several ways. For one thing, the lobsters evidently move into deep water during the winter months, returning to the shallower coastal bays in spring. The Monhegan men set their traps thirty fathoms or more deep, whereas their counterparts in Muscongus Bay, eight or so miles inshore, work in depths of five fathoms and less, on the average. The lobsters shed their shells in June and July and thus are very inferior eating at this time. It is also the period when they breed. So the Monhegan law was a sound conservation measure. Moreover, many coastal fishing ports are beset by ice, or because of the cold weather less traps are set. So in winter prices go up, sometimes twofold. The Monhegan lobstermen are set up to take advantage of this, although fishing at sea in January is tough business, fraught with peril.

I went out lobstering with Doug Odom in fine May weather, and I thought that even then lobstering was as exhausting an occupation as one could put up with. I was a happy man when we ran out of bait and had to return at midday, after only six hours among the traps.

Doug was uncanny. He had the sense of direction of a honey bee. Enveloped in a bright mist, tinted by the rising sun, we cruised from one pot to another, never missing a pickup, even though the compass was of no help in this kind of search, since the pots move with the tides and sea drift. The twenty-eight-foot boat rolled and pitched violently in the swell, but the work went on silently and efficiently. Doug would power up to one of his pots and his helper, Newt, would gaff the warp line and bring up one or several traps on a mechanical winch geared to the main engine. I helped to gauge the lobsters for size, throwing back many that were too small and a few that were too big. Wood plugs shut the claws, the traps were baited, and the diesel engine would roar again. The smell of the bait was quite sickening and, avocational sailor that I am, I never quite got used to it. For my benefit, now and then Doug would tell a story or explain something.

But for the most part, lobster fishing is a lonely business done in solitude, a one-man operation or a silent partnership.

If a man has lived in Maine for five years, he can get a license to set traps. This means that legally he can fish anywhere. However, there is an unwritten law that different colonies or "gangs" of lobstermen have their own territories. Not only is it difficult for a new man to begin fishing on his home ground, it is actually dangerous for him to trespass. The first notice may consist of no more than a few half hitches tied around the handle of one or more of his pots. If he doesn't move his traps, he will probably next find that the warps have been cut. Continued persistence will elicit harsher measures. Shotguns have been brought out on several notable occasions during "wars" between neighboring fishing colonies. Boats have been found mysteriously sunk. The Monhegan Island territory is well defined, since it is so far offshore. It is safely in the hands of the island fishermen.

This is as it should be. Yet if this approach is applied in other places along the coast, the premises will be difficult to explain or justify. The Monhegan people have behaved in a way that will seem contradictory. Having declared that 80 percent of their land is too valuable as open space to become subject to private speculation, they have gone and established a tight set of controls over their fishing grounds amounting to a private local interest. In other words, the land is kept wild for the public benefit whereas the adjacent waters are closed to all but Monhegan residents.

However, it is the only practical solution. Both directives — the open space compact and the fisheries' conservation district — protect a resource in the public interest. Both measures are timely and well-constructed responses to unfortunate trends: overfishing and over-development of the coast in defiance of long-term public benefits. Nobody should want to see the lobsters disappear. Nobody should tolerate the reckless apportionment of the coast between private recreation developments, summer colonists and heavy industry.

Who should own the beach? As much as all of us would love to have a piece of it, under the present conditions and considering the enormous pressures brought about by population growth, the answer must be *nobody*, at least not as ownership is usually defined. The shoreline is a thin margin between two vastly different worlds. As such it contains a natural spectrum of life from both environments and is too fragile and rare to be bargained for. John Hay put it well in his book about Cape Cod, *The Great Beach*. "This is a narrow place, restricted by nature and by men, but foreign lives still fly to it like sparks in the air, and the sea beyond it takes things on their way with more room than analogy is yet aware of."

The goal, then, for Maine communities and for local leaders along the entire U.S. coast, is to accommodate the public in a manner that preserves the extraordinary natural qualities of the coast while at the same time giving *longstanding* private alliances with the saltwater a good chance to thrive under future conditions. And to qualify my earlier dictum, if a Maine fisherman owns a stretch of beach, he is well entitled to keep it, as long as he and his sons go to sea.

How can such a balance be achieved? I see four general approaches that complement one another.

— By outright government acquisition of wilderness areas and parks.
— Through private land trusts.
— Through town zoning or even a combination federal and state master plan that forces towns to act.
— And through open space compacts similar to, or varying slightly from, the Monhegan Associates.

First, let's consider the wilderness protection and park approach. There are three state parks and one national park (Acadia) along the Maine coast. Most certainly there is room for more, but parkland is expensive and Acadia — the largest coastal preserve — is a magnificent park that could never be re-created under present market conditions for such scenic land. For one thing, a few individuals gave the federal government most of Acadia. John D. Rockefeller alone donated more than eleven thousand acres, including miles of carriage trails. No one person, to my knowledge, owns that much coastal property anymore.

Government purchases, however, need not be confined to the state and federal domain. In the future it would be far more fruitful for towns themselves to practice what has been called land banking, whereby individuals donate money, foundations are tapped for matching grants, and the town puts a bond issue to its voters. These are all ways to acquire land before it is priced beyond the limits of public buying power. The land is then set aside, ideally as open space to give solace to future generations, but sometimes for future *controlled* development under strict guidelines established by the people.

A fine example of action by local citizens took place during 1971 in the town of Westport. Spurred on by a group calling themselves the Clough Point Association, the town raised $27,000 toward the purchase of open land with twelve hundred feet on deep water in Wiscasset Harbor. That figure was matched by government funds. It has always been clear to me that once a town makes a concerted collective attempt to define its environmental capacities, it should know best how to provide open space for its citizens. The trouble is that local powerful interests often stand in the way, or people refuse to get together until it is too late. Towns need prodding, but when they are, I am certain they are the units of government best suited to handle the Maine coast's future park requirements.

Among land trusts, the classic organization dedicated to the protection of open space is the Nature Conservancy. The Maine chapter has performed brilliantly through its pursuit of a plan to purchase islands for the Rachel Carson Maine Seacoast, a trust appropriately named for the woman best known for crusading against DDT but who also spent much time along the Maine coast and wrote beautifully about it in *Under the Sea Wind* and other works. Through 1971, the Nature Conservancy acquired some twenty-three island properties through purchase or donation by public-spirited owners. Some of this land is to be fitted into state and federal park systems. Some islands are to be kept undeveloped as places best suited to wildlife — nesting eagles and ospreys, eider duck and other creatures. The leadership and management of the Nature Conservancy is unsurpassed. And this is why the Washington-based group has obtained a potent line of credit from banks and foundations. There is nothing comparable to the Nature Conservancy in action on the Maine coast, although that is not to say other groups can't be formed. If they are, though, such land trusts should focus on select, local ecosystems — a bay or a group of islands, for instance — so that the larger existing program will not be diluted or diffused.

As for the zoning, master-planning approach, in 1971, the Maine legislature passed Public Law 535. It specified that by June 30, 1973, all land within 250 feet of both fresh- and saltwater had to be zoned for different uses in a manner acceptable to the state Environmental Improvement Commission. The law thus applied to some 495 towns. If these communities did not submit an approved plan, then the state would impose its own controls. Not until late in 1972 were uniform guidelines developed in order to assist local lawmakers. Yet these stipulations, drawn up under a University of Maine study grant, were a good step forward, even though it appeared that there was not enough time for most small towns to make the deadline. The guidelines maintained that all new shoreline construction should be set back at least 75 feet from the water's edge (although in my opinion it should be at the least 200 feet). The guidelines suggested that shoreland planning regions encompass six categories or districts for the following self-explanatory uses: 1. protection of natural areas; 2. general purpose; 3. urban; 4. commercial, recreation; 5. fisheries, agriculture, forest; and 6. residential.

Even as the handwriting on the wall became increasingly clear, as Maine coastal towns saw their options going, the old Yankee property ethic seemed to be running strong. Wiscasset boasts that it is Maine's "prettiest village." Yet even in this truly lovely place, with its wealth of historic houses and old public buildings, zoning was resisted at a succession of town meetings.

Nobody understands the situation better than John McKee, who has directed Bowdoin College's Center for Resource Studies and has been an associate member of the Brunswick Planning Board. McKee has spent long hours working out cost-benefit models for coastal developments. His thesis is that the wave of seasonal developments along the coast will ultimately be far more costly than beneficial unless they are tightly controlled, imaginatively planned, and *remain seasonal.* Otherwise, he argues, it will pay for towns to acquire and put their open land into parks. The ideal development, according to McKee's data, would be limited clusters of seasonal housing interwoven with parkland and set back a good distance from the shorefront. Sad to say, nobody in Maine has paid much attention to people like McKee.

Nor, by the end of 1972, had there been any progress concerning state and federal plans to establish a Coastal Islands Trust, an idea broached by the U.S. Bureau of Outdoor Recreation in 1970. The federal planners based their proposal on a lengthy study of the nation's islands. For Maine, the plan was to protect some 30,000 acres through public acquisition, limitations placed on private land use, and scenic easements. The 324 islands of Casco Bay were to become the pilot component of a national system of islands. Financing was to come from federal funds, the National Parks Foundation and private foundations; yet the federals were to rely on local government units to develop master plans and zoning controls. In effect, the federals wanted to spread a big umbrella over any and all actions that would result in preservation of island open space. It was a good idea.

If Maine does create a Coastal Authority, one of its first orders of business will be to set up island trusts for all the big bays along the coast — Machias, Englishman, Pleasant, Gouldsboro, Frenchman, Blue Hill, Penobscot, Muscongus and Casco bays. Such a commission would draft working guidelines toward the object of preserving island open space by *any* means and then would work with already established regional planning commissions and town governments to place what's left of the wild shoreline in "trust" for the people.

Ultimately, perhaps the most promising strategy for coastal preservation is the open space compact. The arrangement of the Monhegan Associates is one kind. A person with strong feelings for the public trust gets things rollings. Like Thomas Edison, he puts his own money or property on the line and in addition solicits contributions from other conservationists. In return, they are made members of an open space association and, if it obtains the status of a nonprofit organization, they can deduct their donations from income taxes. The association may choose to manage the open space or, as in the Monhegan example, turn it over to the township where it is located on the condition that it be kept wild or be managed in a certain way. This is an expensive method of protecting the coast, however, and it is also likely to generate misunderstanding and hostility, since so often the leadership participation comes from outside the coastal community.

Because it is getting late to act and coastal land values are soaring out of sight, the most efficient way to regulate coastal land use is through the scenic easement. And the best example of how it works is shown by the Maine Coast Heritage Trust, an organization begun in 1970 by Mrs. David Rockefeller as the result of conversations with people like John Good, the able, hard-driving superintendent of Acadia. While the national park protected some forty miles of coastline and included a huge portion of remote Isle au Haut, it was most vulnerable to new development along its borders and on prime coastal lands within its circumference. Good tried to convince federal authorities that the park would be enhanced immeasurably and that future needs might be anticipated if landowners in the Acadia environs were allowed to give land to the park while continuing to live on it in their lifetime. Carrying this a step further, Good hoped to see adjacent landowners surrender their development rights so that, at the very least, the existing park environment would not change. Congress would not go along with the first idea and it was left to Mrs. Rockefeller and private supporters to take up both approaches.

This was made possible by an act of the state legislature in 1970 that at long last permitted scenic easements in Maine. A scenic easement is nothing more (or less) than a propertyowner's mandate that henceforth his land can be developed only in certain ways or not at all, so that its environmental assets (scenery and ecological components) are preserved forever. In other words, the owner yields his development rights subject to conditions that are entered on the property deed. You might say that the deed itself only tells a man he owns the land while the easement tells how the land is to be used or not used. Depending on how he directs future use of his land (and it must be extremely restrictive in order to qualify as a scenic easement), an owner continues to live on it, manage it, and pay property taxes. Under the present tax laws in most states, including Maine, the propertyowner receives a break by granting an easement, since no longer is the market value of his land determined according to its development potential. However, in most Maine areas, coastal land assessments are not yet based on realistic market forecasts. If coastal towns have felt that the Maine Coast Heritage Trust is about to talk them out of tax money, their fears are groundless. Only their taxable *potential* is being limited — and, in any event, the costs of future development in these areas will probably outweigh the tax benefits, as men like John McKee have proved with their studies.

An essential ingredient of a scenic easement is that an authority be able to enforce it and fight to protect it in the event of future deviations by subsequent landowners. The enforcement authority acts as recipient of the easement. The Maine law only allows government agencies to act as recipients. In my opinion, it should go further and allow foundations and private associations to be recipients. For that matter, it should be enough for legal stipulations to be clearly inserted in a property deed and then recorded as encumbrances. Under the doctrine of public trust, anyone should have standing to bring suit if a future landholder violates the easement. The point is that while government agencies may be in a stronger position to act, there is a good deal of mistrust surrounding public land use management. It is not always certain that the government will not develop it for its own purposes later on, although I suppose it is as certain as anything, since the government can always exercise eminent domain for any number of reasons.

Anyway, the conversations over the future of the Acadia park region that in turn led to the creation of the Maine Coast Heritage Trust were good developments. The choice of an executive director was particularly brilliant. He was Elmer Beal, son of a Southwest Harbor fisherman who obtained a master's degree in anthropology and then returned to his home ground with strong feelings about what he saw happening to the land and to the native people, particularly along the coast.* In its first year, through Beal, the trust idea was presented to some 279 owners of coastal and island land in Hancock and Knox counties, covering the Penobscot Bay and Mount Desert region. About half of these contacts got a response, and about 20 percent of these owners negotiated easements under the guidance of the Maine Coast Heritage Trust. The recipient was Acadia Park. This is a fair beginning. But there is a long way to go.

In the meantime, federal park planners have discussed still another idea: the creation of the Champlain National Seaway, to be named after the French explorer who first charted the coast. This would be a variation on the National Island Trust idea. It would amount to a declaration that the entire coastal strip, from St. Croix Island Monument to Cape Small on Casco Bay, is of such historic and scenic value that it is in the national interest to follow up every approach possible in order to preserve it. (The Cape Cod National

*Late in 1972, Elmer Beal joined the faculty of the new College of the Atlantic on Mount Desert and was succeeded by Bob Binneweis, former assistant to John Good and another effective leader in coastal protection.

Seashore was conceived on similar grounds.) The federals would provide maybe $20 million initially, more later, toward acquiring land and compensating propertyowners who give up their development rights. While the existence of a Champlain Seaway would not rule out private development, or even attempts by the oil industry to gain a foothold here and there, it would be one more sanction for conservationists to cite when opposing development incompatible with scenic preservation along the coast.

So we're back to that fundamental question: who owns the shoreline? And again, I would answer, the Maine coast is too important to be "owned" in a conventional sense by any individual or self-serving group. For that matter, ownership of land anywhere carries with it an obligation to the land itself, to be good to it so that its uniqueness can be appreciated in perpetuity.

This does not mean that what Nature has wrought all by herself is invariably superior — aesthetically *or* scientifically — to a natural environment altered by the human touch. To the contrary, the world abounds in examples of wild lands that actually were enhanced by humanization. René Dubos noted in an essay for *Smithsonian* how men and goats transformed the Greek landscape from predominant woodlands into sunny open spaces, how French and English farmers created a productive and varied agricultural countryside by careful management of their original "wilderness," and how this trend was continued in the cultivation of the valleys in Vermont's Green Mountains. The forest primeval has a role to play, as I will say again and attempt to demonstrate later in this book. But it should not be overlooked, as Dubos wrote, that "the prodigious labors of settlers and farmers have generated an astonishing diversity of ecosystems which appear natural even though they are of human origin." Intelligent and imaginative land use planning has through the centuries of history complemented the order of Nature, and the results can be seen today in parks and village greens, in the way a farmer lays out and encloses his fields, and in the functional but picturesque simplicity of rural villages.

And so it holds true for the Maine coast. Its primitive appeal will be best maintained through creative stewardship, as is exemplified on Monhegan Island.

116

THREE

The Forest at Work

HARVESTING TREES

IN THE MODERN WORLD, the forest has three equal roles to play.

— It is of critical importance in maintaining worldwide environmental stability. By converting carbon dioxide into oxygen and sunlight into plant matter, the forest both cleanses and cools the air. It influences long-term climatic and short-term weather patterns in a variety of ways. It triggers the rain cycle when the cool, moist air that it gives off rises and meets a warm air mass. By acting as a reservoir for the rain, the forest releases water all year, through brooks, streams and rivers, at a rate equal to our demands. It checks erosion just as efficiently as it checks the winds. Without the forest, floods, storms, droughts, and other environmental calamities would be far more frequent.

— It provides the *only* renewable resource used in construction, in packaging, and in an incredible variety of paper products.

— Finally, the forest has immeasurable psychological value to man. It is a place where the sharp edges of existential confrontation and trauma are dulled and softened. It is an outlet for our animosities as well as our instinctive energies. In this role, the forest has been an allegorical force in history and literature. It is harsh and hostile at a time when we need to recognize our frailty and basic smallness. It symbolizes escape into a secure, impenetrable refuge at a time when we feel crushed by the forces of civilization. And it is where man's stupidity is played out against the pure instincts of the wild kingdom.

The forest is no man's land and everyman's land. We must manage it as a resource and respect it as an environmental influence. But if we tame it too much, by reducing it to the category of a vegetable garden or a subsidized wheatfield, we rob ourselves of a necessary element of mystery and a place of unsurpassed richness and diversity.

These thoughts (or variations of them) have run through my mind many times. Sometimes they are precise, as when I am visiting a timber operation. Sometimes they meander inchoately, as when I am canoeing in the wilderness and can't explain why I feel so good about it. Yes, forests make wood, they make weather.

They also make peace.

I was thinking this again as I sat, tensed for balance, in the front seat of Ken Hughes's red pickup, hurtling through the night, under a sky brilliant with stars, even as snow flurries sparkled in the high beam of the headlights. We were deep in the Maine woods, traveling down a roller coaster of a road, a narrow ploughed strip between snowbanks taller than a man, headed for a lumber camp somewhere near Allagash Lake, not far from Quebec Province whence we had come. In order to be assured of snow-cleared roads into the north woods, we had taken a roundabout route, passing into Canada through Jackman, Maine, and going northeastward over fifty miles before turning back across the border.

Ken Hughes is supervisor of the Greenville District, one of four sections of nearly two million acres of land managed by the Seven Islands Land Company. Let me stress the term "managed." Seven Islands does not actually *own* land. Yet, as a manager, this company has made a reputation unbeaten in the practice of forestry. The trip evolved out of a conversation with John Sinclair, the manager, and Brad Wellman, the president of Seven Islands.

"Our whole philosophy is based on management at the stump," Sinclair said.

"What do you mean by that?" I asked.

"I mean that we're interested in the state of Maine and that we're out there every day, inspecting every acre, every detail, to make sure that land is protected, that it has a future," Sinclair answered.

"Can I go out with one of your men and see for myself?" I asked.

And he answered, "Sure."

But it really all started much longer ago, in 1848, when a shrewd Salem shipping magnate named David Pingree decided that his family — his heirs — would prosper a lot longer from forests than from clipper ships. In his will, he left a million acres of Maine timberland "in common and undivided." This meant that no one inheritor could cash in or sell out his land holdings. The Pingree estate set up an intrafamily management operation, its sole objective being the protection of the forest assets with operations sufficient to provide a steady income for the heirs. It was not a cut-out-and-get-out proposition. It was not forest ownership tied to the production demands of sawmills or, later, pulp mills. The Pingree holdings were managed through various arrangements until the formation of the Seven Islands Land Company in 1964. Such was the reputation of their previous management that Seven Islands assumed responsibility for over three quarters of a million acres of forest owned by others, ranging from small individual holdings to the lands of Dartmouth College and tracts jointly held with big companies like Great Northern.

By the 1880s, the Pingree managers had abandoned the traditional approach to lumbering — high-grade, selective cuttings, taking the biggest and best pines and spruce — and inaugurated an enlightened method of selective cutting known as the diameter cut. A permit is sold to a woods operator, a jobber. It specifies that, according to the species, only trees within a certain diameter range can be cut down. The idea is to leave a healthy number of fine specimens to seed the succession. Call it forest genetics, a science that still seems to baffle the experts. Sinclair puts its better. "It leaves the trainers," he says.

At the time this method began, millowners complained that they couldn't make money when forced to accept a lot of small, inferior trees. But a century later, the Pingree forests, mostly in the Allagash and St. John watersheds, were the envy of the forest products profession. "The best-looking woods in Maine," I was told more than once by other company men, forestry officials and a university professor.

By following Ken Hughes on his regular rounds, I hoped to develop at least a crude appreciation for good forest management. We would pass through woods in various stages of growth and sections of the wilderness that had been treated quite differently by other land managers.

The winter road in from St. Juste appeared well suited to the lumbermen's purposes. It had not been salted or sanded and was therefore free of the potholes and frozen ridges that invariably result from such treatment. The banks were ploughed up so high that they formed a soft safety barrier on either side.

Hughes drove fearlessly. He kept up speed on the turns by deliberately directing the skidding motion of the pickup, skillfully flicking his wrist on the steering wheel just enough to regulate the sideways drift of the machine's back end. I was impressed.

We crossed two branches of the St. John River as well as the Allagash Stream and passed a multitude of lakes that were frozen solid and, like the floor of the forest, were covered by more than four feet of snow. Somewhere between Allagash and Eagle Lake, forty miles from the border and just west of the Allagash Wilderness, we pulled into the camp of Edmund Roy, an independent lumberman who was working under a Seven Islands permit.

The camp stood in a large rectangular clearing. It was well lighted, and I could hear a generator in the background. Two cabins, a large bunkroom, the cookhouse, Edmund Roy's cabin/office, and a storage shed stood in that order at one side, and lined up next to them were the parked trucks and cars of the loggers. It was only 8:30, but as I walked to the toilet and washroom behind the main sleeping quarters, I could see that every last one of Roy's crew was sprawled out on his bed asleep. The lights were still on and the kerosene heaters must have been set high, because most of the men were in T-shirts, lying loosely covered by their blankets.

In *Forest Life and Forest Trees,* John Springer over a century ago extolled the combination of hard work and clean living that prevailed once the lumberman was deep in the forest. At night, he wrote, "They need not court the gentle spell, turning from side to side, but, quietly submitting, sink into its profound depths." It was true right here in the 1972 camp of Edmund Roy. Besides Hughes and me, there appeared to be only three others awake. Edmund Roy; his office manager, Jean Marie Ste. Hilaire; and Mike Dann, a Seven Islands forester. Gathered around the bottle of bourbon I had brought, the five of us talked until nearly midnight in the cabin regularly assigned to visitors. The two Canadians were charming and enthusiastic, delighted to have company and the chance to explain their operation and way of life. Roy spoke only French, so Ste. Hilaire was the interpreter.

Edmund Roy, at fifty-three, was a short, wiry, handsome man. Tipped back in a chair, arms folded, legs crossed, an aquiline nose, lantern jaw creased by a ready smile, and still wearing a green cap (a bit like a golfer's, called a calotte), he was the picture of confidence and insouciance. Unhesitatingly, he laid bare every detail of his arrangement. He paid Seven Islands different rates for stumpage — in other words, so much per thousand board feet of cut tree, varying by species. For white pine and yellow birch, the rate was $25; for top-grade spruce and fir (over a hundred feet), it was $21. At the bottom were spruce and fir suitable only for pulpwood, worth $6.50 per thousand board feet.

Roy had six two-man crews out cutting. Each team consisted of a cutter, who felled and limbed the trees, and the skidder operator, who bunched them, hauled them to a yarding area and cut them into sawlogs. At the yards, which were no more than clearings with turning room, trucks arrived to haul the logs to the sawmills in Canada.

This close to the border, the Canadians dominated the business. And as a result of market and transportation factors, the only big sawmills within several hundred miles were Canadian. Otherwise, wood that was processed in northern Maine went almost entirely into pulp. To the men of Quebec Province, the pay and working conditions were attractive. A man could clear $10,000 if he worked hard. These lumbermen owned their own equipment, from chain saws to skidders (which cost as much as $18,500 new, but could perform the work of five horses). Until 1967, Edmund Roy used his own horses and he was sad that those days were gone. He liked animals, the rapport that a man had to develop with his team, and the neat and tidy job that a horse could do in heavy forest compared to the machines, which damage trees and the fragile humus ground surface wherever they go.

The men paid Roy for room and board; in turn he paid each team according to the amount of wood it cut: $11.25 per thousand board feet of softwood, $13.25 per thousand of hardwood. One crew stood out among the rest, Roy said. A skidder operator named André Lessard and a cutter named Rock Veer. He insisted that I watch them in action. One week they had cut 105,000 board feet and they were averaging over 65,000 a week.

Every Friday at three in the afternoon, the camp broke for the weekend, everyone driving home and returning by eight Monday morning. This was quite a change from Springer's time a hundred years ago. Then the camp broke only once, when the cutting was over in the spring and the river drivers appeared to take the logs downstream to the mills. So after three or four months in the forest, the loggers came to town and celebrated, parades by day and carousals by night. "Grog shops were numerous, and the dominion of King Alcohol undisputed by the masses," Springer reported.

In those times, timber cruisers spent the summer surveying prospective cuts while farm crews made hay for winter fodder, first for oxen and later horses. Throughout the Maine woods today you come upon areas once cleared for hay now being reclaimed by the woods, where a farmhouse, barns and other outbuildings still stand: Pittston Farm, Grant Farm, Chamberlain Farm, to name some. The houses are civilized and incongruous — nineteenth-century rural architecture in the middle of nowhere — but handsome. I have thought many times that these outposts could become jumping-off places for fishermen, canoeists and hunters—a recreation opportunity for the forest products companies.

In early fall, roads were laid to the cutting sites, a process known as "swamping" because of the wet, boggy character of the flat, low ground. Before the first snows camp was built, a sleeping shelter containing kitchen and mess table, where men sat, socialized and sang songs on the celebrated Deacon's bench, and a shelter for horses called a hovel. (I saw Edmund Roy's hovel. It was turned into a garage.) With the freeze-up and heavy snow, cutting proceeded in earnest until the river drive both ended and resumed the cycle.

The seasonal changes still exist to some extent. Camp closes when the snow becomes too deep for skidders and Caterpillar tractors, and summer is the best time to make roads and survey timber prospects. Usually there can be no heavy work done in the woods in the spring and late fall because the ground is soft and roads turn into quagmires. But if the woods do not present a fire hazard, some cutting operations are resumed in summer.

The machines have changed life and work in the woods just as they have changed everything else. While economic factors clearly have dictated the surrender to "progress," only time will tell whether this is not another example of the hastening of man's own environmental doom. New technology has made other resources, other materials — aluminum, steel, plastic and fiber glass — competitive with wood products. As long as the environmental costs — resource depletion, the energy factor and pollution — are not accounted for, the lumbermen will have to modernize too, save on labor, increase efficiency and yield. (Of course, the pulp and paper industries have been polluters from the very beginning of their technology.) Already skidders and Caterpillars, then a second generation of work-savers — chippers, delimbers, stackers and pulp tree harvesters — have made an awful mess in the woods. And their arrival has justified different methods of cutting, taking larger and larger blocks or strips of trees: massive clear cutting. As a result, the forest to a large extent has lost its looks, its natural diversity, and its capacity to resist wind, erosion and disease.

Certainly the lives of the foresters have changed. It is now possible for Edmund Roy to keep an eye on his farm in Ste. Germaine, where he has eighty-five Holsteins producing 1,200 pounds of milk worth $84 a day. And while Roy and Ste. Hilaire boasted that the men were as tough as ever, when I saw all those vehicles parked outside in the moonlight I recalled the contemptuous comment I had read in Stewart Holbrook's *Holy Old Mackinaw*. "The highways, in fact, have done as much or more than the women," he wrote, "to reduce the logger to proletarian status."

Not a word was spoken in the mess hall during breakfast, an enormous meal consumed in silence.* Orange juice, apricot pie, jam layer cake, doughnuts, head cheese, fried eggs, bacon, diced potatoes and coffee. The men straggled out as they finished eating and rinsed their paraphernalia in the sink. It was not yet seven; the day was only beginning to break.

I went off with Mike Dann, a 1968 University of Maine forestry graduate and one of two foresters who reported to the district supervisor, Ken Hughes. Mike spent as much time in the woods as the loggers, scaling, inspecting operations, and surveying for cutting

---

*While I first imagined the absolute lack of conversation had to do with the ravenous appetites and workmanlike attitude of the men, I later learned that it went back to an old logging camp rule: silence prevents arguments or real fistfights.

permits. While Seven Islands had begun to employ a new mechanical scale that actually weighed truckloads of logs, from which board footage could be computed, 10 percent of the loads still had to be scaled by hand in order to obtain data for calibrating the machine (in other words, to maintain accuracy in equating load weight with wood volume). Scaling is a traditional term that actually has nothing to do with weight. The scaler uses a measuring stick inscribed with figures that indicate the board footage of a log according to its diameter and length. Yet a good scaler does not judge by the stick alone. He must take into account the log's taper as well as the amount of rotten or useless wood it contains. It takes keen judgment. After a morning's work, two scalers of differing skill may be thousands of board feet apart.

Seven Islands' permits are based either on a diameter limit or a marked cut. The limit usually applies in a forest stand where the mixture of trees, by both size (age) and species, follows a consistent pattern. In this case, Mike Dann will presume, after analyzing a part of the stand, what its entire content and yield is likely to be. Moreover, after it is cut, the stand will look the same throughout. There will be no gaps or thick clumps after cutting. So the permit will specify that trees exceeding a certain diameter can be cut, depending on the species — pine, spruce, fir, birch or another hardwood. A marked cut is necessary where the trees have not grown up in a consistent or uniform pattern. If diameter limitations were followed in such an area, the forest would end up being decimated in some places, still dense in others. As a consequence, the stand of trees would be left vulnerable to wind damage, and conditions would be poor for continuing growth. When Dann comes upon a section of forest where this could happen he walks through the entire stand, taking a strip at a time. He marks with orange paint only those trees to be felled, making certain that the forest's regenerative capacity — existing seedlings, small trees and seeding potential (the trees Sinclair called "trainers") — will be preserved.

Seven Islands' policy follows the longstanding practice of previous Pingree estate managers: encourage uneven growth, a sound mixture of trees of different generations, so that selective cutting always will be followed. Some areas of northern Maine were decimated by the spruce budworm, most heavily during the 1920s. Where a large area of forest was thus wiped out, an even age stand was the successor. The only way to encourage uneven growth is by improvement cutting, hard for a big corporation to justify economically. Yet ideally, with the long term in mind, trees would be cut down for the express purpose of opening up the woods, allowing sunlight penetration and selective growth. Instead of a lot of small-trunk trees sprouting up thickly like weeds, there would be a lesser number of thick, healthy specimens. And in the gaps of sunlight new generations of seedlings would stand up and join the growing army.

Seven Islands is not the only Maine land manager to cut trees selectively. But the others have been forced to cut more aggressively and have left far fewer high-grade trees, since they own their mills and have to meet production demands. Seven Islands, with no mills, can wait out market developments. "We're free to do what is right for the trees, not just what is economically necessary," Dann said. "Every time we cut the woods, we're trying to improve it."

Guided by the tracks of a skidder and the angry snarl of a chain saw, Dann and I found the team of Lessard and Veer, the pacesetters. Behind them the forest had already been cut. Tops and branches, the "slash," were quite evenly distributed, and the overall effect was not as devastating or ugly as I'd anticipated; a uniform pattern of trees remained standing. Dann pointed out that seedlings, and trees not quite ready to be taken, were undamaged so far. "If the pulp market improves, this stand could be cut again in two years," he said.

I asked what he was looking for as he inspected the operation. He briefly mentioned six criteria.

— Diameter limits must be followed.
— Small, merchantable trees cannot be harmed.
— Stumps must be low.
— Tops cannot be cut farther down than where the trunk diameter is four inches.
— The road system (i.e., skidder trails) must be efficient, so as to make the most use of the machine (e.g., its winch cables reach out fifty feet) and the least damage to the woods.
— Forest breakage all around must be prevented by skillful cutting technique.

If Dann saw excessive violations (a few mistakes were inevitable), he would speak to Edmund Roy and let the boss handle it his way.

To my unpracticed eye, it appeared that Lessard and Veer were every bit as resourceful as Roy had said they were. Maybe I should have watched an average crew. It took Veer only thirty seconds to drop a large spruce, notching it on one side so as to aim its flight precisely down an opening in the forest, then cutting all the way through from the other side. In less than an hour there were eight fair-sized trees (around three hundred board feet each) fallen and limbed, ready for the skidder that had returned from the yard. Lessard maneuvered his machine with extraordinary economy, getting off to fasten a choker cable to each log, then snaking them all together on a power winch. (There were ten choker cables, room for two more logs.)

We followed Lessard to the yarding area, watching him drag the wooden carcasses so as to avoid damage to the remaining trees in the cutting area and along either side of his road. Even with care and skill, though, the skidder is far less considerate than a horse, particularly in the summer when the ground gets churned up. (This point can be demonstrated dramatically by looking at aerial photographs of forest stands logged by machine and by animal.)

In the yarding area yet another motorized monster, the loader, took the bunch of tree trunks (aptly called a "twitch") and stacked them into a bank. Then Lessard got out his chain saw and began to make sawlogs. Dann explained that a clever man could make money by judging correctly where to make cuts so as to take advantage of the way the trunk tapered or was swollen in certain sections. Under the Maine Log Rule, the scaling stick was calibrated to favor longer logs, yet a smart man might find it as productive to cut shorter logs when the taper was sharp. Then again, maybe he could get a long log with seemingly less taper by cutting the narrowest end on a bulging point of the trunk. This was a game played between the scaler and the man with the saw.

That afternoon, I rejoined Ken Hughes and we headed south through the lands of three other companies. Along one stretch, the roadside had been bulldozed in such a manner that the trees (spruce and fir) were badly undermined and weakened. Storms had knocked many of them down and they lay toppled outward or in sharp recline against the forest, damaging the other trees and posing a threat as blight carriers by decaying and attracting bugs and worms.

Once we stopped to gaze upward and ahead through a corridor of white pine — one of the few concentrations of these giants left, Hughes told me. The white pine was once wilderness gold, prized by the king for ship masts and by the settlers for fine lumber. In old farmhouses you still see floors, wainscoting and tables made of pine boards over two feet thick, clear-grained and devoid of knots. When pines grow old in a stand, their lower branches die and drop off, and the trees continue to put on thickness over the knots, making clear pine all the way outward from a core maybe two feet in diameter. You find few such specimens anymore, although the trees we saw were candidates, some being more than four feet, breast height diameter.

The white pines formed the transitional zone, or southern edge, of the North Woods. By the middle of the last century, they were gone as large stands — in Spencer's chronicle, "doomed by the avarice and enterprise of the white man, gradually to disappear from the borders of civilization, as have the Aborigenes of this country before the onward march of the Saxon race."

I stood on the engine hood of the pickup with my camera, looking ahead at two of the biggest white pine I had ever seen, flanking the road like two black columns feathered in green. A patch of clouds had filtered the sun to a distinct yellow ball that sat right above and between this pine portal. Perhaps these two were pumpkin pines, a variety that grew along brooks and in ravine bottoms; they probably were so named because they grew fast in wet ground, and in old age their cores turned soft like that of a pumpkin, and their wood was golden-hued too.

That night, at Great Northern's Scott Brook Camp, I talked for nearly two hours with Ken Allen, another Seven Islands forester. I had heard that the previous summer, fresh out of school, he had held a temporary job taking the public on bus tours of the Scott Paper Company's controversial clear-cut operations at Spencer Bay. I had circled the area in a seaplane, had read about it — both sides — and had heard the opinions of other Maine foresters who were generally critical.

Clear-cutting! Discussion about this method is inevitable and unavoidable in the light of the national public controversy and congressional hearings concerning it — and in the light of economic pressures and increasing mechanization in forest industry.

In general, clear-cutting is the taking of trees — everything standing, except for maybe a few scattered seed trees — in solid patches, blocks or strips that are as small as three acres or as large as three thousand acres. This method is in direct opposition to cutting only mature trees or a certain variety (e.g., smaller fir for pulp) on a select basis. As it applies to the forest landscape, then, clear-cutting is a descriptive term. Selective cutting amounts to a thinning-out process. As the virgin forests have disappeared, as mechanization has increased, and as new seeding methods have been developed, clear-cutting has been justified increasingly by all the forest products companies. However, all the arguments I have seen boil down to economics. A company can't afford to build the solid roads needed for the new logging equipment just to take out a select percentage of trees. It is easier to seed an open area and even fertilize and spray it from the air than it is to wait for seedlings to grow and young trees to mature in selectively cut forests.

It is argued that in sandy or soft soil, in bogs or wet ground, where the holding quality of the ground is weak and unstable, if you cut selectively you simply expose the remaining trees to the possibility of windfall. And indeed, in certain cases this is a valid point, and probably the trees should be cut in patches or small blocks in such a way as to minimize erosion and storm destruction. And if wood must compete with other materials under present marketing conditions, compromises will no doubt have to be made with clear-cutting methods.

Yet, to look at history, there are telling arguments against widescale application of clear-cutting, beginning right with Gifford Pinchot, father of the U.S. Forest Service. Pinchot was the man who articulated and refined the collective principles of enlightened forestry for this nation. In *A Primer of Forestry*, a publication of the Bureau of Forestry in its first year, 1905, Pinchot advocated what he called "conservative lumbering." The loggers, he stated, should take no more out of their woods than will be matched by existing growth rates.

Today the forest industry says it is doing just that. But if Pinchot were here to guide us, I bet he would ask the industry two questions. First, if your growth matches your cutting, then why are you asking for millions more acres of U.S. Forest Service land? Second, when you balance your growth against your consumption of trees, are you counting just your own land holdings, where you will contain and practice your operations *forever*, or are you taking into account public forests that have not yet been cut or have been logged only sparingly, lands that the U.S. citizen might prefer to keep as wilderness?

Pinchot probably did not foresee how forest economics and technology would be changed nearly seventy years later. He always insisted that the forest should be cut "in such a way as to leave standing trees and the young growth as nearly unharmed by the lumbering as possible." But if it seems that I am reaching into an old hat, then there are plenty of present-day advocates carrying on the Pinchot tradition, men who say out loud and feel in their hearts that present trends toward clear-cutting have gone much too far.

Since 1970, the forest industry has been pushing to get the Forest Service to open up millions of acres of additional land for clear-cutting. Their demands have resulted in congressional hearings and government-sponsored studies. The most telling report was presented by Arnold Bolle, dean of the University of Montana School of Forestry. He coined the descriptive term "timber mining," and he accused the Forest Service of doing just that by allowing the Bitterroot National Forest to be ruined by clear-cutting. Mainly he felt that the lumbermen should be forced to recognize the forest's *other* values, both environmental and aesthetic. "The combinations are limited only by particular situational factors and the ingenuity of the forester," he wrote in an article.

The industry has for years used the term "sustained yield management" as a way of describing forestry that matches the cut with the growth. Yet as Dr. Robert R. Curry, also at the University of Montana, testified regarding the way private companies have abused their cutting rights on public lands, "multiple use–sustained yield is being patently and overtly violated if that yield is not, and cannot, be sustained beyond one to four cuttings, after which the soils of the national forests will be unable to support merchantable sawtimber until replenished by slow, geological weathering in five thousand or more years."

This is a complicated business. New terms and new justifications keep popping up. In Professor Curry's testimony, the term "multiple use" was coupled with "sustained yield." Well, multiple use describes a requirement under the law that, before public lands can be contracted to the forest industry, their entire use potential must be considered. Often it may serve the public better to let the land sustain itself naturally, as a wilderness area, even if the forest rots and wastes away, as the industry claims will happen. After all, when you enter the wilderness it helps your psyche considerably to find dead trees and wood rotting on the ground. So maybe the forest has grown so dark from the canopy spread by mature trees that wildlife has diminished from a scarcity of lower vegetation and sunlight. The point is that nobody has been there manicuring and "improving" and "managing" and so forth. We need places like this. A few years ago the Great Northern Company came up with the term "working wilderness" to describe the happy balance of public recreation, environmental protection and enlightened forestry that was achieved on its lands in northern Maine. Unfortunately, there is no such thing in the truest sense as a working wilderness.

In my view — and I am brash enough to think Gifford Pinchot would share it — good forestry should consider four criteria.

— Growth should *exceed* the cut, in order to anticipate future demands for wood products as well as the likelihood of damage from disease, fire and flood. Moreover, growth projections should not depend on receiving additional land through government bid or lease.

— Loggers should keep in mind that a forest's environmental health is in proportion to its biological diversity. To be sure, a climax forest, an ultimate stage of natural evolution imposing a narrow range of life conditions, may lead to a disaster as great as indiscriminate clear-cutting. For example, since we put out the forest fires that were caused by lightning and that used to wipe out millions of acres of woods, maybe our climax forests will succumb to disease or just rot away. Yet I think we should let a good number of them decide for themselves and concentrate mainly on controlling our bothersome tendency to overexploit. Foresters I talked to in Maine told me that uneven age stands showed greater resistance to disease and also produced better trees, as long as they were managed selectively.

— The cutting should not damage the character of the soil either by causing erosion or by increasing the evaporation rate so that the forest loses its capacity as a natural water impoundment. In the Canadian Northwest I once saw a steep slope so cleared of trees that its topsoil had washed down into an ocean inlet below and it appeared unlikely that cedar or fir would cover that mountainside ever again. This can happen, and in some places already may have, in Maine. And what if a clear-cut makes such an open spot that the evaporation rate is accelerated greatly from increased sunlight penetration and the forest floor loses moisture that was counted upon to sustain the succeeding growth? I could never get a satisfactory answer to this question, nor have I read one.

— Finally, good forestry preserves natural beauty. This is the toughest of the four criteria to treat because it is so subjective. It involves taking into account the public needs for park recreation *and* wilderness escape. It raises the question of how soon? Although cutting destroys forest aesthetics according to the number of trees left standing, the clear-cut advocates say that if you wait long enough, the woods will look green and wild and succulent again. And I'm tempted to say, sure, just when you're ready to cut it again. Perhaps the only way to resolve the problems caused by this fourth consideration is somehow to insure that the public has a voice in determining how forest lands are to be managed and maintained, even if these lands are private. For the doctrine of public trust has embraced all kinds of laws in the past. It is the basis of zoning and is one of the reasons a factory can be shut down for dumping noxious exhaust gas all over a community. The public has a large stake in those North Woods of Maine, an area comprising over half the state. Mismanaged, the public is denied a resource as well as a wilderness that must exist, even if access is limited.

Ken Allen and I went over this ground, talking about some aspects longer than others. It was I who kept pressing, who kept becoming contentious. He was open-minded and polite. He wasn't at all *sure* about any of these things, though he hoped that on the job he'd learn. Considering the conditions of the soil and the forest, he felt on the whole that Scott Paper Company was justified by clear-cutting at Spencer Bay, opening blocks of the woods no more than would sustain a fifty-year cutting cycle. The soil was extremely soft, so selective cutting might lead to windfalls. While the trees were cleaned out completely by a frightening mechanized duo, a Beloit Harvester and a Slashmobile, seedlings grew up soon. The entire area had been blighted by the spruce budworm in the twenties, so by 1971 it was an even age stand, the trees growing in dense stalks, jammed together like people leaving a football stadium. This was the way Allen explained the Spencer Bay operations en route on the bus from Greenville. There the people could see for themselves how the forest was regenerating.

Allen did not criticize Scott. But I still felt I was right when I suggested that the company was really backed into a corner by economic events. Since the forest had not been thinned out long ago, since Scott did not have holdings nearly as adequate or diverse as other companies in Maine, and since Scott had to keep pulpwood going to its big mill on the Kennebec River, there was little choice from an economic standpoint but to clear-cut Spencer Bay. Would increased evaporation from the opened slopes throw a monkey wrench into Scott's growth projections? What if there was another blight? Would the soil eventually be drained of nutrients? Why did Scott get tied down to such a limited market anyway? I had interviewed an official of the International Paper Company a few days before, and he had noted that his operations were marketing sawlogs for the moment since paper prices and demands were down. Clearly, other forest operations in Maine did not share Scott's problem. To these reservations Ken Allen refrained from comment and I didn't press, because the answers weren't simple and maybe there weren't any at all, at least as far as Scott was concerned.

I walked outside and down what passed for the main street of Great Northern's Scott Brook Camp. I could see through the cabin windows (no shades needed) that most of the men had turned in. Even so, here as at Roy's camp, the place was brightly lit, the rationale being, I suppose, that since there was a big diesel generator good for 30,000 kilowatts, you might as well use it.

Rounding a bend, in two minutes I left all the hubbub behind and was heading east into a full moon and down a one-lane highway that was so brightly lit from the moon and stars that you could pick out the shadows cast by small clumps of snow and spot the footprints of animals. Around another bend, I raised my wool cap above my ears and strained to catch the slightest sounds. Silence. I stamped my foot on the packed snow. I slapped my hands. Still silence. So I shouted. "Hello. Hello." Not much better. No echo at all, and my voice was swallowed up by the snowdrifts. I hallooed and hallooed again — Indian whoops and rebel yells — but no sound that I could make would transform my insignificance.

As the road twisted, the moonbeam came on and off and on again. At times I could clearly read the second hand on my watch. A lone pine stood out against the sky ahead, and at my feet there were different sets of tracks, a rabbit's and something larger that maybe caught the rabbit, although there was no sign of a scuffle.

On the way back, rounding one of those bends again, coming out of the darkness, a sudden light flashed on me from behind. Quick, a truck's coming, I thought, and jumped aside. But it was just the same old moonbeam. Round the last turn was the reassurance of Scott Brook City. Naked light bulbs, a television set flickering through the window, the parked trucks, the barking of the cook's German shepherd, three men strolling toward me as if we were about to pass and mutter hello to one another in a small town, which indeed we were.

Ken Hughes and I drove out of the woods on a road that had just been plowed after a lunch with Charles Nelson, the district supervisor for Great Northern at the Lobster Camp. I was depressed, thinking about what Nelson had told me. Sensing that maybe there was a shift in the attitudes of young people toward work in the wilderness, Great Northern had run a four-month training school in the forest near Telos Lake. With 50 percent federal financing, the trainees were paid three dollars an hour for a forty-hour week, learning all phases of forestry production work. Some dropped out early, more dropped out as the summer lengthened, until less than half a dozen completed the course. Nelson didn't know what had happened, whether the students got bored or the work was too tough.

Then he told me about the new machines coming into use, one of which could cut down a hundred trees an hour, eight to twelve inches thick, delimbing each tree and depositing the slash right back on the ground where it would do the most good. As the companies encountered labor problems, as the machines became more efficient, some form of clear-cutting would become necessary, probably strip harvesting, giving the machine a straight line to run. Since the river driving was over, the supply of logs for the pulp mills had to be kept moving, day in, day out, by trucks over new road systems. I wondered what this would do to the woods. From horses, to skidders five times as fast, to one-man-operated harvesters that would be even faster. I sensed that Nelson was wondering too.

We left the wilderness at Kodajo, which Hughes said was pronounced Ko-*dád*-joe. We drove past the Spencer Bay area and I looked through a thin veil of trees; I couldn't miss one of Scott's celebrated clear-cuts. (The forest companies think their public image is protected as long as they leave a strip of trees to conceal the destruction. A friend of mine calls this "peekaboo cutting.") I thought how I had seen seedlings, young trees, middle-aged trees, not-quite-ready-to-cut trees all growing side by side, when Edmund Roy's loggers executed a cut. There was always growth — generations overlapping — this way. Mike Dann had explained that it was best when at least three cycles grew side by side. But the clear-cut was like an A-bomb blast.

Hughes saw my expression and issued his only comment on the subject. "I guess it'll take a while to get a forest in there," he said.

THE LAST LOG DRIVE

THE SUN HAD JUST APPEARED, still a pale yellow glow through the overcast of the day and night before, when the last log drive was commenced on the West Branch of the Machias River. My watch showed that it was fourteen past eight on the morning of April 27, 1971. Dick Albee, the St. Regis Company's river boss, gave the word to start paying out the thick wire cable that closed the boom above Great Falls. The boom consisted of a string of logs chained together and secured to trees on opposite banks. Behind it strained one and a half million board feet worth of sawlogs, over a quarter of a year's production for the Passamaquoddy Lumber Company mill six miles downstream in Whitneyville. The wood filled every chink of the river and stretched back out of sight for half a mile.

Moments earlier, Albee had slithered down from a branch fifteen feet up in a big white maple where he had slung still another cable that was attached to the near end of the boom. As the tension was eased on the first cable, this one took up the slack until the boom was opened about sixty feet, a third the width of the river. The idea was to allow no more than a few logs at a time to pass through that mouth. This way they wouldn't jam up again as easily on the rocks and snags downstream. Since the wire that regulated the mouth sloped down from the tree branch, the logs were able to pass beneath it. The first group moved slowly, as a pack; then they were separated in the eddies and swirls of the free water.

A small and agile man, Albee hopped across the front of the log-jam and stationed himself on the end of the boom. Here he began to prod the logs along through the mouth. But most of the time he seemed to be leaping out onto bunches that were tangled up like jackstraws, heading in all directions. He jimmied them loose with an implement known as a Peavey * and then jumped back onto another bunch or the boom, controlling his moves perfectly to avoid being pitched into the cold water and its dangerous and unpredictable burden.

It was precarious business, but everyone in Albee's crew seemed to know just where he should be and what he should do, and there was scarcely another word spoken after his first order. Some men went out on the jam farther back from the opening. Others used Peaveys to keep the banks running free.

Stevie Kilton, assigned by St. Regis to be my escort, pointed to the first logs floating slowly into an eddy not far above the white water that marked the beginning of the falls. "Come on," he said. "And we'll be in time to catch them coming through. It's a good sight."

We took a trail along the river, a few yards back in the trees which climbed right down among the ledges and boulders along the falls. The din of the pounding water drowned out all other sounds. The forest was damp and pungent from the rising spray. Crowded to the brink by the trees, we stood and waited on a big rock. Suddenly there was a sound like an artillery cannonade, a distinct percussion against the roar of the river, and in the gorge beneath I could spot the logs tumbling over the rocks. Kilton beamed. "That's what makes log driving so enjoyable," he said. "You find a nice comfortable spot to lie down in the sun and you don't have a worry until you can't hear those logs any more. Then you know there's something wrong and you're stopped up again somewhere."

I had asked to come along on this drive because it was the only one still held in Maine that compared to the operations described by John Springer in his 1851 classic. "No employment that I am aware of threatens the life and health more than river-driving," Springer wrote. "Many a poor fellow finds his last resting-place on the bank of some wild stream, in whose stifling depths his last struggle for life was spent, where the wild wood skirts its margin — where, too, the lonely owl hoots his midnight requiem."

Springer had run his own timber business. In those times, there

---

*So named for Joseph Peavey, the Bangor blacksmith who invented it in 1858 only to file too late for a patent. Fortunately, he was a prolific inventor, successful in other projects.

was still plenty of white pine left to be sent downstream to the saw-mill. Then, in the 1880s, the supply of pine dwindled and large spruce logs were floated out, in lengths ranging from twelve to twenty feet, known as long logs. These drives petered out during the early 1930s and, except for the Machias long-log drive and a few other small operations, sawtimber thereafter was taken to the mill by rail or truck.

Then the pulp drives prevailed. These were messy operations. The long-log drive had begun sometime in April and ended in June. So during summer the river was clear again for the people to fish, canoe, and enjoy as they wished. The pulp logs were cut in short four-foot lengths and at least 6 percent sank or got caught up somewhere. More-over, the period of the drive was extended well into late fall in order to sustain the demands of the pulp and paper mills. Impoundment dams were built to hold back water that was released whenever it was needed to keep the pulp logs going. As a result, rivers and tributaries throughout Maine were damaged. The great mass of lost waterlogged pulpwood wiped out fish spawning beds and depleted the rivers' oxy-gen supply as it decomposed. It destroyed the tiny bottom organisms that trout, salmon and bass like to feed on. As the waterways were dammed, the natural flow cycles that the fish depend upon were dis-rupted.

By 1971, all kinds of log driving were under attack by environ-mentalists. That summer, the Great Northern Paper Company held its last drive on the West Branch of the Penobscot, where in recent years 150,000 cords annually were transported to the big mill in Millinocket. On the Kennebec, log driving was threatened by both court and legislative action. It would surely be discontinued.

The Machias drive came to an end not so much because of the environmental outcry as because of the dwindling supply of long logs that could be conveniently dumped into the river. Like the other forest operators, St. Regis had found that it was probably more eco-nomical anyway to use trucks to get deep into the woods for *both* sawtimber and pulpwood. A new system of roads was being built even as I participated in this river event.

I wanted to see how conditions had changed, or persisted, since Springer wrote about them, and St. Regis was most accommodating. All told, only 4 million board feet would be moved, most of it in the first two days, and a final million and a half board feet during a summer cleanup. When Springer was on the West Branch of the Machias, nearly 35 million board feet worth of logs were moved. Some twenty sawmills converted 18 million board feet into long lumber and fourteen lath machines made 16.8 million board feet into laths, the thin strips that were laid behind plaster walls and ceilings. There were 475 men and 400 oxen and horses employed in these particular operations.

Kilton led the way farther down the trail. It wound back into the forest where the thick spruce blocked out the thunder of the falls and the moving logs. It had been a tough winter, and in the dark hollows there were still deep patches of snow on the ground where we sank in up to our knees. We came back to the river by a logan where the river made a big turn away from us and created a back-eddy. On a promontory across the logan stood a cabin that Kilton said was leased from the company by a retired and well-liked logger known as "Hunk" Hurlbert. "This is a good place to fish and relax in the summer," Kilton said.

We crossed over to it on a pontoon made of logs lashed together. We could look upriver and see the end of Great Falls and a steady stream of logs floating our way. About half of them shot into the back-eddy where they spun around lazily before being caught up again in the current. These logs and others moving out in the main current were driven under terrific pressure right at the point of the promontory, where they were caught on a rocky ledge that extended underwater. Two men were stationed there with pick poles to keep the logs moving before they congregated in one jamup. If this situation was not watched carefully, the whole river might turn into an impasse of logs.

Willie Mitchell and Joe Launiere, the two men, worked with Peaveys and a much longer pick pole. They were so sparing but efficient in their movements that it seemed like an immensely enjoyable job. But it was hard, exhausting work, as I soon found out when I took hold of a Peavey. There would be long moments of being entranced in the view upriver, watching the black specks of logs disappearing and bobbing up again. The sun was invigoratingly warm as it broke the cold grip of the winter and there was a fragrant scent in the air. But then, without warning, a log would break from the pack in the back-

eddy or come shooting in from the main current like an errant tor-
pedo.

I was embarrassingly clumsy with the Peavey. Several times, I
pried too vigorously and lunged forward, desperately lashing out at
the log to keep myself from diving in. Once I was unable to pry
loose an enormous log, fully two feet in diameter. Within seconds, a
bundle stacked up behind it and even with help from the others it still
took fifteen minutes of frantic exertion to break the mess apart.
"You'll feel lame through the shoulders tonight," Kilton warned. I
was sore long before then.

Launiere told stories about life in the woods in a guttural, broken
English. He was part Indian, part French-Canadian, and his seamed,
aquiline features made him look older than fifty-six. He wore a base-
ball cap with the initial M for Machias, and he'd taken what I later
learned was a common precaution against cold water leaking into his
boots. His heavy work trousers were stuffed inside, and over the tops
of the boots he folded down tucks which he sealed with a red rubber
band taken from a homemade preservative jar. He was immensely
happy, grinning broadly all the time. "I like it out here," he said. "I
could get a job in a factory, but it wouldn't be the same. No moose,
deer, or beaver."

Kilton and I went back up the trail to the boom-opening to eat
lunch. Without much thought, I had expected it to be provided. In
Springer's time, the river drivers had eaten hot and hearty meals
four times a day, at 5, 10, 2 and 8 o'clock. The cook and his helpers
had kept up with supply boats called "wanguns," the Indian word
for bait. I learned from Kilton that this custom had prevailed until
very recently. He didn't know why it had stopped. Like other U.S.
businesses, I thought, maybe the forest companies felt that the pleas-
urable traditions were out of keeping with demands to step up the
revenues and the profit margins for the stockholders.

Kilton generously insisted that I share his shrimp sandwich and
thermos of coffee. We sat on logs beside the aluminum outboard we
had used to come downriver while he filled me in on the extensive
and colorful jargon of river driving.

"You call the logs that are behind the boom a *body of logs*," he
said. "Today we broke down the body and turned it over Great Falls.
The logs you saw piled up on the bank by Smith's Landing, where we

started, that were dumped there by trucks, were *rolling tiers*. When you tip them into the river with Peaveys, you're *watering the logs*. When you let the boom go, you *cut it*. The logs are moved in the woods by great big tractors called *skidders*."

"Are those the machines that gouge up the woods and make such a mess?" I asked.

"Yes, when the ground is soft." He continued with the glossary. "The logs that get left behind are what we call *the rear*. At the end of the drive, the men go back upriver and *rear down* what's left; some say *pick up* or *clean up the rear*. When they leave off at the end of the day, they report the rear was at Smith's Landing tonight or wherever it was."

A big body of logs had refused to join the others that Albee and the others had been prodding toward Great Falls. This stubborn flotilla, referred to by Kilton as a *break*, clogged up the river next to where we sat drinking our coffee. We could see two men sent up to pry it loose. The idea was to find the *key*, the one or two logs that had caused the whole mess to get bound up in the first place. I had read of frightening moments in river-driving history when such a logjam developed in turbulent water in a narrow gorge and a man would be lowered by rope to unloosen it. As he found the key, he would be jerked out of the avalanche he had started. But often it was too late. Dead river drivers were buried in flour barrels joined together. Many of them were then memorialized in ballads sung in lumber camps and on the river drive.

Kilton was an ex–river boss and all day he'd been chafing to get in on the action. Now he moved swiftly out onto the jam and I found myself joining him. The three men probed along the leading edge of the logs, jumping from one to another, and it was not long before they found the key.

"She's moving," Kilton shouted.

All of us sprinted back across the logs, but in a few minutes the body was jammed again and the three men returned to the congested middle. I sat on the shore this time and watched. They worked silently until they finally unlocked it again. The only sound was the clank-clank of the Peaveys and the splashing of logs as they jumped off.

That night the men motored by boat back to Smith's Landing where they'd parked their cars. If the drive had covered a longer distance and taken up to a week instead of two days, they would have camped out and there would have been at least two hot meals in the woods. Albee told everyone to be back at six-thirty the next morning.

The second day's work would clean up the river until much later in the spring, when the remaining million and a half board feet would be "watered" and driven to the mill. The eight men under Albee were to cruise by outboard upstream a few miles, breaking off to follow a tributary called Old Stream to where the body of logs lay behind a boom. Kilton was detailed elsewhere so I was on my own. He said the stream was narrow and there would be some excitement.

The day began clear and cold. I arrived early, but not before robins, red-winged blackbirds and white-throated sparrows were striking up everywhere. I watched a male hairy woodpecker fly into a cedar tree and drum for insects, rat-a-tat-tat. He was matched upstream by an even louder member of his clan.

Lynnwood Archer was the first to arrive, in a pickup truck. He had been helpful the day before, pointing out different types of hardwoods, particularly the maples, and explaining the varied uses for wood. In the fall he was a hunting guide, but he had little use for the modern hunter.

"There are too many people in the woods now," he said. "And they'll shoot at anything. They don't really enjoy the woods and they don't even like the taste of the deer. It just means something to be able to drive back with one on top of their car."

I rode with Archer and Willie Mitchell, the stout, near-deaf old-timer who had teamed with Joe Launiere below Great Falls. We were assigned to patrol the *front end,* which meant that we were to cruise back and forth among the front ranks of the moving logs, making sure they didn't get caught anywhere. We carried rope to *tie in* logs to trees along the bank where there was a snag or an indentation that might cause a jam. The secured log would act as a barrier to deflect other logs.

As we whined upstream, the sun warmed the west bank and Archer moved to that side of the river. The other side was as cold and dark as night. Old Stream was about twenty yards wide and twisted back and forth in abrupt oxbows. The beavers had chewed down trees on several of the low points that jutted out between the loops in the stream. A porcupine huddled high up on the branch of an elm and moved his head ever so slowly to see that we were safely past him. We spotted a beaver swimming and Archer got out a movie camera he'd brought along. We tried in vain to get closer.

After we watched the boom being cut, we went in pursuit of the logs, battering through them when there was no clear passage. The boat withstood the shock well. The shaft was not locked in place, so it would bounce up if it struck a log. Only once did we have to replace a sheer pin when a crash came without warning at high speed. Archer was skillful in butting the logs into the current and directing a channel, and we helped with long pick poles or Peaveys.

Albee cruised past, inspecting the logs' progress. He was grinning. "They're going good," he said, as he went by and repeated as he came back.

Bob Wright, a St. Regis officer, had shed his business suit to take station at the mouth of the boom. An old river driver, he was as graceful as Albee. "You get all the pictures you want," he told Archer, "because this will be the last one."

The trouble commenced after lunch. We had eaten our sandwiches on a narrow point dividing Old Stream from the river. Archer noticed that there were no more logs passing us.

"They're caught up somewhere," he said.

We found them at a sharp bend. On the outside of the turn, an overhanging maple tree had stopped all movement. On the inside, where the river turned to the right, logs had gone riding up into low brush and scrub that was awash in the spring high water, and a jam had developed. The middle had filled in, the logs rolling over each other until they were stacked deep down underwater and were jammed back upriver a long ways. We tied up the outboard in an inlet below the maple where it would not be damaged when the logs moved again. Grabbing a Peavey, I joined the two others.

For ten minutes we grunted and sweated, prying logs loose near the maple, the advance edge of the logjam where the river pressure seemed directed. We set free a dozen logs, but as they popped to the surface and took off more crowded in from the rear. A big head of water was building up, for the river was blocked nearly to its bed. The entire raft of logs quivered and rose and fell as the stream gushed out from underneath. It was like squeezing a high-pressure hose with your thumb, only the constricting force was provided by the weight of the logs.

Archer crossed to the far side, jumping across gaps of river, and I followed. Once I toppled over my Peavey and had to fall down over a log, drenching my feet and arms, to avoid being totally immersed. Oblivious of the hazards, I became absorbed in the operation. There was an acquired rhythm to it, and while I knew I had years to go, I imagined that I was cutting a respectable figure for a visitor. We had pried loose plenty of logs but still had not found the key that would release the entire flotilla. The smart procedure was to stand near the center of the log you were working from, where it was most buoyant. Otherwise, when it was set free, you would sink to your knees in water, the log dropping under you like an unbalanced seesaw. I had several narrow escapes for forgetting this natural law.

We seemed to be getting nowhere; the futility of the effort made it more tiring. We were reinforced by two more drivers, but another twenty minutes passed before someone found the key.

"Get back," Archer shouted, as he leaped across the front edge of the break, which was accelerating fast under a wave of water. The logs swung free and slowly straightened out to the direction of the current. I ran after Archer, avoiding a fall simply by keeping up my momentum on the rolling logs. I grabbed the maple and landed in shallow water up to my knees. I looked back and the logs were moving past as if there had been no delay.

We motored upstream to join the whole crew for a break. Bob Wright, the St. Regis officer, took the movie camera and got footage of Archer, who turned away until he'd emptied all the chewing tobacco from his mouth.

Except for picking up the rear, this drive was over. In the late spring or summer St. Regis would release water from one or more of its nine upstream dams in order to bring the river up high enough to float down the logs that the skidders had not yet reached. For some of the men, this might be their last work in the woods; for all of them it was their last tour on the river. They would not suffer materially because they would have other jobs for St. Regis or another company during this season.

Yet I sensed that for a moment, as conversation lulled, there were thoughts about the passing of a tradition.

Wright was the only one who said much. He told me quietly what the others might have been thinking too.

"It's a fever, working on the river. It gets into your blood. You're out on your own and it's a good feeling not having someone standing over you. Now we all sense that it's going out of our lives and it hurts a little."

PAYROLL OR PICKEREL

THE ASSISTANT SUPERINTENDENT of a big paper mill, a good friend of mine, was talking around the campfire one night about what would happen to the forest industry. "We may keep the mills open a while," he said, "but as the standards toughen, and they have to, and we lose all our competitive advantages, there will only be two mill complexes left in Maine, Great Northern's in Millinocket and International's in Jay."

Because of its increasing value for recreational and wilderness pursuits, Maine's forest land is becoming more expensive than the vast acreage in the southern states that is being put into trees. Moreover, once the southern conifers are through the seedling stage, they grow several times as fast as their North Woods counterparts. My friend cited these facts and then predicted that southern tree growers ultimately would produce nearly all the nation's pulpwood, growing trees fast in short cycles in a highly scientific manner comparable to the revolutionary techniques of agribusiness. "We'll use our woods instead to milk the tourists," he said. "This is a great wilderness, with brooks and rivers running all through it and mountain ranges in some parts. You can canoe in the spring and summer, climb and hike in the fall and ski in the winter or go snowshoeing and cross-country skiing."

Other men in the pulp and paper industry have concealed such thoughts, if indeed they even share them, and have talked instead about the rising demand for both lumber and paper products and how Maine forest companies had better hurry up and develop ways of growing trees faster and utilizing more of the tree. (The state of the art in 1972 was still so crude as to waste 35 percent of every fir, spruce or pine that was felled.) These men saw both paper and lumber operations expanding in the North Woods along with new manufacturing installations to process waste matter such as roots, bark, branches and treetops.

The more I traveled across the Maine woods, the more I came to think my friend in the pulp mill had a point. Installations like his were old, some of them with buildings and even production equipment that were antique. Scott's plant in Winslow was built in 1891, and the one picked up in the merger with S. D. Warren at Westbrook went back all the way to 1854. The average mill consumes well over 20 million gallons of water daily, and when this water is cycled back into a river, at the same rate, it carries a pollution load equal to that of a big city. In fact, three fair-sized pulp mills can outdo all of the domestic and municipal sewer systems in Maine in terms of the biochemical oxygen demand of these wastes.

The Council on Economic Priorities, a New York investigative group with a decidedly liberal bias, and a team of Ralph Nader's raiders conducted independent studies of Maine's forest companies. Both presented findings that indicated that the state might reap greater benefits in the long term from putting the wilderness to a use other than forestry. The CEP study, part of an overall look at the U.S. pulp and paper industry, predicted that hundreds of millions of dollars would have to be spent on pollution controls and waste treatment facilities just to meet the 1976 water quality standards. The focus of the Nader investigation was misuse of forestland and unfair advantages gained in wildland taxation.

I could see that even if the studies were hatchet jobs, when the subject was put in proper perspective there was plenty of hard evidence being gathered to show that my friend in the pulp mill was right. Maine's woodlands would continue to be harvested, but not by so many operators. Instead, modern forestry techniques would be applied throughout the woods in order to satisfy the production demands of the new or renovated mills managed by the big companies, quite likely IP and Great Northern, as my friend predicted. The resulting forest management would *rotate* operations *along* with recreational uses of the same lands. Yet in order to be economical, the harvesting would probably be almost entirely mechanized and very destructive. Cut-over forestland would be opened to mobile recreation units installed by the forest products company or by a lease operator. The logging roads might be improved for public access, so that camper trailers would also appear on the scene. The results could be very bad unless the Land Use Regulation Commission or some other arm of the state government exercised planning control. But if it were well done, rotation of the woodland areas between sustained yield production and recreation could be an ingenious solution to public needs and a real opportunity for Maine.

Nobody felt the pinch more than the Scott Paper Company. There was talk about closing down the old mill in Winslow, because a multi-million dollar capital investment was required if the plant was to meet the pollution deadline for the Kennebec. Scott's markets were suffering terribly. In terms of its overall priorities, the company did not appear ready to spend capital on a mill that dumped some 21 million gallons a day of untreated pulp wastes into the river—fibers, chips, sulfur and bleaching chemicals that used up enormous amounts of oxygen in the process of being broken down biologically. If the mill closed down, it would mean a loss of roughly a thousand jobs in the immediate area, not to mention its effect on the woodlands pay-roll.

Up there, around Moosehead Lake and Jackman, where Scott's 850,000 acres are located, there was also a crisis. No other paper company had to move wood such a distance to the mills. Having de-veloped a transportation system depending almost entirely on water-ways, Scott was faced with more costly adjustments, because the river drives were no longer going to be allowed.

The company's behavior was confusing. On the west shore of Moosehead Lake, there was evidence in the Squaw Mountain area that Scott was phasing into recreational use of the wilderness. Yet across the lake at Spencer Bay, massive clear-cutting operations were stepped up as the water quality and log-drive deadlines got closer. At the same time, neither Scott, the communities that would be affected, nor the governmental authorities that might help appeared to be actively in search of solutions to the economic and social dislocations that were surely coming.

This was sad to both me and my friend, the pulp mill superinten-dent. There was always the chance that he was wrong, and that in spite of the competitive advantages predicted for southern pulp and paper operations there would always be a future for the paper companies in Maine, not just the two with the best setup. Yet if that were the case, then the companies were wasting time by complaining about environmental costs, particularly when it was shown by the White House Council on Environmental Quality that these national firms and their counterparts in business all over were spending very little on pollution control. For example, the council noted in 1970 that to install secondary treatment facilities by 1974, a basic step in the right direction, all the companies would have to spend no more than 1.6 percent of the value of their 1967 shipments.

So there was no way that the paper industry could complain, as it did back in the heyday of the Industrial Revolution, that the whole question boiled down to "payroll or pickerel." To be sure, Maine communities faced great short-term hardship. But if the companies accepted the future as seen by my friend, or became realistic about their environmental responsibility, everyone would get over the hump soon enough.

THE WILDLANDS

EVER SINCE people banded together to form settlements, the doctrine of public trust has been a governing principle. Sometimes it is expressed in written law. But more often it is implicit and assumed. The doctrine holds that the way property is used should be reasonably consistent with the public interest. Usually it has been applied to environments that are fragile or limited and have unusual scenic appeal, such as lakes, rivers and the shoreline. But all land really should be treated as if it were a trust. After all, any one person's ownership is only temporary, and once it is abused or degraded the land may never recover. The owner of private property is a steward, no more.

In the United States, public trust underlies the most basic measures to prevent pollution from being a health hazard as well as a nuisance. In communities where zoning is established we say that a factory cannot be built next to a residential settlement except within a planning framework approved by the community and if the factory satisfies environmental requirements. It is public trust that is invoked, even if only implicitly, when we tell industries that they cannot discharge their air, water and solid wastes in a manner injurious to the people or the people's environment.

Consequently, the rights of private ownership are not absolute. They are subordinate to the common good. A man's home is his castle only when he does not turn it into a fortress to take advantage of his neighbors. There's nothing "un-American" about this. Deep down, it is everybody's wish to be assured of stability in his surroundings, to know that the land around him will be used in a way that enhances the enjoyment and value of his own property. Historically, it has been the rich man who has hollered loudest and longest about the rights of privacy and property when his neighbor began to subdivide or a new road was planned or when the noise from traffic became intolerable.

I hate to be didactic and repetitious about this, but it is a concept that is so obvious that it seems to have been overlooked, with the result that throughout the United States, not just in Maine, improper land use has become one of the major violations of public trust. And I'm still not sure that the principle is properly understood by the dozen or so private landholders — corporations and several families — who own over half the land in the state of Maine and are subject to absolutely no local government controls whatsoever.

These few landholders form a bloc of private ownership that almost entirely serves a single interest — forest products. It is a situation that is unique in the patterns of land ownership and management in the history of this nation: so much land owned privately by so few, used basically for the same purpose, within one state. The only remotely comparable case is dominant ownership by the federal government, as in Alaska, but there the public has at least a theoretical say in how the land is managed.

The results of this ownership bloc for Maine have been both good and bad. Good in the sense that so much land, virtually wilderness, has remained mostly intact by a unified commitment to forestry. And good in that now the public, through the state government, can concentrate on a small number of landowners in order to deal with the problem. And further good in that, once the public has secured leverage, there is so much potential for enlightened — even prototypical — solutions in land use to be developed.

The results have been bad in the sense that the forest products industry frequently has been abusive and indiscreet in wielding power, has naturally been guided by the profit motive in responding to present trends in land development, and still seems bent on resisting applications of public trust that ultimately will serve the good of both landowner and the people. Public servants unfortunately still seem bound by the notion that profits in paper and timber are essential for the entire economic well-being of Maine, and so attempts to channel these landholders down enlightened, new paths are all too often tempered by compromise.

The situation was well reflected in a report presented in 1969 by the

152

103rd Maine legislature's Subcommittee on Wildland Use Regulations. "While these lands represent the basic raw material resource of the *economically indispensable forest products industry* of this state," the report said, "the legislative Research Committee feels that the use to which these lands is put *should not be left to the vagaries of corporate policy*" (my italics).

As a result of this legislative study, and under the leadership of Harrison Richardson, the bright and forceful house majority leader at that time, a law was enacted that established a Land Use Regulations Commission to develop guidelines for wilderness management.

At its inception, LURC was a compromise. Its jurisdiction covered only 4 percent of the wilderness, even though this included most of the land where the pressures were the most immediate. It had virtually no enforcement power and a pitiful budget. However, in the spring of 1971, after an extraordinary campaign to muster public support, Maine's environmentalists succeeded in getting a law passed to strengthen LURC and to require that by 1973 all the unorganized territory had to be subject to a master plan that encompassed zoning controls and various land use guidelines.

All this came none too soon. Big paper companies like Scott, Great Northern and International Paper already were beginning to plunge into the recreational business, particularly Scott and IP, which set up second-home subsidiaries. These wilderness landholders realized full well that forest, lake and river frontage and valley property with a view was far more valuable developed for people than for paper. What is more, they were now paying property taxes that reflected the new value of such land.

And if it wasn't a big company, it was some franchise operator or lessee that was going ahead with wilderness development on the big company's land. Throughout the woods it was happening, and it was almost always aimless and ugly. Already, in the incorporated parts of Maine that border on the wildlands, this kind of development was abundant and dreadful. Examples of such indiscriminate, ticky-tacky construction were painfully obvious around Moosehead Lake and Kingfield, the town nearest the Sugarloaf Mountain ski area.

The pressures for recreational use were not the only forces at work in the wilderness. One day while driving near Caucomgomoc Lake, I met a crew of geologists who had spent a good deal of time in this region scouting the prospects of mineral exploitation for the Humble Oil Company. In my presence, they were never explicit about their findings or even about their hopes, but I knew from conversations with state people that more than one large U.S. corporation was looking for low-grade metals in the Maine woods — such increasingly scarce resources as copper, zinc and iron. And there was talk of open-pit mines as large as 30,000 acres.

Moreover, at the same time that industries were forced to reduce their discharges of pollutants in order to comply with the 1976 water quality deadline on the big rivers, it was obvious that the pressures for recreational development would be felt in the headwater regions of these same rivers. This land was almost entirely in unincorporated townships where there were no controls on land use. So as fast as pollution was being cleaned up downstream (and it wasn't all that fast), more pollution of a new kind was becoming a threat upstream. To be sure, it would take a lot of recreational development to equal the effluence of a paper mill. But the intrusive ugliness of such development was just as bad, a realization that was uppermost in the minds of the people who fought so hard to create LURC.

One of these leaders was James Haskell, the red-headed, outspoken, and refreshingly idealistic executive director of LURC. Whenever I stopped to talk with him in Augusta, he was frank and informative, one of those rare officials who are not afraid to speak their mind. Haskell was often accused of being too brash and cocksure to deal effectively with the wildland powers. Yet by constantly putting his case to the people and by being consistently outspoken, he had made more headway, I thought, then if he had spent more time reasoning in the back room.

"There are over 400 of these unorganized townships and plantations," he once told me and added, half seriously and half in jest, "nobody really knows the exact number because lost townships keep popping up. A government that doesn't know how it divided itself is a pretty sad state, don't you think?"

I agreed.

The fact is, most of northern Maine had been given away before statehood, in gratitude to war veterans or to pay off debts. Over the years the big interests had gradually consolidated the whole territory. In each unorganized township there was set aside a thousand-acre public lot that was to be divided four ways if incorporation ever took place: for the parsonage, the church, the grammar school, and for education in general. One of the gambits employed by both the state and the landholders was to use the public lot as a trading card. When it was located in a place considered more suitable for logging or development, the major owner of the township would simply move in.

But most often the location was unspecified. So the trick was to offer cheap land in trade. If the township did in fact incorporate and the public lot had to be designated, then the landholder would transfer the lot to his ownership and give the town land somewhere else.

The state got into the act by selling its public lands in unabashed violation of the public trust. You would suppose that an aggregation of some 400,000 acres of public lands, *an area twice as large as Baxter State Park*, would give the state a valuable trading card for applying pressure on private landholders in order to obtain parkland or space for public recreation. But the state did not see it that way and instead sold its land dirt cheap for timber rights, recreational camps, and other uses. In at least several instances, public lots were found to be designated in areas that were under development for skiing and winter colonies. In each case the public was cheated as the state allowed the developers to transfer the public lands or acquire them outright.

Such shenanigans incensed Haskell, and he did much to expose the loopholes and inadequacies in the state's supervision of the wildlands as well as the total lack of a comprehensive plan to protect the wildlands far into the future. The 1971 LURC law gave him what he needed, although it certainly could not be applied without great resistance on the part of the landlords. That was evident at the very outset as the forest products people talked about zoning and the 1973 deadline as if it were yet another example of creeping socialism, the big government takeover.

It is unfair to the little man, the small campowner, the fisherman who has leased a lot on paper company land and should be allowed to use it as he pleases, was what the companies were saying. And this was effective propaganda. But in fact, the LURC mandate was the only way to restore public trust in the wildlands by bringing some harmony to individual land use developments. Moreover, LURC went about its business through public hearings, giving all interests a chance to be heard.

Haskell set about to break down all of the wildlands into four different land use categories or districts — protection, management, holding, and development — listed according to the extent that each kind performs a conservation function. A protection district is an environment where ecological damage will likely result from any kind of development. Management districts would be lands harvested for timber and agricultural purposes. Holding districts would serve as land banks by reserving property that might have different kinds of potential. Such land might be used for a recreational colony, a new town, for additional timberland, or simply to receive the expanding growth of a contiguous development district. A development district, the least preserved from an environmental standpoint, is for residential and commercial development, from recreational colonies to the expansion of existing communities in the midst of wildlands, like Greenville, at the foot of Moosehead Lake.

If the landholders got smart they would set up their own land use committee and then work closely with Haskell. In my own mind I could see these forest managers going about it like this. First they would take an inventory of the environmental characteristics of their aggregate holdings, singling out the most important assets to be preserved — lakes, mountains, brooks, rivers, whole watersheds like the West Branch of the Penobscot next door to Baxter Park. Next they would inventory existing developments and road systems as they related to present and future patterns of growth in the wilderness. Then they would try to determine within this enormous patchwork of private lands where recreational areas and access roads could best be opened to the public in a way that would preserve the wilderness experience, a sense of mystery and solemnity in the woods. Finally, they would meet with Haskell and try to match their own ideas about land use districts with his notions.

Only then would public trust come to the North Woods of Maine in time to prevent a great deal more damage being wrought by uncontrolled or uncoordinated land use development. Here is a chance for Maine to produce a model for wilderness management and protection. Yet even as I write these words the entire matter hangs in the balance.

FOUR

The Maine Woods

BAXTER: THE IDEA AND THE VICINITY

WHILE THE LOGGERS were the first white men to appreciate the woods, this vast, still primitive portion of Maine has a greater worth than that counted in wood products revenues. I speak of its value as a natural *refuge*, an outdoor *experience*, and as an *idea* having to do with both nature and the savoring of it.

John Kauffman, a planner with the National Park Service who is as comfortable in the woods as anyone I know, likes to use the words "magical quality" to describe the appeal of the forest environment. That may seem romantic and literary. But it is so. The very term "the woods" is so all-encompassing as to suggest that it has many different contents and purposes, none of which can be easily grasped. In truth, as folklore has always presented it, the woods is a great harbor of mystery. One has to *be in it* a while before the details sink in, before environment that is superficially hostile to man takes on that "magical quality" that Kauffman and now I, his convert, love so much.

"Nature was here something savage and awful, though beautiful," Henry Thoreau wrote about a spot somewhere below the summit of Mount Katahdin. "I looked with awe at the ground I trod on, to see what the Powers had made there, the form and fashion and material of their work. This was the Earth of which we have heard, made out of Chaos and Old Night. Here was no man's garden, but the unhandselled globe."

In all my visits to Maine, before I began researching this book, I had stayed close to the coast, where picturesque towns and the arrangement of bays and islands are a landscape architect's dream. Not until I went into the woods could I understand the paroxysm that must have induced Thoreau to convert a simple word like "unhandled" into "unhandselled."

Having read Thoreau's journal, *The Maine Woods*, I decided to try his "third trip," deviating from his route only by skipping its first and last sections, which long before July 1971 had been well penetrated by civilization compared to over a century ago.

Beyond its literary value, Thoreau's account is a model of sound journalism. There was little he could have missed or didn't record about the country, people, plants, fishes, birds and animals. I was interested in seeing how his route had changed. If it was still quite the same, by carrying a copy of *The Maine Woods* with me, I could refer to the book quite literally as a guide and compare Thoreau's observations with my own. And I hoped this comparative perspective would influence my understanding of what was happening to wilderness areas throughout the United States. Thoreau wrote when much of the continent was still a wilderness and there was not yet a need for parks and natural preservation. Yet I believe that for all his elitism, his attitudes have an application today.

Thoreau, an unnamed companion, and Joe Polis, the Indian guide who has become a kind of folk hero to modern-day Maine canoeists, launched their 18¼-foot birchbark at the southern tip of Moosehead Lake at four in the morning, July 24, 1857. It took only eleven days for them to reach Indian Island at Oldtown on the Penobscot. The route followed some forty miles of Moosehead Lake to the Northeast Carry, a two-mile portage to the West Branch of the Penobscot. After following this for twenty miles and crossing the head of Lake Chesuncoak, the party poled up the Umbazooksus Stream and into the lake of that name. Then they slogged two miles across the wet and buggy mud Pond Carry, taking the Mud Pond outlet to Chamberlain Lake. After making a side trip up to Pillsbury Island in the Allagash–St. John watershed, they headed back southward, down Chamberlain Lake and through the Telos Thoroughfare (where the present Allagash Wilderness Waterway begins). Then they entered the short canal that was built to reverse the flow of the lake into the St. John watershed by connecting it up to the Penobscot, thus avoiding Canadian log duties. The canal flows into Webster Lake, from which the route follows the Webster Brook to Grand Lake Matagamon. After carrying around the dam at the southern end, the party was on the East Branch of the Penobscot, which merges with the West Branch well above Oldtown.

That Thoreau covered nearly three hundred miles in less than a fortnight — exploring on foot (getting hopelessly lost once, and then losing his friend), collecting botanical specimens, and taking such detailed notes — is a considerable feat.

We chose to do 125 miles of the same route in five days, and felt throughout as if we were pushing hard. We stopped at most of the same places, finding that the natural features had changed remarkably little, if at all, and that the woods along the water had largely recovered from lumbering.

"It is somewhat like navigating a thunderspout," Thoreau wrote of Webster Brook. Indeed, on this very wild stretch, a rock ledge tore through the stern of my canoe and we very nearly filled up. During a stop on the Webster Brook we penetrated scrub and bramble thickets to come upon the remains of an old cabin and, in the middle of a clearing, the bleached skeleton of a bateau, fully forty feet long and exquisitely shaped like a dory. This was the essential craft that bore the loggers on their drives and, according to Thoreau, "properly manned, shoots rapids as a matter of course." The long-abandoned encampment had, by dint of natural forces beyond my understanding, held out against the succession of the forest that had seemed so relentless everywhere else we passed. The bones of the bateau, the decaying cabin, and the wild flowers in the grass gave the place a degree of sanctity. Throughout the trip, like Thoreau, we had bemoaned the slaughter of the white pine and had hoped to see some signs of a primeval forest. Yet in this place, the passage of man had actually been an enhancement in that it had added an historic dimension.

There were, however, places where I felt differently about the presence of people.

In one instance, we had just entered Chamberlain Lake in midafternoon and had stopped for lunch at a point with a gravelly beach where Thoreau had walked out into the lake to wash his muddy clothes. Now it is a campsite on the Allagash Waterway. It was littered with food remains, papers and tinfoil, even though the state wastebarrels were less than half full. The forest floor was trampled to a concrete hardness and was eroded near the banks.

Later, we paddled down Chamberlain as storm clouds gathered and as the wide-open lake surface began to kick up in our faces, heading for an island "campsite" that Don Fletcher, our "scout," had an attachment to. When we arrived, we saw two tents already set up. Out of one emerged a shaggy youth and a girl. Obviously, on this two-hundred-foot-wide dumpling there was no room for us. We saw no boat of any kind.

"How'd you get here?" Fletcher asked.

"Oh, we're just hitchhiking our way down the Allagash," the youth said. "We've been here three days. Came to Telos by truck, left off here by boat. We'll take anything that comes."

I was furious, but I kept my feelings hidden and we moved on.

A mile farther on we explored a sheltered spot with good potential, but it was not a registered site, and after deliberating we decided not to break the law.

It was late when we finally reached the Telos Thoroughfare, a mile north of the Allagash check-in station. The campsite was a gross magnification of the lunchtime scene. The ground was gouged and scruffed; tree roots were exposed. Trees all around had been crudely hacked down for firewood. An enormous log crib stood a hundred feet behind us, overflowing with rubbish. The tin cans, papers and plastic materials composed a shocking abstraction against the quiet tones of the woods. Just as we finished supper, the storm broke, and the wind picked up the loose refuse from the dump crib and scattered it through the camp. There was no sunset, but it didn't matter because this was no place in which to enjoy it.

Our experience that night clearly demonstrated the ill effects of "regulating" the choice of campsites in the state preserve. Since restrictions of some kind are a realistic necessity in the face of people pressures, I thought how much better it would be all around if the state issued wilderness permits, with strict rules governing both the equipment and behavior of people who came to a place like this. We'd seen other campers with only the most expensive gear, like the fancy tents and packs of the young people back on the island. So a permit fee would not be a burdensome expense and it would give the state the funds desperately needed to check and clean these campsites.

The permit would contain a checklist for three categories of campers: backpackers and canoeists, day-tourers, and those who drove to a base camp and only wanted to fish and picnic with their families. For each category there would be an equipment checklist that the bearer was honor-bound to observe — and would be liable for violating if accosted by a ranger.

The list would be brief for a picnic party, but for travelers like us there would be such necessities as a knife, compass, topographical maps, flashlight, basic first aid kit, a light ax and folding saw, life jackets, clothing and footwear suitable for the season, tent, sleeping bag, and a folding shovel to dig and cover latrine holes in the forest. If a primus stove was carried, you could stop anywhere. Otherwise you'd have to spend nights at a designated site or in an area specified when you obtained your fire permit (already required), in order to aid ranger patrols and fire lookouts. Perhaps most important of all, at any of the various points of entry to the wilderness, you would be provided with litter bags with these instructions: *Make no more waste than you can carry back out, and then return the filled bags to us.*

It is unfortunate that such a system has to be created, but it should prevent what we encountered that night on the Allagash. The state would not have to set up nearly as many garbage cans and dumps, if any, and park personnel would be free from janitorial duties to keep an eye on the entire waterway, even assisting campers by providing interpretative guidance about natural phenomena.

These were bad moments. There were great moments as well.

Two nights later, having gone a short way down the East Branch of the Penobscot below the dam of Grand Lake Matagamon, we set up camp on a bluff looking across lowlands to the grand prominence of Traveller Mountain, behind which the sun would soon drop. The dying light moved gradually across the valley, up the spine of Traveller's long ridge and three summits, and suddenly dusk descended. The final minutes of daylight were like a curtain being lowered. Just as it was about to close, it illuminated a beaver twenty yards across the river in a swampy depression that Fletcher called a "pughole." The only sounds were the river, swirling on a rock, and the crackling of our fire, the center of a very small and comfortable world. The bugs didn't bother us and we sat around for a long while, watching the night come up over Traveller and speaking with lowered voices.

The next morning we carefully covered all traces of our presence, burning papers and food residues and packing a squashed aluminum tin. We felt pretty good about it.

Later we skirted the edge of Baxter State Park, several times catching glimpses of Mount Katahdin (5,267 ft.), Maine's pinnacle as it appeared through gaps in the peaks in the foreground. Park planner Kauffman lamented that the north section of the park did not include the region from Webster Lake to the East Branch, connecting with the Allagash Waterway, because he was fearful that the paper companies would abuse it. Ideally, he said, Baxter would also be extended eastward to include the corridor in which we were now traveling.

However, the accomplishments and intentions of park creator Percival Proctor Baxter remain unique in the history of the conservation movement. I cannot understand why he has not been more widely heralded outside of Maine because, by contributing so much to the wilderness movement, he is in a league with men like John Muir.

The son of a successful Portland businessman, Baxter entered Maine politics without any obligations to the vested interests. As a representative, state senator, and governor (from 1921–1925), he repeatedly pressed in vain for the creation of a great sanctuary surmounted by Katahdin. So what he failed to do as a public official he undertook to accomplish as a private citizen.

He began by purchasing from the Great Northern Paper Company a 5,690-acre tract that included most of the mountain. Right away he deeded the property to the state on the condition that it "forever be used for public park and recreational purposes, forever left in the natural wild state, forever be kept as a sanctuary for wild beasts and birds, that no roads or ways for motor vehicles be constructed thereon or therein."

By the time he died in 1969, at over eighty, Baxter had repeated his first gift many times, on one occasion tripling the park area, so that it finally totaled 200,000 acres. By then, too, several other things had happened. A three-man commission had been created to administer what became the Baxter Park Authority. It was composed of the heads of the departments of Inland Fisheries and Game and of Forestry and the state attorney general. With the consent of the Baxter family, access and perimeter roads have been allowed. Yet a year before he died, and apparently unknown to the old man, snowmobiles were granted use of two park trails.

"Everything in connection with the Park must be left simple and natural, and must remain as nearly as possible as it was when only the Indians and the animals roamed at will through these areas," Baxter said in his lifetime. But the state was blatantly neglectful, even printing in a Biennial Report that winter travelers in Baxter Park had switched from "snowshoes to powered snowmobiles."

When the snowmobilists pushed for increased park mileage a year later, defenders of Percy Baxter's idea waged a successful counterattack, and now only official persons ride the machines.

Baxter shrewdly took unusual precautions to guard against encroachments. He deeded each new parcel, no matter how small, in a separate agreement with the state, each time repeating the original stipulations. In so doing, he felt he would firmly establish the trust precedent, since a succession of governors and legislatures would be on the record as upholders of Baxter's will. He once said that a map showing all his purchases "would remind you of your grandmother's quilt which finally, in some mysterious way, came out of the confusion into one large piece."

The people of Maine were to be the prime beneficiaries of Baxter's life work, and today they are given due priority by the park's reservation system for campsites. He feared that if it had become a federal preserve, the Katahdin region would have been turned over to concessionaires and treated as a recreation center for the entire Northeast. For that matter, time and time again Baxter warned against what might happen to the park, even under state management.

"I seek to provide against commercial exploitation," he said, "against hunting, trapping and killing, against lumbering, hotels, advertising, hot dog stands, motor vehicles, horse-drawn vehicles and other vehicles, aircraft, and the trappings of unpleasant civilization."

With a small group that included my Maine canoeing comrades, Fletcher and Zip Kellogg, John Kauffman, and Buff Bohlen, a ranking federal parks official, I set out to climb Mount Katahdin in October 1971. But the summit area was struck by wet snow the night before and the trails were made dangerously icy, so we were told to stick to lower altitudes.

In two and a half days we hiked over twenty-six miles, camping on the island in Wassataquoik Lake and at the southern end of the Upper South Branch Pond. It drizzled or rained hard most of the time, yet the fall foliage seemed all the lovelier for the weather, glistening with wetness on the trees and spread rich and thick over the ground. Kauffman and I remarked to each other how we became heady and lost our sense of depth perception from staring at the brilliant carpet in front and all around us as we walked along, bowed under our packs.

We were struck by the distinctive glacial characteristics of the lake and ponds. Unexpectedly, and only for an hour, the late sun broke through the clouds up at Wassataquoik, glinting off the steep sides of South Pogy Mountain where a long time ago logs were snubbed down into the lake below. Up above Green Falls, to the west, Fletcher pointed out a stand of ancient spruce that the lumbermen missed. I wondered whether it was too inaccessible or too beautiful. Maybe both.

After this trip I sent my companions a questionnaire, asking them to tell me their impressions of Baxter Park, whether they liked the way it appeared laid out and managed, and what they thought could be improved.

All of us, it seemed, were pleased to find that the spirit of Percy Baxter had not been dishonored, at least from our vantage.

"I was struck by the fact that Baxter very nearly fulfills my idea of a true national park," Kauffman wrote. "The visitor enjoys the park on its terms, not his, and thereby enjoys it more deeply. In the park he meets new requirements and encouragements of mind and body, a new dimension of living. Baxter should be managed for a North Woods 'man in nature' experience of the highest quality."

All agreed that the campsites should be kept as primitive as possible, located so as to attract only backpackers or day-hiking families. "Show me architecture as pleasing as a tent, an appliance as satisfying as a rock fireplace, and a 'planned' area as exciting as Wassataquoik Island," responded Fletcher, apparently still thinking of Thoreau.

Baxter dreamed that all of the Maine woods would someday be managed as a wilderness park. "I want hunting with cameras to take the place of hunting with guns," he said.

But he was forced to make some concessions to paper company people in return for getting land, concessions such as logging rights-of-way and permission to continue sustained-yield cutting in certain areas. Yet it seems implied in the spirit and tone of what Baxter said and wrote that he never thought his legacy would ever fully be taken advantage of. An optimist about people, he thought that an idea could snowball into a reality.

As I write now, the reality is something else and Baxter Park once more is threatened. This time the Park Authority revealed that it would trade a section in the south, where Great Northern Company cutting rights still exist through December 1973, for an area in the north with a cutting extension until 1975. The reason given was that logging in the south section would pose a safety hazard to hikers and campers who came in greater number to this part of the park. But the circumstances were questionable. It appeared that Great Northern would not have as much time as it needed to harvest the allowable cut in the south, and the topography, as conservationists noted, was more difficult than in the north.

There were also mutterings that the Baxter Park Authority was hoping to take over the logging roads made by Great Northern and harvest valuable timber on its own under a "scientific management" clause of the trust agreement. On these matters, members of the authority remained obfuscatory and secretive so the governor intervened by ordering a delay in making a decision.

Percy Baxter showed his understanding of business and politics, after all, when he issued warning that "as time passes and new men appear on the scene, there may be a tendency to overlook these restrictions and thus break the spirit of these gifts."

The National Park system dates back to 1872, the year that Yellowstone was opened to the public. In 1972, the centennial was marked by intensive debate over the role of parks and primitive areas. The most intensive study was conducted by the Washington-based Conservation Foundation, under contract to the National Park Service. Papers were assigned to different experts on park management. Task forces met to formulate policy on such subjects as outdoor recreation, the function of parks in education and culture, and urban open space. Finally a symposium was held at Yosemite, the second park in the system (1890) and unquestionably the most beleaguered.

The CF report's most prominent conclusion would have pleased Percy Baxter, but it touched off controversy and hostile reaction among some government park people. "The National Park System can best meet the future needs of all Americans," said the report, "by reasserting its original mission — the preservation and interpretation of natural landscapes and ecosystems."

The critics of the CF study (which was published in paperback form as *National Parks for the Future*) said that the needs of public recreation were not stressed as much as the preservation of environmental values. I think that these critics have missed the point and that they had better strap on their packs and get out to see for themselves what is actually happening, what even their own rangers will tell them. It all goes back to John Kauffman's observation that the challenge and excitement of a park comes from accepting it on its own terms.

The recommendations of the CF study strongly reflected that viewpoint. For example, one proposal was that "recreational use in all parks should be based on natural assets, not constructed facilities" (such as golf courses or swimming pools). The increasing development of road systems and mechanized conveniences in general were decried.

As a group, young people have caused the most confrontations in the parks during the past ten years. There was the widely publicized battle between rangers and youths in Yosemite, when the valley seemed lost to the carnival madness of the hippie culture. Edward Abbey, author, occasional ranger and a fire lookout, was appalled when he went out on night rounds with a Yosemite ranger. Even though he is a liberal man, Abbey wrote bitterly in a *Life* article about encountering drug scenes, drunkenness, noisy parties and vandalism involving young people. While he was shocked to find that Yosemite had a jail, a full police calendar and a force of rangers in prowl cars who carried .38-special revolvers, MACE and handcuffs, he agreed it was necessary. "For the basic trouble in Yosemite," he wrote, "is urbanism."

Places like Baxter State Park still serve the people as well as the woods. The state would do well to keep in mind and even reaffirm occasionally why this is so.

REPORT FROM THE ST. JOHN

THE UPPER SECTION of the St. John River — 160 miles from St. John Pond to Fort Kent — is probably the most remote, least impeded watercourse east of the Mississippi. It has no dams. And when the river is full and flowing fast, an experienced canoeist can run all of its rapids without having to make a portage.

It is quite the opposite of the Allagash Wilderness Waterway that runs almost parallel to the St. John, a short distance to the southeast. Allagash is hardly a river at all, composed as it is of a string of lakes and ponds that take up 47 of its 92 miles.

The route that we planned on the St. John — putting in at Baker Lake and taking out at Negro Brook, just below the confluence of the Allagash — is 115 miles of unadulterated river; a moody river, fed by seeps and sidestreams too numerous to count, gradually adding might from five fair-sized tributaries; a river bounded by the forest, bridged only three times by logging roads until the crossing of Highway 161 at Dickey, the spot where the slide rule beavers, power advocates and politicians envision a monstrous hydroelectric dam.

The thought of that dam, called Dickey-Lincoln, in fact, was one of the reasons we wanted to travel this river by canoe. We wanted to see what it was like as a wilderness waterway, or at least to confirm our emotional preconceptions that no more free and wild rivers should be dammed in this country.

The history of Americans gouging and filling the land, blocking and diverting rivers, stripping mountains while piling up the rock refuse on the flats that are left, is a sad old story. It has been recorded by many, from de Tocqueville in 1831 to Edward Abbey in 1968. There have been isolated moments when the national penchant seemed ready to change, as when Missouri Senator George Vest argued eloquently that Yellowstone should be a "great breathing place for the national lungs" and the U.S. Congress agreed, denying a railroad a right-of-way through the park in 1886 by a vote of 107 to 65.

But these moments of sanity never lasted long. An historic and sad confrontation between conservationists and development interests occurred beginning at the end of the last century, when the city of San Francisco asked the federal government to dam Yosemite National Park's high-walled Hetch Hetchy Valley to make a reservoir. For two decades, debate raged. Men like Robert Underwood Johnson, editor of *Century,* and John Muir, founder of the Sierra Club, championed the opposition. Noting that throughout civilization men had been making gardens and parks, Muir deplored the destruction of "a grand landscape garden, one of Nature's rarest and most precious mountain temples." But Woodrow Wilson finally approved the dam in 1913, siding with an earlier president, Garfield, who had declared that "domestic use" of water was the highest value of a river.

Here there is comparison with Dickey-Lincoln, since a large private utility eyed the valley as a means of dominating California's hydroelectric resources. Advocates of the project, including some well-known conservationists, saw the reservoir for San Francisco as a wedge for public resource ownership and management.

The fight over Hetch Hetchy was not in vain, for it consolidated the conservation movement. And as a specific issue, it was revived during the congressional debate over new dams in the Grand Canyon in the early 1960s. This time, led by David Brower, the Sierra Club prevailed. But those who would save the remaining free-flowing rivers must be ever active. The dam builders only change their pretenses, not their plans.

At the most, hydroelectric power based on damming rivers cannot provide even a fifth of the U.S. demands for energy in the coming years. In fact new hydro projects cannot even equal the growth rate alone of projected power needs.

Moreover, while dams don't cause air or thermal pollution or present a radiation threat, they most certainly are not free from ecological side-effects and adverse environmental influences in general. The Maine woods depend for stability on a remarkable network of brooks, rivers and ponds that move and store water, absorb runoff, and in general keep the wilderness suitably wet and spongy. Already the lumber and power companies have abused this region enough to meet their water requirements, and now the loggers' dams are no longer really necessary because the log drives are over.

While public trust should be given far more consideration in wilderness planning, a public hydroelectric project is not the answer. If it is to be justified on recreational grounds, a fragile environment and, above all, a wilderness whose crowning asset is its appeal to the individual and his sense of privacy will be ruined by motorized hordes. If lowering Maine's power rates through the introduction of large public utility competition is the justification, certainly there must be better ways of dealing with the all-powerful private power bloc. Imaginative leadership on the part of the Maine Public Utilities Commission will help.

The power companies like to argue that present trends in electrical consumption dictate that more and more generator facilities should be built right away. Yet it has been shown in studies and maintained again and again by experts like S. David Freeman, former director of the White House Energy Policy staff, that the growth rate argument is fallacious since it is untenable in the long term. These men emphasize instead that the growth rate could be halved by simply imposing some austerity or energy conservation, acting as if the supply were finite and not unlimited. Reverse the utility rates and penalize the large-volume users, the so-called "end block" electricity customers, suggest experts like Freeman. Slap "dis-incentives" (the nice word for taxes and special levies) on new methods of technology that demand increased amounts of energy. Of course, taking this approach means that the politicians will have to bite some big, hard bullets. But the result would be real energy savings and the planners would have time to think of something else besides a stopgap like Dickey-Lincoln or an improperly conceived nuclear plant like Maine Yankee, which has consistently failed to live up to its own engineering projections and to site location standards recommended for similar hot installations.

The place for hydroelectric power appears to me to be in Eastport, as I have said earlier in this book, where a Washington County Authority might be established to develop large-scale prototype tidal power in conjunction with the administration of an aquaculture industry and the county's priceless recreational lands.

Aside from my inclination to prove a point in the cause of conservation politics, I find it difficult to explain or analyze why I have an urge in the spring to take to the woods and the rivers. I have the *most* trouble answering the question during the moments of discomfort that invariably come up on every trip, when my spirit is let down and I realize that I have no obligation to prove anything in particular to anyone.

It is pouring rain. The flies, mosquitoes and noseeums are making their strafing runs, often without a warning buzz, and always coming from all directions, impervious to insect repellents. Or it is cold and spongy, and my feet are wet and my fingers are numb.

Or we have been three hours hunched up in the back of the pickup, lurching along a logging road, gulping down red wine because the fiber glass shelter doesn't stop the mud and saturated air from blowing in and something has to be done to help raise the spirits. Washouts everywhere, road falling to pieces, potholes to China. It is amazing that the truck can do it.

The question is equally baffling to park planners. They want more wilderness, but as fast as they get it they add improvements: more and more access roads, lunch sites and campgrounds. The backpackers, the canoeists and the fishermen are as mistrusted by park officials as they are coddled.

Aldo Leopold over fifty years ago said that true wilderness should be able to "absorb a two week's pack trip." In 1962, the Outdoor Recreation Resources Review Commission defined a wilderness as an area over 100,000 acres with no public roads. Under the 1964 Wilderness Act, it is "where the earth and its community of life are untrammeled by man, where man himself is a visitor who does not remain."

Leopold's test and the 1962 definition both hold up in the Maine woods, although only when you discount the presence of the lumberman, who is as persistent as the black fly. But neither is really as bad as reputed. The lumbermen have at least done a good job of keeping the woods green and dense, even though their cuttings are at times

172

abusive and will become far more destructive with increasing mechanization. As for the flies, you've got to give them credit where it is
due. They are the inland equivalent of the coastal fog — Old Nature's
means of crowd control.

But getting back to my own attitude toward the wilderness, I have
these deep but undefined feelings about the woods, at least the woods
that I know by canoe. "It is even more grim and wild than you had
anticipated, a damp and intricate wilderness, in the spring everywhere wet and miry," wrote Thoreau back in 1846. Yet the more you
are in it, as your civilized feelings subside, the more you become
attracted by the forest's power. The sense of isolation is overwhelming, and you are left with no choice but to accept Nature on her terms.
With this acquiescence comes an appreciation of the subtle diversity
of this mysterious environment. The evergreens that at first all looked
alike reveal different characteristics. Along the banks where the
river's rise and fall has created a precious and narrow world, you
look for wild flowers. You anticipate the changes ahead, downriver.
The forest cover turns from spruce to cedar or birch and poplar
where there has been a fire. (There are several species of spruce as
well as fir and, less frequently, white pine.) And the fall of the river,
its swirls, eddies, upwellings and various interruptions, are just as
absorbing. The water becomes still and you know that ahead a rapids
is holding things up. The course that twisted among boulders widens
and races over gravel shallows, making a pleasant, calming sound.
Back in the deadwaters there are meanders and inlets, called logans,
where the true beavers, not engineers, have created a security of ponds
behind mud and stick dams.

All this may be familiar to the lucky Mainer, but it never ceases to
put me in a new mood, an easy, lazy state of wonder that is worth all
the trouble of getting there and the discomfort with the wetness and
the bugs.

Then too there is the aspect of friendship that we rediscover as men
and boys, some of us strangers to each other. We never seem to argue
or fidget in this place. We have this atavistic feeling that it is good
for the male human species to be set loose for a week, falling back
on the basic instincts. To eat, push on, explore, eat again and sleep.
"Though you have nothing to do but see the country, there's rarely

any time to spare, hardly enough to examine a plant, before the night or drowsiness is upon you," wrote Thoreau.

It is a kind of ritual. One man awakens and assumes leadership of the breakfast. As he thrashes with the wood and the first flames of the fire crackle to life, a pan slides on the rocks, and the others, low down in their sleeping bags, can no longer make pretense. The day is young. Yet even as the last riser finds that he has inherited the dirty dishes, others have folded tents, stuffed clothing and sleeping bags into their packs, and are loading canoes. By eight-thirty we are on the river and the air is still crisp from the night.

There are stops wherever there is interest. A brook enters the river and we must fish its mouth or the back-eddy just below it where trout may congregate. There is an old lumber camp where we can hunt for artifacts (like the ax blade in good condition that I found where the river had washed out a bank at Seven Islands). Or we find a sand or gravel beach, and the sun is warm, and we decide it is time for a swim. There is a sudden opening in the woods, created unexplainably by natural forces, or it is a meadow once cleared to provide hay for the lumbermen's horses now giving back ground to the forest.

Since we are in no hurry we stop at these places, at one of them eating a light lunch of tidbits or peanut butter and jam on hardtack. We camp according to where on the topographical maps we think we can read a natural site or where the state and lumbermen have designated one.

For example, the map shows a shelf of open ground or a bluff on a meadow. A stream enters the river. The view is east to the rising sun — or the other way, to a promising sunset. The distance to this place is about right, twenty miles or so, an easy day's run with plenty of time to fish and explore.

But, as Thoreau said, business catches up on you fast. No sooner have you stopped than it seems urgent to get the tents set up, fire going, supper done in time to sit around the hot coals with a good cigar.

There are nine of us. So five men put up tents. One builds a fireplace out of rocks from the bank. Our Natty Bumppo is Don Fletcher, a Mainer all his life, outdoors most of it. He makes a rock cooking range worthy of study. A thin slab in front to bridge a gap between two other rocks creates an oven. Rock ledges are provided around the rim for keeping pots warm. A high back contains the heat. A pole of green wood is laid across two forked stakes so that the pots may be hung at just the right height for cooking.

Another man searches for wood. Yet another helps where he can, opening the food packs and laying out supper. That leaves one or two to go fishing, and maybe there'll be trout for side orders.

By the time it is all done, the sun is in its dying glow. Zones of red merge with the ascendant tones of night and the constellations appear directly overhead, gradually merging with the horizon.

Fletcher's father, Walter, a wiry, grizzled Mainer who bridges two eras, stretches out his wooden leg, a memento of the assault on Monte Casino. "I didn't go into the woods with the old-timers, but I was fortunate to hear them tell all about it," he says. And the day's final act begins.

Early in the morning the cycle resumes. It is not long after six when I go out with one of the boys to look for the moose whose enormous hoofmarks are all over camp — the biggest duclaw (hind hoof) imprints that Walter has ever seen — and other wildlife whose signs are numerous. We have no luck, although the moose could not be far ahead of us — its tracks on the muddy trail are so fresh that water is still seeping into them. Then we come upon a victim. It is a deer, apparently slain by the bear whose tracks are also evident in the muddy wash of an abandoned logging road. There is not much left, a leg with meat and hair intact and the head, cleaned to the bone. The hide lies flat on the ground beneath two spruce, a startling sight. Struck by the morning sun it looks like an abandoned doormat.

We had begun our trip on the St. John by launching four canoes into the Baker Branch of the St. John's River on a cold, bleak day with light rain falling on and off. We might have started on another tributary or taken the traditional route from the Northeast Carry, poling up the North Branch of the Penobscot until striking favorable current at Fifth St. John Pond, where the water starts to run toward Canada. But we didn't have the extra week or so to do the St. John the old way.

The weather cleared the second morning as we awoke at Knowles Brook. The sweat inside the nylon tents had turned to ice droplets, but before long the sun took over. We hung our wet clothing and damp sleeping bags on an old camp shelter frame and didn't get going until well after nine.

The river widened as we met the Northwest Branch; it was running maybe three feet higher than normal for the season. So instead of having to pick our way through a winding channel, evading boulders, skirting ledges and dragging the canoe over bars, we halved the distance and cheated on the corners. All the same, we had to watch out. There were plenty of rocks lurking just beneath the surface, given away by boiling and rippling where the river rolled over and around them, and some nasty ones that gave no warning at all. With such a volume of water running so hard, getting hung up most likely would have resulted in a serious capsizing.

This year, all of Maine had received unusually prolonged spring rains. Since it is fed by brooks running out of the forest, with few lakes or ponds to hold back the runoff (unlike the Allagash and the branches of the Penobscot), the St. John can become an angry river overnight. Its regular fluctuations make it only so-so for trout and on our trip the conditions were the worst, although we didn't go without fish.

Moreover, the bad weather had produced two bonuses: a river that was mighty and fast, a joy to run; and a delay in the opening of the black fly season. Not until the sixth day did we get attacked and then only Don Fletcher was bloodied.

The river surprised us pleasantly by the force of its current, its varied temperament and by the loveliness and changing character of the forest on either side. Just as it seemed we were on an endless promenade between strips of spruce and fir, there would come a clump of towering white pine or a graceful stand of poplar, leaves shaking in the wind. Then there were logans, quiet domains unto themselves, and islands where we spotted sandpipers and killdeer. Once during lunch the air suddenly was full of nighthawks. And twice we saw ospreys keeping ahead of us.

We had two visitations with official personages. The first time we were set up on a grassy knoll overlooking the derelict piers of the bridge that Helen Hamlin wrote about when her husband was warden there. I had enjoyed the book, *Nine Mile Bridge*. No longer in use, the bridge was washed out during one of the river's most memorable rampages in 1970. Our visitor was a forest ranger, a man of common sense, we soon learned, who had lived all his life beside the Nine Mile Bridge, and had seen all kinds of travelers. He had landed by canoe and came up the bank, hesitant, waiting for us to make the first move. Acting like a stinker, expecting trouble, I prolonged his uncertainty and stared back. Finally he told us in an embarrassed, friendly way that we were in an illegal place, property of the Fish and Game Department. We replied that we had conferred with the ranger at Baker Lake during a miserable rainstorm. Since the woods had already been wet for weeks, he had told us that we could camp and light our fire anywhere on the river.

The visiting ranger said we wouldn't have to move, but he asked us to leave the site immaculate when we left. Fair enough. This exchange being quickly done, we talked a while about the history of the place. Since he had been raised there and knew it well, even remembering the Hamlins, he was saddened that the state had bulldozed their cabin into a rubble twenty yards behind us and that a truss of the ruined bridge had been taken to Canada. Both were historic and should have been preserved.

"All that was gone in the cabin was the floor," he said, "and that would have been easy to fix."

This meeting with the ranger put us in a good frame of mind. It confirmed my feeling that if there were more competent rangers and less roads in primitive areas, the public would be better served. But my optimism did not last out the next morning.

The second state man had scouted us for quite a while from back in the trees across the open meadows of the long-abandoned Seven Islands Landing, once a bustling lumber depot. Walter spotted him at once and told us this would be one "square" and tough warden because he was dressed in full regalia, gray-blue suit with badges, official knapsack and the familiar Smokey-the-Bear hat. First he inquired about our fishing licenses, but when I said I had to rummage to the bottom of my pack to get my wallet and promised that the license was there and in order, he was reasonable enough and said not to bother. However, he insisted that one of my longer-haired companions empty his pack. The license check was passed, except that one had to be revalidated because the man who issued it had made a small mistake on the dates.

The warden stood by for a while and watched us prepare lunch.

When a photo was taken of me standing next to him, he grew suspicious. "Now you're trying to flatter me," he said, in a serious manner.

Then our other long-haired member arrived from a promontory a hundred yards distant, where he had been exploring momentarily with two companions. We had already shown the warden that we had the required total of life jackets, but when he saw three in the canoe, he rightly suspected that for such a short ferry trip we would have forgotten to shift a jacket from another canoe to account for the third man. A twenty dollar fine, payable in cash on the spot. We held back our anger and protested as politely as we could. But it was in vain.

"I realize that you only violated the law for that short distance," he conceded, "but the law clearly states that there must be a life jacket for each person in the craft at all times."

The law does not read that the life jacket has to be worn or even has to be accessible. As long as it is Coast Guard–approved, you could screw it in place and encase it in clear plastic, visible but immovable. We paid the fine and the warden marched away into the trees, after promising us that there would be tougher encounters with more of his kind downstream. Only six months a warden (he had told us), he was clearly hard up for a ticket or had lost his head.

It was also at Seven Islands that we realized we were entering a stretch of the St. John that would cease to exist and instead would be a lifeless backwater if the Dickey-Lincoln Dam were built some fifty miles downstream. With a rise and fall of fourteen feet, this artificial impoundment (the engineer's word) would have little value for recreation. Northern Maine needs another lake like Los Angeles needs another freeway. For the rest of our travel we couldn't put this troubling thought out of mind.

The river became even more varied and challenging. We ran four exciting rapids: Priestly, Big Black, Schoolhouse and Big Rapids, and at least four other good whitewater stretches. Big Rapids, the last run, was climactic and beautiful. The river did a tight loop south and then back to the north. Before entering this two-mile descent, we spent the night on a gravelly island in the bend, where the wind kept away the black flies we'd seen that afternoon and their escorts the mosquitoes.

The morning brought low, dark skies. Just before we entered the difficult water, we saw a handsome, square farmhouse on the left, a curtain blowing out an open window, the glass mostly gone, and no sign of an inhabitant, although two of us thought we saw a light upstairs. On either side the land rose up in rounded hills. You could see the river's steep drop in the gorge ahead.

As stern man, I stood up to pick a channel, what there was of it, and we started to wind down between enormous boulders with the river boiling and thundering and no time to look out over the entire wild scene. My bow man leaned out to either side, executing powerful draw strokes to pull the canoe out of the reach of rocks that appeared at the last second, and I followed his lead, pulling or backwatering the stern out and around the obstacles. On the last half mile, he suggested we veer right, out into the middle.

"The hell with it, let's just dodge them as they come," I yelled back, and we both laughed because we knew we were too exhausted at that moment to care. A brook dropped in on the left, and there we stopped to drink the sweetest water I've ever tasted.

There wasn't far to go now. The sun broke through the morning mists. The river widened on its way to meet the Allagash. How did it rate as a wilderness waterway, I thought to myself? The answer came easily. Very high. Four stars. It was a clean, clear river with a compelling history and diverse natural character all the way. In my mind's eye I again saw our campsites: the lush meadow beside Knowles Brook, a swift pebble-bed down which the runoff rushed to the river; the grassy bluff at Nine Mile Bridge with its view of the sunrise; a night in the dense trees above Big Black Rapids where we'd thinned and manicured ourselves enough room to pitch tents and have a campfire; the classic idealness and purity of the Chimenticook Stream where we'd remained a day to swim, fish and explore; and the last night on a gravelly island out of reach of the bugs. All first-rate places and, best of all, no competition with other campers.

Just before the end of the trip, Highway 161 crossed the river. Under the bridge the current still ran fast, but we all knew this was where they wanted to drop the gates that would flood over 88,000 acres and back the river up for forty-seven miles. We hoped we'd be back before that happened, to run this river when it was in yet another of its moods.

"I would have liked to come across a large community of pines, which had never been invaded by the lumbering army," wrote Thoreau. And after that time, nobody ever got the chance. Sad to say, a century later, similar comment could be made about our wilderness rivers.

FIVE

The Farm

LIVING OFF THE LAND

THE FIRST NEW ENGLAND FARMER was the Indian, even though most modern historians convey the impression that the white settlers introduced agrarian self-sufficiency to a region previously populated by hunting people. After telling us that Squanto introduced the Pilgrims to corn and how to grow it, the historians say little or nothing more about the Indian farmer.

Yet the journals of such men as Samuel de Champlain, William Wood, Roger Williams, and John Giles, who was a prisoner of the Maliseets from 1689 to 1696, reveal that Indians were wonderfully adept at growing enough food to supplement their fishing and hunting diet. In fact, one has the impression that in coastal estuaries and inland river valleys, it was hunting that was supplemental.

According to historian Clarence Albert Day (*A History of Maine Agriculture 1604–1860*), the Indians had elaborate cornfields in the vicinity of such present day towns as Berwick, Wells, Fryeburg, Brunswick, Topsham, Durham, Auburn, Bethel, Winslow, and Bangor. The Indians even put up paling fences to keep small animals like raccoons, woodchucks and skunks from raiding the crops. Though their tools were extremely crude, the Indians compensated in other ways. For example, after using dead fish (often alewives) as fertilizer, they would grow beans and corn together so that the cornstalk would support the bean shoots and the bean plants would also spread on the ground to keep out weeds. Blueberries, other fruit berries, corn kernels and peas were dehydrated by being spread out on wood under the summer sun. In the winter, these garden products were reconstituted just as we prepare freeze-dried foods today.

It was only when the Indians found it easier to barter furs with the English and French (often in return for the settlers' corn), and when their lands were constantly being taken, that they abandoned agriculture. By then, as I will explain later, the Indians' entire system of life support was destroyed. But historian Day gives them full credit. "Indeed," he wrote, "the English frequently found Indian methods of tillage better adapted to their use than the skills that they had learned in the homeland."

Hugh McLellan, an Irishman who put down stakes in Gorham in 1733, typified the early white farmer. He cleared out the forest, put the debris and stumps to fire, and then planted in the "burn," finding that the ashes made the soil fertile and relatively free of weeds. He grew corn, pumpkins, potatoes, and peas at first and added variety later. Eventually he had made his own gristmill in the end of a block of maple, using an overhanging tree limb as a pestle, since it would spring upward after each stroke and save McLellan's back muscles. He also kept cows and a pig.

But subsistence was in itself a full-time job, as McLellan soon found out. In a year when he made a side income from cutting mast timber, his family came perilously close to starving to death.

The settlers apportioned Maine's salt marshes, meadows and upland clearings. They built low-eaved frame houses to replace log cabins, and hewn-frame barns to replace the crude animal hovels. As they improved their tools they took on new crops: rye, oats, barley, and buckwheat and flax, from which they made cloth.

By the middle of the nineteenth century, subsistence farming was at its height. Sheep were grazed extensively. Oxen were kept for hauling plows and wagons. Most farms had an apple orchard. And quite likely there was not only a shop in which tools were forged and repaired, but a butcher shed where the farmer killed, cut, and packed his own meats.

Up until the turn of this century, just before the advent of the motor car, ten dollars a week was all that a family required to supplement its own output. This money could be earned from the sale of wool products, garden foods or meats to the nearby (and sometimes, by ship, and rail, to distant) market centers.

The typical farm a century ago was as well set up for the good life as it would be today with all the modern conveniences that cost money and thus have undermined the subsistence principle. The farm household was the embodiment of efficiency and careful forethought.

Let's start in the attic. Hanging from the rafters were onions, corn, squashes, pumpkins and different herbs. In the pantry or kitchen storeroom were barrels of flour and sugar, all-important staples. The cellar was yet another reflection of the farm's state of readiness. If it were well stocked, there would be tins of beans and dried peas, kegs of lard and butter, boxes of carrots, beets, potatoes, onions and apples (insulated with autumn leaves), and many shelves crammed with soups and juices, jams and other preserves. Outdoors, such vegetables as parsnips and brussels sprouts remained unspoiled by frost, and with a mulch cover, even kale and Swiss chard could be revived in the early spring.

What more could a person want than food, clothing and the security of his land? This is the crucial question. There is no one answer. It is perfectly clear that the subsistence farmer quite naturally succumbed to the era of convenience and luxury that resulted from the increasing application and spread of technology. As I say elsewhere in this book, Maine and other New England states surrendered some of the natural advantages they had possessed before the development of the West and South, and in order to compete even in a minimal way, the subsistence farmer had to acquire machinery.

It has been a temptation to idealists like myself to imagine that the New England farmer, from Hugh McLellan to his nineteenth-century successor, had achieved the ultimate state of happiness. I like to think that this picture of farm life is manifested in many ways. For example, the lovely rural villages that evolved out of farm life. The church steeples put up in these settlements blaze a trail today through the upcountry reaches of Maine, New Hampshire and Vermont. Stone walls in the woods evoke the nostalgic vision of the stoic, strong individual clearing his land and defining his margins with the rocks that defied his plow. I think of a life based on the family unit, and the cooperative spirit of a community made up of many families.

Yet obviously there were practical considerations. A man needed his sons to stay and help him, and the community was bonded together out of the psychological need to ward off a sense of isolation as well as strange "outside" influences. Even so, at a time in our history when localism has been stifled in a sort of numbing conformity, it is easy to find appeal in the notion of a resilient rural people who are stoic and tough, gentle and wise, earthy and enduring.

One cannot, however, overlook the fact that subsistence conditions coincided with an incredible rate of alcoholic consumption. In fact, the Maine Temperance Union, in 1851, obtained the first prohibition law in the United States. It became known as "The Maine Law." But in the perspective of cultural changes, as one looks back in 1972, I willingly will bear the risk of stating that a life of subsistence is a happy goal for a great many people, farmers and nonfarmers alike.

Moreover, it will not do to argue that it is too late to sustain or revive the concept. It can still be done to a greater or lesser degree, depending on a family's willingness to make sacrifices. I will concede, too, that some other source of income is also often needed to pay for much modern necessities as medical care, transportation, and the public services that one is forced to support through property taxes. Yet modern tools also make it possible to subsist without putting in the long hours and toil of Hugh McLellan.

Even the conservative Maine Department of Agriculture had this to say in a recent prospectus:

> For the subsistence farmer, the only limit to what he can do to provide his own food is his ability and state of health. On a small farm with five or six acres of pasture, a similar amount of hayfield, a small woodlot, and a good sized garden, a man can raise most of his family's food. He can keep a few hens, pigs, sheep, a milk cow, a couple of beef animals, raise berries, fruit trees, and all manner of vegetables. This means work, of course, and a certain amount of expense to start with, but the result can be a healthful, happy, productive life, with ample time to enjoy all the pleasures which vacationers travel many miles and spend hundreds of dollars to find.

This is a straightforward avowal, an assertion that something can or cannot be achieved. The subsistence idea goes beyond that, however, and becomes a state of mind, a philosophy. In my opinion, nobody has expressed the idea with greater eloquence than the late Henry Beston in *Northern Farm*, a simply written paean to life on his place near Damariscotta, Maine. Beston was immersed in the seasonal rhythms and the unending drama of small events and small surprises on his countryside. To him the farm cycle was the most real kind of demonstration of what life was all about.

186

"What has come over our age is an alienation from nature un-exampled in human history," he wrote. "It has cost us our sense of reality and all but cost us our humanity."

By 1973, it seems to me, the farm idea has become to many people what it was to Henry Beston — a reaffirmation of the natural cycle in harmony with the spirit of man. An increasing number of people will agree, even if they have not tried it, that a farm is an ideal place to test themselves and raise children. Or, as Beston put it, "Under today's disorders there is something at work among the nations whose great importance has not yet been adequately realized — the need of men for a community to live in and live with."

THE FARMER'S SON

WENDELL BRAGG had been described to me as one of a vanishing breed, a farmer who tested his ingenuity by providing for his family on a small place, who took orders from nobody and did just about everything — managing a woodlot, putting up vegetables and selling milk. His cucumber pickles were mentioned with particular enthusiasm by those who directed me to his place in Sidney, overlooking the Kennebec River about ten miles north of Augusta.

Rather than take the Interstate a few miles to the west, I decided to keep the Kennebec in sight, even though the narrow River Road was treacherous. There were about six inches of snow on the fields and it was so cold that the ice slick had not melted. But a brilliant sun made the countryside clear and intense. Even if it had not been icy, this road would never have permitted fast going. There were too many houses along its borders, too many deep dips, sweeping curves and driveways and country lanes suddenly entering from the side. Though not spectacular, the view was tempting. I'd imagined the farms would be down in a valley just above the flood plain, looking toward the river across fields that would be rich and green in June. Instead, the floodplain was narrow, and the farms that I could see on both sides stood on high bluffs or steep slopes, several hundred feet above the Kennebec. The neighborhood was too close to Augusta to be entirely rural. As one would expect these days, there were quite a few nondescript houses built along the route by people who appeared to have no compunction about littering their backyards. In several places, the bluffs and hillsides had been rent open for sand and gravel pits, and I could see wide tire imprints where trucks lately had been turning off to pick up loads of sand.

Bragg's was the first farm of real character. Looking north, the white wood house stood to the left of the road, a handsome two-story front section joined behind by what appeared to be older wings, although I'd have guessed from the trim and the narrow high windows with large panes that the front part was late nineteenth century. Opposite, across the road on the right, stood an assemblage of barns, a shed and an old tractor. Nearest and parallel to the road was a big hay barn with a gambrel roof. Beyond it, across a yard, stood a low cow barn. I could tell that because of the steam coming from the warm animals inside. Joining the ends of the two, to make the yard, was a storage barn with a sliding door. The cow barn was open and I spotted a figure moving inside. I couldn't distinguish his features because the sun beat into my face and bounced off the barns and the ground, making the yard pleasantly brilliant. The barn interior was dark as a cave by comparison.

"Are you Mr. Bragg?" I asked.

He walked toward me as I entered. "No, I'm his son," he said. "My father had to go to a funeral. He felt bad about you coming and him being away all of a sudden, but he didn't know where to get you." I'd telephoned Wendell Bragg the week before and asked if I could visit his place, but hadn't left an address or number.

I stood for a moment, wondering whether I should come back another time and talk to both of them. I looked around at the neat arrangement of the barn, the Holstein cows kept in their stalls by steel yokes, and then at the son who was feeding them grain and hay. He was slightly built, short and boyishly handsome with curly red hair and a splendid drooping russet moustache in the style of Mark Twain. What stood out most, though, was an alert expression and confident manner.

"Do you mind if I stay and look around?" I said.

"Heck no, I like to have somebody to talk to."

I thought I'd better find out right away whether the son planned to work for his father, start his own farm, or turn to a different kind of life entirely, like most of his counterparts. His answer would determine the drift of our conversation. He did not hesitate. "So far as I know, I plan to stay on the farm and farm this land right here," he said. "The Braggs have always lived here, since the early 1700s when the family got a grant. Now we farm this whole neighborhood."

Wendell had turned sixty-one, and this son, Wayne, who was twenty-four, had been helping out since he left high school. He planned no further schooling. "If you have questions, there are government dairy specialists who'll come and answer them," he said. "You learn how to help yourself."

On this farm there were 62 head of cattle; 38 presently were giving milk. All the farmland in the immediate vicinity along the Kennebec was owned and worked by the father, two uncles, four neighbors and a brother, Howard, who had his own larger spread up the road. Now most of Wendell's cows were Holstein. Six years before they had been Jerseys, with rich milk, high in butterfat, that became unpopular when the doctors tied cholesterol to heart disease. But the Braggs still kept a few Jerseys whose milk they mixed with that of the others in order to bring the butterfat content up to a respectable average of 4.2 percent. To keep efficient, they had invested $4,500 in a pipeline system that took the milk from a machine that fit right over the cows' udders. The pipes, made of clear plastic, conveyed the milk all the way to a shiny stainless steel 375-gallon tank in the dairy. That had cost $1,000, after trading in an old smaller tank for $200. Every two days, the tank was emptied by a tanktruck from the Purelac Dairy in Winslow, four miles up and across the river. If there was any surplus milk it went to the big Hood plant up in Newport, thirty-five miles away.

There was no extra labor except in the summer, when students were paid to help put up over 15,000 twenty-five-pound bales of hay. Otherwise, Wayne Bragg and his father did everything. The day began in the barn at seven sharp. "I get up at six-fifty," Wayne said and grinned. "We like our sleep; we don't start as early as some."

As a rule, Wayne told me, he and his father milked the cows first, each moving down a row of stalls, attaching the machines to two cows at a time. As the animals were sucked dry, the men cleaned the udders of the next two. This took about two hours. Breakfast was at nine in a kitchen that was warmed by a big wood stove. Afterward, Wayne went just down the road to the barn where the heifers and dry cows were kept. He fed them grain and hay and put down fresh bedding. Around ten-thirty, he got back to the milk barn to help his father finish the same chores.

Lunch was from twelve-thirty to one. Then Wayne liked to read the newspaper. Sometimes he had to attend to breeding records and the other bookkeeping. "We don't have a bull," he said. "Like everybody else we use artificial insemination." The second and final milking came at five. The family ate supper together at seven.

This was the basic routine. However, there were plenty of regular small details to take care of. All the dairy equipment had to be constantly cleaned and kept sterile. The machinery had to be oiled, greased, and overhauled. There were maintenance jobs, inside and out.

Wayne had been refastening the big hay barn when I arrived. It had stood for well over a century but it looked as if it had plenty of life yet. The hand-hewn timbers were joined together beautifully. Where some foundation beams had sagged, a friend had provided assistance with a house jack. Wayne was able to reuse most of the old siding. It was unpainted and had been bleached by the elements to a silvery gray. He put the boards up vertically. "The water follows the grain and the wood will last longer," he said. "I think it looks good, weathered like that, but a red and white barn is pretty too."

He pointed to the storage barn that enclosed the yard. "They moved it from over there during the Civil War," he said, swinging his arm to a bare corner thirty yards distant where a stone wall met the road.

The present-day Braggs have at least one trait in common with their forebears and other early New England farmers. They have banded together in a cooperative effort with their neighbors whenever it is desirable in order to achieve what is called today "an economy of scale." I suspect that these farmers go their own way a good part of the time too, but the moments of sharing or being helpful are important. Wayne himself has bought sixty-one acres two miles away, where he raises Holstein steers and makes hay for his father and to sell to neighbors at $25 a ton, a very fair price for the times. Tractors,' plows, seeders and harvesting equipment are loaned during crises. When his brother's Allis Chalmers tractor was out of use with transmission trouble during the critical spring months, Wendell's ancient loader tractor was available. "He helps us in ways and we help him in ways," Wayne said. "As long as we've got a good group here, we'll do okay. Me and my father, we get along well together. I make a good living. He put me on a salary, $100 a week, and I have my room and board free with my family. I'm all set."

As he told me all this, he moved easily through his chores, stopping only to face me when he wanted to emphasize something. He was proud of the way the barn looked, of the way he and his father had kept everything working smoothly, and of the way the animals were looked after and kept clean. Some of the cows' tails were held up by string. His father had done that because these particular animals would switch their tails more obnoxiously than others, whipping the men in the face. Extra hay was laid on top of the manure that the cows dropped in the cement gutter behind them. This was to keep their tails clean, but it didn't always work, and a tail in the eye might not only be painful but foul.

The Braggs spread the cow manure on the fields late in fall, allowing this fertilizer a whole winter and early spring to seep into ground and have a good effect. The manure was kept piled up just below the barn. It was conveyed there by a chain belt with rungs that was pulled around the gutter by a small motor. "The health inspectors hold it against you if you don't dump that manure in the spring," Wayne said. "They say it breeds flies. But it doesn't make sense to spread it then. I have to give those inspectors some credit though. They keep us in good habits. If it weren't for them, you'd have some awful sloppy dairy farms."

The Braggs pretty much subsisted on their own land and products. Wayne's mother had a large vegetable garden from which she preserved string beans, corn, beets, spinach and peas. His father reserved a quarter of an acre for the cucumbers he pickled and sold locally. They set aside a calf for veal and a steer for their own beef. There was plenty of milk, cream and butter. The farm made enough money to take care of excess needs with some left over. You could tell that by the tidy, prosperous looks of everything. "If you've got to work out in order to live on a farm, you're not doing it right," Wayne said. "But it's a seven-day week, and that's what is getting to a lot of farmers and they're quitting. If you're alone and you have the flu, you've still got to get out to those animals and get those chores done. It's an awful drag sometimes, but it works good with my father and I."

Wayne's father let him take time off every once in a while, but he didn't want much. In the past year Wayne had taken four days. He and a friend had fixed up the back of a pickup truck for sleeping and driven off to the big farm exposition in Springfield, Massachusetts. Then they'd headed north, having dinner with a cousin who had a dairy farm in New Hampshire, before visiting still another farming relative in Vermont. From there they went to Montreal and found that the World's Fair had shut down the year before. But that didn't matter because the scenery driving back to Maine was in its full fall finery. "We just took our time," he said. "There was no hurry. It was beautiful."

On weekends he might take his snowmobile and join friends in Skowhegan. At night he might drive off in the snowmobile too, and stop for coffee and a meal somewhere. "All I want now is a little motorcycle," he said. "That will get me around here pretty good."

"Do you ever walk much, just to get the feel of the place?" I asked naively.

He smiled. "You come here in the spring, when I'm fixing the fences. You'll do plenty of walking."

From mid-May to mid-November, the cows had been in the fields, and the Braggs had been out with them, putting up the bales of hay and cutting the grass up fine into "green chop," which they put in feed boxes outdoors when the grazing got sparse late in the summer. In the woods west of the house, the father practiced forest management on a small scale. And there were always trees to be cut back that were encroaching on the fields. "I hate to see them return to the bushes," Wayne said. "We spend a lot of time on this farm just trying to make it look good."

As I turned to leave the farm couldn't have looked much better. Solid, trim and bright, with the snow dazzling all around and the river running half a mile below us at the foot of a long steep slope. As I turned on my ignition and sat with the door open to take a final look around, I couldn't refrain from saying what I'd felt from early in the conversation.

"You know I have nothing but admiration for what you're doing."

He looked surprised. "I wouldn't want to work here if there wasn't money in it," he said, "but I wouldn't want to work here just for the money. Me and my father will make it work. Now you make sure you come back, you make sure you do."

He waved and walked back to the barn, and I drove off to the north, past his brother's impressive-looking place and through farm country for another five miles before I hit Waterville.

A DIFFERENT STORY IN AROOSTOOK

IT WAS DAWN IN CARIBOU. I'd spent the night in an upland farm, and when I awoke I could look across the gentle valleys and spinal ridges of Aroostook, all the way to Canada some forty miles distant to the east. There the hills of New Brunswick were outlined against the brightening sky. It was breathtaking countryside, the more impressive to me for having been cleared from a dense wilderness by hardy farm settlers. That was back in the early 1800s, when Aroostook was virtually cut off from the rest of Maine by a fifty-mile cordon of forest.

Then the U.S. Army built garrisons during a succession of border disputes and, as no other political force could, obtained roads to the north country. By 1870, Aroostook was covered by farms. Hay, buckwheat and oat crops were planted; horses, cattle, sheep and pigs were raised. Before potato farming spread from southern Maine, grass seed was the main commodity. One year a Presque Isle farmer produced 5,800 pounds of clover and 230 bushels of Timothy seed.

In the eighties, when the railroad finally was pushed all the way to Caribou, potatoes took over. *Solanum tuberosum;* it was discovered in the Andes by the Conquistadores, introduced to Spain, became the staple for man and beast in Ireland, and was brought to North America by Scotch-Irish immigrants. Seed potatoes, potatoes for the table (per capita consumption still is 112 pounds a year), potatoes for starch: the potato was king up here, and farmers made fortunes. But it was a fickle business. Prices would triple in one year, then fall back lower than ever the next. Other crops held out for a while. Wheat production was 167,323 bushels in 1919.

194

Yet during almost all of this century, Aroostook has reverted to a monoculture farm economy and the local rhyme holds true.

> When the price is high enough,
> we have a little cash;
> And when the market's on the bum
> we eat a lot of hash.

When Caribou, known as the "hub" of Aroostook County, became a city in 1967, the man chosen to be mayor was Gilman Albair, a potato farmer whose family had worked the same land during four previous generations. Already he was the chairman of the City Council, and he typified a personality long identified with the region: honest, independent, tough and outspoken. In Gilman Albair these basic traits were blended with other attributes. He was compassionate; he had a sense of humor; he felt a deep commitment to his community, and he was as respected as he was well liked. Although Aroostook farmers had suffered five straight years of losses, although farms were going under by the week, Gilman Albair was still considered an example of reliability and steadiness. The big question was whether such a man could remain a leader and a prototype when drastic changes were taking place in agrarian society and when economic and technological developments threatened to disrupt entirely the world of the American farmer as it had existed for more than two centuries.

When I introduced myself to Gilman, he was having trouble. His machines wouldn't work. He lay on his back on the raw earth, wedged under a big red harvester, trying to trace the latest breakdown. Towed by a diesel tractor, his harvester had scooped up potatoes for half the distance of one row before the conveyor belt motor stopped. Gilman was furious, for throughout the previous day he'd been plagued by mechanical stoppages. Now the morning was barely begun and the nightmare continued.

Two factory service representatives had been called, but they couldn't decide what was wrong and stood by helplessly. When he spotted me Gilman came over and we shook hands. He had to shout, to be heard over the racket of the idling tractor motor.

"This is enough to give a man a heart attack. Life's too short to have to worry all the time about things like this."

The harvester was a new model, the entry of FMC, a highly reputed California firm, to the potato business. It cost $6,000, and Gilman had bought two. Apparently they were full of bugs. One night early in the season he and his son, Ricky, stayed up until one-thirty in the morning composing a letter to FMC that recommended detailed changes to be made on the harvester. The company agreed with most of them, but nothing was done in time for the 1971 harvest.

It was a short period, this harvest, no more than three weeks. It was absolutely critical to waste not a moment, or the potatoes would be ruined by the twin dangers of rain or frost. As Gilman looked over at his neighbor's field, he could see two Lockwood harvesters going full tilt. They had been at it all week without cessation, Gilman lamented. It was salt on the wound of his frustration.

"I think we don't go to the right church. Or say the right prayers," he said.

The service reps looked around sheepishly. "Nobody's listening, that's your problem," one of them ventured.

I spent the forenoon hurrying up to keep pace with Gilman. There was a trip to his machine shop to fetch a battery. Then, when a truck transmission gave out, there were calls made to see which could be done more economically, considering the immediate need for the equipment, repairs, or a trade-in for another truck. There was another breakdown in the mechanized conveyor carrying potatoes into Gilman's warehouse along the railway tracks in Caribou, and he was needed in person to fix it.

Nevertheless, I seized every available moment to learn about Gilman's own farms and potato growing in general. We would talk in his pickup, riding between troubles. I would hang on to the tractor when Gilman took the controls now and then. I supposed that his personal involvement inspired confidence in his help. And I could clearly tell that his operating skills were very necessary to keep the harvest moving. There were rare intervals when he stood still, and then I asked him even more questions.

From his account and what I had read, the picture in Aroostook County could not have been painted more darkly. The farmers began 1971 in the wake of five straight years when production costs averaged higher than sales, and only twice since 1960 had they averaged profits. It was astonishing, but true, that potato prices for growers like Gilman Albair were in the same range as forty years before and were far less than revenues during good years in the fifties. To lump growing, handling and shipping costs, the farmers were out of pocket around $2.40 per hundredweight (cwt), whereas in the most recent years the price per cwt seldom averaged more than $2. Because of this gap, more and more farmers were forced to mortgage land, homesteads and equipment. Many couldn't bear the load and went under. The banks and the Farmers' Home Administration, the predominant backer, issued foreclosures in the spring when new loans were needed for fertilizers. Throughout the summer the FHA had sponsored auctions where confiscated tractors, truck, harvesters and other implements were sold cheaply. It was sad to hear about the proud farmers pacing in the crowd, watching with strained faces, as their finest machinery and their homes, usually in the family for many generations, were sold out from under them to the highest bidder. And as I've said, it was a buyer's market.

The Northern Maine Regional Planning Commission conducted an investigation to see what had gone wrong, and its report issued in the spring was pessimistic. The main problem, it appeared, lay in the character of the growers. Individualistic, proud and traditionally attuned only to the conditions of the field while remaining ignorant about the market, the farmers quite simply had failed to keep up their homework. "They have skirted responsibility by waiting for some vague national solution and undefined outside leadership, rather than taking the situation in hand on the home front," said the report.

As a result, several things happened, and the farmers were understandably bitter when they saw their potatoes selling in supermarkets for more than four times as much as they received. (A ten-pound bag that brought the farmer 18 cents was selling for as much as 80 cents in the market.) First, the number of dealers had increased greatly, so that competition among dealers lowered prices paid to the growers. Then the dealers, in turn, would buy ahead for speculative purposes, not only pushing down prices again but increasing spoilage claims. Strangely enough, growers were responsible for their potato shipments until these carloads reached the market. It was generally known that too often, when it was expedient, a false damage claim would be filed against the grower. And since he was tied down to his farm, the grower was unable to check it out. Dealers resold carloads, always taking a slight profit, and often they created the false impression of a potato oversupply, as a dozen or more brokers might be on the phone all trying to sell the same carload.

The planning commission report recommended that the farmers get together to develop their own pipeline to the markets or follow the example of Canadian growers by establishing a single marketing agency, owned and run by the farmers, to pay a fair price for potatoes, then take care of all the handling, shipping and distribution problems. It all boiled down to a lack of business savvy and disorganization on the part of the farmer. "What the potato farmer has to be today is a pretty good banker," a Maine politician told me. And this may have been an understatement.

There were other problems. Overfarming with just one crop had depleted the soils so badly that acreage yields had dropped way down. Southern and western states with milder climates were able to put their potatoes on the market long before Aroostook's were even harvested, so in order to get the best price Maine growers held their shipments back until late March or early April. Ideally, they should have even waited until May, but that would have left them no time to begin planting in the middle of the month. It was a strange sort of a business. When there was activity, it was frenzied and disorganized, with the farmer taking it upon himself to perform too many functions. But the activity only extended for half the year.

Gilman fought the same odds as all the rest. It was too late to avoid them. His family was part of that soil, the "Caribou loam," that is so well suited to potatoes, because it is sandy, drains well, doesn't bake hard in the sun, and has an underbody of limestone that helps it to recover naturally from cultivation.

Gilman's father had 60 acres, 43 planted. And he had three sons. One became an agronomist, another a chemical engineer. Gilman, the youngest, had a scholarship to Dartmouth and was all set to prepare for a medical career, but his father hoped he would stick by the farm for a few more years. He needed at least one of his sons in this tough business.

Gilman stayed. He even bought his own place, 80 acres for $3,200, planting 50 acres in potatoes and sharing his father's equipment. Within a year he made good, paid off bank notes on the land, interest charges and taxes, and a loan for a car. Before he knew it, Gilman

Albair was a full-fledged potato farmer and there was no turning back. He acquired five farms in all and was so respected in his work that he was made a member of the potato council. He traveled to the other potato-growing regions, like Idaho, the state that took over the production lead from Maine in 1957. As a farmer, pure and simple, a practitioner and not a theoretician, Gilman knew or had access to most of the answers. His 300 acres of potatoes showed it.

Yet he was never prepared for the bad times or the trends in farming, developments that forced farmers throughout the nation to make bedrock changes — in character as well as business outlook. By the fall of 1971, Gilman had a quarter of a million dollars tied up in land and machinery, $90,000 just in big machines: including four tractors, four trucks, two harvesters. These major investments stood idle between November and May.

When hard times hit, Gilman felt the pinch. In 1971 he did something he'd tried hard to avoid ever since his first year in farming. He went to the bank. This time he obtained mortgages on all five farms. Yet he seemed hopeful that eventually he would buck the tide, even as he fumed pessimistically about the changes in farming.

"Here in this country I'm considered as good a grower as anybody," he said. "I don't mean to brag. The only luxury I've got is a Cadillac in the garage."

And as far as I could tell that was true. The people I talked to had a high regard for Gilman's farming ability. And it didn't appear that he had let his past success go to his head. To be sure, he had a summer cottage up at Lake Madawaska, but in Maine such an arrangement is not a luxury; it is considered quite usual for rural people who naturally enjoy going into the nearby back country to hunt, fish, canoe and rest up from field labors. It is really their only outlet.

"It's just like a prescription," said Gilman about his lake sojourns. "Sometimes I have to get out from under the potatoes."

So far, 1971 was not shaping up as a good year. All indications pointed to a continuation of prices around $2 a cwt.

"If we could only average $2.50 to $3," said Gilman, "we could take all the mortgages off and pay our bills."

I hoped the way this particular day was going was not an advance warning that trouble lay ahead. By the end of the morning, after repairing the sprocket on the warehouse conveyor, Gilman was be-grimed. His hands were caked with mud and slimy with grease, his jacket stained with both. Seldom had he stopped for breath; he gave orders to his crew, explained problems, and did most of the trouble-shooting himself. Though he should have become tired, his reserves of energy seemed limitless. He spat out a wad of chewing tobacco before he entered his house for lunch: a very commanding figure.

The afternoon began smoothly. The day had warmed up to Indian summer and so had the machinery. Both harvesters moved into a field west of the homestead. They squealed raucously as they scooped up both rocks and potatoes, sorted them out, and fed the potatoes through a side conveyor that dropped into a big truck moving alongside at the same pace.

At the controls of one of the formidable John Deere 4020 diesels was Gilman himself, constantly playing on a row of levers that acti-vated their incredible ganglia of hydraulic lines while he kept the harvester moving evenly. In the morning I'd watched Ricky at the same job. He was eager, intent and very careful, though not quite as assured and casual as his father. Ricky had quit college. He was a hard worker and he was determined to stay on the farm just as his father had, although Gilman couldn't understand it.

"I like the land," he said. "But we're all going to go broke. If I had to do it all over again, I'd go into a profession, be a lawyer and make twenty-five thousand. How can a young feller start farming today? He's got to have collateral."

Another son, Mark, was an alert towhead who seemed older than his ten years. He wanted to be a veterinarian. Like all Aroostook schoolchildren, he was let out during the harvest. He worked, too, although much of the time he stayed right with his father to run various errands and carry messages. Older schoolchildren manned the harvesters, picking out by hand the rocks missed by the machine process. They also drove trucks and did other field jobs. There ap-peared to be an easy relationship between Gilman and these helpers.

Behind the harvester rose a lengthening plume of dust and chaff. The machine and its trail looked small, though, in the vastness of the open rolling country. It might have been a scene on the midwestern plains.

Troubles resumed at two-thirty when a big rock suddenly jammed the elevator of one harvester. It took fifteen minutes to clear it. Then either the clutch slipped or a drive chain came undone, and the steel lags of the conveyor belt got jammed again. This time Gilman had to cut them loose with an acetylene torch that he kept ready in his pickup truck.

Unlike his mood in the morning, his reaction now was philosophical. "These things happen. It isn't the machine's fault."

The other harvester got jammed at four-thirty, the same way, and again the torch was needed.

"That's about thirteen dollars in lags I've had to cut," said Gilman.

The dusk came early, but the harvesting went on. Many farmers work well into the night to take advantage of good weather, and you can see their lights eerily probing the dark landscape miles away. Gilman planned to keep going until he'd got in at least twenty loads.

But then there was an electrical failure in one harvester. Once again he was terribly dejected. A chill descended over the field and the lights came out in the town of Caribou lying below, some three miles away.

I said I had to go and I wished Gilman luck. He shrugged. "I've heard people say this country would grow up in bushes again."

What could be done about it, I asked.

"Nothing, unless the farmers get together and tell the dealers we're through with this malarkey, that either you give us something for our potatoes or we're through."

I walked away, then stopped and looked back. Gilman had climbed up on the dead harvester. He pushed the starter and all I heard was a clicking sound. It was long past six o'clock.

Before I left Caribou, I talked with one man who was optimistic about the future — with qualifications, and provided that adjustments were made. Dick Keenan, in his thirties, a newcomer who was raised on a farm in upstate New York, was head of the Aroostook Federation of Farmers, a cooperative that sold fertilizers and other farm supplies. Keenan was convinced that Aroostook farmers could enrich themselves and their land if they would diversify and rotate their fields between potatoes, bean and vegetable crops. He was also confident that this was good country for apples. The combination of cold nights and warm days in late summer gave an apple like the Macintosh a premium red color.

On his own, spurned by the banks, Keenan started an eighty-five-acre apple orchard. He also planted experimental plots of dry beans, soy beans, sunflowers and corn. He hoped to extract the oils from these vegetables to serve the needs of local potato processors who presently go outside Maine for their vegetable processing oils.

"I'm doing it to build pressure and I think it's working," he said.

The main obstacle, as I have said before, was skepticism on the part of local farmers and a traditional reluctance to organize for any reason whatsoever. Moreover, the state encouraged sugar beets in 1969 with disastrous results. Although sugar beets were grown successfully in Maine back in the 1870s, the latest effort was conducted under inept and irresponsible management. The operator of the sugar refinery was a celebrated failure. When he went broke, he took with him a whopping sum of state money. So the state was unenthusiastic about diversification in Aroostook County.

As Keenan saw it, the potato farmer would have to become a business manager as well as a field boss. He would have to become more involved in research and development, not only to improve the quality of the Maine potato but to explore crop alternatives. Until that happened on a wide scale, Keenan predicted that potato farming would drop off, the acreage would diminish from 145,000 to 125,000, and land holdings would consolidate in larger blocks, 250 acres in size, more than twice as large as the average farm in 1971.

"The efficient operator will make it; Gilman Albair will make it," said Keenan, when I told him of my fears. "The market price is going to come back."

It took another year of hardship. But in 1972, as the harvest was in full swing, farmers were averaging $3 and as high as $5 or $6 per cwt. It was going to be the best year since 1965; the Aroostook crop was expected to bring in $81 million, an increase of $20 million from the year before. Competing regions slumped in production. So did Aroostook, but this made the national demand go up. Aroostook potato acreage had already dropped, as Keenan foresaw, down to 133,000 acres.

One of those who didn't plant again was Gilman Albair. When it came time for him to order fertilizer, the banks foreclosed on Gilman. They took over his five farms, bringing eviction proceedings to force him out of his homestead. On the auction lot, the farm machines Gilman was so proud of stood out by virtue of their clean appearance and fine maintenance, but they went with all the rest, with equipment that had had a lot more time to deteriorate. This hurt Gilman and he showed it. Yet he was still a respected citizen, and for the year of 1972 was even again chosen to be mayor. But he was too deep in debt to inspire business confidence. Embittered and shocked, he went to his lake cabin while he looked for a new job. He hoped he would be hired to manage a farm; that was one thing he knew he could still do well.

ALPHABET SMITH'S VISION

BY COMPARISON with the agricultural regions west of the Mississippi and down in the deep South, where the climate is milder and the soils more rich and less rocky, Maine is limited as a rural farm state. That is to say, it is limited in terms of what it can contribute to the agricultural production of the nation as a whole. Much of the land out West is leased from the federal government dirt cheap. Free irrigation and low-cost power come from the big public hydroelectric and reclamation projects. Growing seasons are longer. The character of the land is conducive to big and efficient spreads, with vast open stretches being cultivated by machines. In Maine, by contrast, the farm valleys are cradled by forests and steep hills, confined by rock ridges, marshes and streams. Nationally, the average-sized farm has grown from 150 to nearly 400 acres during the past three decades, and it will grow to 1,200 acres by the year 2000, so they say. Consolidation. Mechanization. These have been the bywords.

Maine doesn't fit very neatly into this picture. In 1970, farm receipts accounted for only 10 percent of Maine residents' total income, farm employment had dropped 29 percent in the decade, and the number of farms was also way, way down. State planners interpreted these trends superficially. Right on up to the governor, they had washed their hands of farming except for poultry and potatoes, which fast were becoming agribusiness industries anyway. Farming didn't figure in Maine's future; it would be better to use the rural open space for industry, recreation, and residential developments, or so the official view seemed to be.

The state policy was myopic because it led to rampant land speculation, even far inland, and Mainers whose families were rooted back into the centuries were forced to sell out. Moreover, it seemed to me that one of these days, as more and more open space was gobbled up throughout the land, Maine's agricultural acreage would not be considered so inferior that it wouldn't support some forms of farming again. Finally, from a psychological standpoint, it seemed that the loss of all that farmland was tantamount to the loss of a vital part of the whole idea that is Maine.

In 1969, Maine's "Cash Farm Income" broke down as follows: $110.4 million in poultry meat and eggs; $60.8 million in vegetables (of which $55 million were potato products); $40.2 million in dairy products; $8.3 million in fruits (almost all apples and blueberries); $7.2 million in red meat; and $1.8 million in feed crops. The poultry men seemed solidly assured of a good future. They were close to the market and the crisp Maine air kept disease vectors low. Moreover, a special pattern of operation applied. Five major processors controlled all of the state's broiler production and paid the costs of supplying chicks, feed, medication, fuel and litter to the growers. The same contractual arrangement held for egg production, with about a dozen big operators providing hens to small farmers. Most egg operations averaged around 11,000 hens, although some hatcheries ran many times that big.

For the moment, too, the dairy farmers were holding on, with 45 percent of the state's milk production demanded by the Boston market. Yet rising land prices, general lack of interest on the part of coming generations, and high initial capital costs ($1,750 per cow) put the curb on growth in the dairy business.

The problem with farming, as with so many other lines of endeavor, was the insistence of the planners and economic development people always to think big, to look at economic situations in terms of major movement and major policy influences instead of considering small innovations that collectively might solve the problems.

Alphabet Smith was one man who knew better. He had a plan, a vision, I was told by different people. The part-time farmer, the small farmer, the traditional rural landholder, was the key man in Smith's scheme. The main strategy was not only to perpetuate farming but, really just as essential, to preserve rural open space. Smith noted how so many men who still lived on their family farms no longer had anything to do with farming. They fell into two general categories. First, the natives of Maine. They were electricians, plumbers and so forth, men providing services, or they worked somewhere in a plant or in an office. Thus, there were no longer any effective constraints, apart from pure sentiment, against the sale or subdivision of the family land. In the second category were outsiders like Smith, who loved the Maine land so much that they bought a farm on it where they lived part time as "rusticators," or year-round, retired or undergoing a change in life style.

In other words, Smith conceived of *farming as a strategy for preserving Maine's open spaces*. In itself, production on a particular farm might not be profitable. But, as he saw it, when you added the value of this kind of a life plus the payoff to Maine from saving farmland from development, then farming on the whole was well worth being perpetuated.

On his own hook, Smith pursued a farm activity that he felt would work in Maine, regardless of other considerations: the raising and marketing of beef. He was not its only advocate. I had read in several places that Bruce Poulton, highly regarded dean of life sciences and agriculture at the University of Maine, also felt that Maine's soil conditions, climate and location were good for beef cattle. But Smith's approach *was* novel. His idea was to persuade the nonfarmers with farmland — natives and newcomers alike — that it would be to their benefit and their land's if they would let him graze his beef on their property during the summer months. He would offer them in return a price based on the fattening of the animals — for example, 20 cents per pound of weight gained during the grazing period. At the same time, on his own lands, Smith would grow the winter feeds that were otherwise so costly to obtain from the Midwest and other outside growing regions. In short, as Smith provided nonfarmers with an incentive to maintain the quality of their grazing spaces, they were enabling him to overcome one of Maine's handicaps for beef farming, the high expense of winter feed.

You don't have to consult the consumer market reports to know that there has been a dramatic nationwide rise in beef consumption. Maine has a healthy climate for raising animals and is close to the concentration of Northeast markets, particularly the restaurant trade.

Alphabet Smith's approach seemed to me to make excellent sense and should have been encouraged by the state.

Yet, sad to say, he was considered something of a fanatic in state offices where he had advanced his plan and had suggested its widespread application to beef production and even other forms of agriculture as a means of keeping Maine farms alive. "Oh yes, we've had no end of correspondence from *him*," was what I heard from at least two officials.

When I finally visited Smith's farm on Wolfe's Neck in Freeport, I found that my sympathies were entirely justified. It was a pleasant confirmation. To begin with, from his nickname alone, I had harbored a lingering suspicion that he was indeed a fringe character, as the state people had implied. If so, it is only to his credit. For if his farm is an indication, he has come a long way toward proving his point.

The place was neat and lovely, with vistas of green meadowlands rolling up from Casco Bay, fine old farm buildings, cattle grazing in one field, the others in different stages of cultivation, and a large vegetable garden handy to the main house.

Smith and his family were finishing breakfast in a room that was radiant with sunlight streaming in through high glass windows. He readily invited me to join them, and we sat there for an hour or so talking about his farm.

L. M. C. Smith is a distinguished Philadelphian, an entrepreneur who has interests in five different companies (including the city's classical music station). He has a wide background in both business and law. As a young man he clerked for two Supreme Court justices, helped write the sweeping Investment Act of 1940, and conducted extremely high-level and sensitive business missions for the government during the Second World War, including the purchase of the fuel oil that got Patton's tanks rolling again across Germany.

His wife is an ardent conservationist who is particularly active in the field of historic preservation. It was she who acquired the place on Wolfe's Neck as a summer retreat back in 1946. They are elegant, enthusiastic people who seem to be involved in all kinds of things. It is a happy, hectic household.

As for the farm operation, from November 15 to May 20, Smith said, he had to winter-feed his 600 head of beef, "but we're growing

85 percent of it right here." During the summer, he sent most of the cattle away to graze on leased land in nearby Brunswick and two "affiliated" farms in Skowhegan and Ipswich, Massachusetts. His farm was entirely organic, fertilized from chicken manure, of which Maine has plenty. Since demand for organic meat had skyrocketed, he was back-ordered well beyond his present capacity to provide beef. "This kind of operation is far better for Maine than industrial parks and shopping centers, which are just parasites," said Smith. "Our money is put right back into Maine, like the money from lobsters."

At the time of my visit, Smith was experimenting with a hybrid called Sudax (a cross between corn and sorghum) as a winter grain substitute. So far the yields were high, 15 tons an acre for two cuttings, and he was hopeful that the substitute would give his animals plenty of energy.

As Smith saw it, the main obstacles were development of marketing outlets and getting state support. For a year, due largely to apathy by the state, there had been no U.S. Department of Agriculture inspection station in Maine. Thus Smith and other beef producers had to sell within the state through direct channels. If he were able to ship out of the state, the rates were favorable, only seven cents a pound by air to New York.

Alphabet Smith termed his approach a "land use supplement," which, as I have already explained, is a way for rural landholders to use their open space to supplement nonfarm income. He envisions sixty-acre affiliate operations proliferating throughout the state in arrangements with farmers like himself. Maybe the initiative and the main capital will have to come from people like Alphabet Smith, well enough supported from other channels of income to be able to absorb the high outlays of launching this kind of farming in the absence of government support. But if the state would at least provide moral leadership, this open-space strategy might go a long way.

"We've been at this for fifteen years and we haven't turned the corner," Smith admitted. But Wolfe's Neck Farm was beginning to make money, and the demand for organic goods had become tremendous. "Don't forget," said Smith, "we had to find out how to do this all by ourselves, we had to foot all the research and development costs. We've made mistakes, don't kid yourself."

He drove me around the place for another hour. We looked at the "open" silos that Smith had patterned after English farms. (They are now quite common in the United States.) The silage was covered with a tarpaulin, which in turn was weighted down with old tires. Then an industrial vacuum cleaner sucked out all the air left trapped beneath the tarp so that the silage was anaerobic, i.e., unable to ferment with bacteria. In the winter the tarp was raised and the animals ate their way through the pile by spring.

I met Smith's manager, an energetic and jovial man named Charles de Grandpere, who lived in one of Smith's handsome old farmhouses and had become an associate in the beef business. The two men bubbled over their success with cross-bred Black Angus and Charolais cattle and how they had come up with a marketing package of beef that included a full assortment of cuts and eliminated inventory problems.

Then we drove along the shore through a private campground that Smith operated for the public. "Recompence" was the name Smith gave the site. ("It's a favorite eighteenth-century word of mine," he said.) The camp was imaginatively laid out, with an unusual amount of privacy and open space for the people who came in trailers or truck-campers. Litter and other wastes went into special containers that were picked up and replaced regularly. It was late in the season and near midday, so there were not many people or vehicles around.

The way Smith described this campsite gave me the feeling he was trying to prove a point, as with farming. In this case, he was showing how a certain segment of the public — the motorized campers — could be accommodated in a manner that would still preserve coastal values. This was not the first time Alphabet Smith had led the way. I remembered that he was the person who had quietly purchased Popham Beach at a reasonable price and then had sold it, at cost, to the state for a park. The state could never have pulled it off, particularly without condemnation power for recreation. And he was also chairman of Landguard Trust, Inc., a nonprofit association that provides counsel in land use practices throughout the state.

Our last stop was at an old house, weathered and quite rundown, that the Smiths had acquired for the purpose of historic preservation. Long ago it had been a trading post, and Smith led me down a rough dirt road to the hollowed-out stone between some trees where Indians had ground their newly acquired corn. It was quiet and warm, standing there in the sun, with Alphabet Smith still telling me how he and his farmers created drainage depressions or sodways (that were also planted) running through his fields so they could get to ploughing early in the spring.

Alphabet Smith said he'd made mistakes. And no doubt he had. But his successful ideas were what mattered most. These are the ideas that the state and the people of Maine ought to pay a lot more attention to.

BACK TO THE LAND

BACK IN 1932, in the depths of the Great Depression, Helen and Scott Nearing left New York City for Vermont's Green Mountains and what they hoped would be "a simple, satisfying life on the land, to be devoted to mutual aid and harmlessness, with an ample margin of leisure in which to do personally constructive and creative work." That's the way they described their intention in *Living the Good Life,* an account that has become a sort of operating manual for the new pioneers. In this and another journal, *The Maple Sugar Book,* the Nearings demonstrate that it is still possible, by making material sacrifices, to escape from the bondage of discordant, dreary urbanization and incessant, incomprehensible technology. For them the solution was to subsist simply and joyously in a rural environment comparatively unaltered by the modern pace and pressures, where they could recapture an essential measure of living on their own terms.

The Nearings said they went to the country with three express objectives: economic independence, improved bodily condition, and philosophic liberation. "Instead of exploitation, we wanted a use economy," they wrote. "Instead of the hectic, mad rush of busyness we intended a quiet pace, with time to wonder, ponder and observe."

Their success has served both as an inspiration and a model, even though it took a long time (a period of three wars, the last barely ended) for their outlook to gain credence. By the time their books had become hot sellers, the Nearings had begun another farm in Harborside, Maine. With humor and patience they still counsel many visitors who want to see firsthand how nineteenth-century-style New England farming is a fine solution for life in the seventies.

I was aware of the movement back to the land long before I read the Nearings' books. Probably it was because I had myself become so unhappy with urban and suburban life. I do know that I treated with the utmost optimism the occasional reports that rural life in places like Maine would somehow become the basis of an American Renaissance that would blend the best of our traditional values with a new awareness about the essentials of a peaceful, positive life. I really put full faith in the Nearings' rallying call, expressed in *The Maple Sugar Book,* that "the Good Earth with its fertility, its resources, and its eager response to cultivation and conservation holds out to all comers its horn of plenty — in exchange for forethought, planning and well-directed labor."

In the *New York Times,* in the *Washington Post* and *Wall Street Journal,* in my copy of the *Harvard Bulletin* and in the environmental journals, I read about the homesteaders and pioneers of the seventies. Few were as well organized or as dedicated to a strict seasonal routine as the Nearings. Many were unwilling to readjust their lives totally by sacrificing the modern conveniences they were used to, not counting the family car and electric lighting. And there were few who followed the extreme of Elliot and Sue Colemen, who were featured in a *Wall Street Journal* piece.

The Colemans acquired forty acres near the Nearings, put up an 18- by 22-foot cabin, hauled water from a distant spring, and sat down to eat on tree-stump stools. Despite Maine's growing season of only around 140 days, the Colemans grew about 80 percent of their food. In the first few years of their new life they were able to earn almost all of the $2,000 they needed to supplement their production by taking on part-time jobs and selling surplus vegetables.

In the face of all kinds of obstacles, the back-to-the-land movement, or whatever you want to call it, was making headway. And for every couple who actually took the hard step, there were others consciously working up to that state of mind. Antitechnological, even antiintellectual, the New Naturalism was an emerging social philosophy. It stressed the absence of complication and hypocrisy in a way of life that was direct and sensory, in the acceptance of conditions imposed by Nature, conditions that one could feel and understand on the most basic terms.

My first *real* contact with the movement came in mid-November 1972, on a raw, chilly day that spoke of the rush of fall into the harsh Maine winter. The sky hung low to the horizon, colored pale orange, tinted and screened by thin overcast, through which snow flurries came driving with unexpected suddenness. For three balmy days I had been lulled into the feeling that, even with the trees bare, the land would always be soft and golden. Now I was reminded that it would soon turn hard and unyielding, and the night winds would rattle loose shutters and send chill darts into even the warmest habitations.

Shepard Erhart and his wife, Linnette, were far more sensitive to the climate than I. They were participants in the race to be ready for winter. And when I drove up to their small, two-story wood farmhouse in Franklin, they were at work on a cold frame, where vegetable plants might be sustained during the freeze-up and where seedlings might be started before the spring thaw. It was a simple but efficient-looking affair. Three walls made out of granite blocks formed an enclosure against the side of the house. This rectangular pit would be lined with manure, the side of the house would be sheathed with metal foil, and the whole unit covered with a window frame. Thus the sun's hot rays would be magnified, then radiated and retained within. Both the manure and the rocks would hold heat, Shep explained.

I had learned about the Erharts from Shep's sister, a school friend of my wife. When I wrote him a note asking if I could stop by, he replied on a postcard, giving me directions to the place and indicating in a few cordial sentences that he and Linnette would be delighted to tell me what they were doing. I ended up visiting them twice. Each time we huddled around a small kitchen table, close to the kerosene stove, devouring the most delicious preparations from their amazingly varied vegetarian menu; and I was totally caught up in their enthusiasm and happy expectancy about what the seasons would bring forth.

The first time Shep took me down through his fields to the edge of a tidal inlet. On the way back, we came upon the burial plot of previous landowners. Overgrown by alders and scrub oak, the finely chiseled and inscribed granite monuments were reminders that life here had always been difficult and solitary and that eventually the land had prevailed.

For the soil was not uniformly fertile. It was shallow, full of clay and bedded on the rock ledges that once made Franklin a busy granite center. Where the ground looked rich and black it was sodden from lack of drainage. Rising above the place were blueberry barrens strewn with enormous boulders. A geologist would call it a fine example of terminal morrain, a natural slag pile deposited by some receding glacier millennia ago. Glacial action made Maine second-choice farmland, so when subsistence farming was no longer necessary, over 40 percent of the early homesteads, along with their cleared lands, were abandoned.

If the farming is so bad and the climate so severe, compared to other undeveloped rural sections of the nation, why did the Erharts and others like them come to Maine? Under what sort of self-created system did they think they could exist? What were they looking for in their lives? Did they have a long-term plan?

These were some of the many questions I asked, sitting in their kitchen, just the three of us and a cat who would move from lap to lap. The food was unbelievably good, there was much to learn, and such was my own enthusiasm that it took two afternoons for the answers to accumulate. Even then, no prototypical picture emerged, because the Erharts were ready to own up to the basic human traits that all too often most people consider weaknesses: an open mind about the future, not to mention uncertainty about the present, and a determination to assemble all of the available knowledge about different possibilities in charting a way of life. These were candid people with a refreshingly clear outlook and a sense of humor about themselves.

Buying the land in Franklin six months before was the culmination of a two-year on-and-off search that had taken them to Nova Scotia, to the valleys of northwestern Pennsylvania, through the vastness of the western prairies and mountains and along the Pacific Coast. The land in South Dakota was perhaps the most beautiful they saw, and the price was right, but gradually they realized that they were searching for countryside that had a community caring about it and, in a sense, complementing it, a countryside where the best cooperative instincts of people had already created the basis for a strong rural revival. It was clear to them that New England offered the most likely opportunities. Having established this in their own minds, once and for all, it was natural that the Erharts should come back from the West.

However, the two years were constructive and formative. While together in New York, both studying at Columbia, they became vegetarians. At first it was a spiritual decision. They were influenced by a man who told how the after-effects of a violent death spread throughout an animal's system and thence into the systems of people who ate the flesh. "New York was a violent city and we wanted to cool our vibes," Shep said. Then it became a carefully thought out matter of establishing a more balanced and healthy diet.

They lived in an old mill not far from New Haven. Linnette studied Sanskrit at Yale, Shep took on carpentry and became apprenticed to a cabinetmaker, and together they grew an organic garden. Casual and unquestioned love of the country turned into an affirmative philosophy. It was more than a pleasant place to live or rest in, it was a place to work, to be and to feel practical with your whole body, and it was the source of the food that they had come to feel strongly about.

Living a while in San Francisco, Shep worked as a full-time cabinetmaker, producing the desks for an office renovation, and together the two lived in a macrobiotic study house where the science of both organic gardening and dieting could be fully explored. Yet as they coursed over the western lands, the Erharts missed the contact with their families and the New England people they felt comfortable with. This wasn't snobbery on their part. Rather, it was the yearning of all persons who have a strongly developed root feeling for the place they knew when they were growing up.

Back in Connecticut, they finally decided to buy a farm. Shep's father suggested they look along the Maine coast, and they did, finding the place in Franklin through a realtor after they concentrated in that area. Twice they had become excited about acquiring land in Nova Scotia, but each time they were pulled back to New England by forces within them that they can't explain — a sense of patriotism, perhaps, of wanting to prove that it was still possible in America; or maybe the force of conscience that often seems to lurk in the New Englander's soul. "Having spent all our college years rejecting the Puritan ethic, we realized that it worked," Linnette said.

By the time they moved to the new twenty-eight acres, it was spring. If they planned to subsist, there was no time to lose getting the land plowed and planted. They had hoped to find a place with a stream, the most reliable source of running water, and where there was enough land so that eventually they could launch a community. But the scrabbly Franklin property would do while they were as yet experimenting. They paid $16,000 for it, drawing on Shep's savings and getting some support from his father. Skeptical and uneasy at first, Mr. Erhart was increasingly responsive as the couple worked out their plans and became more intent about it. "He was like the father who wants to give his son a boost in starting a business. He saw we were serious about this, so he wanted to make sure we did it right," Shep said.

Their first priority, considered as one of the acquisition costs, was hiring a man to plow and harrow fields that had become impossibly hard, uneven and streaky with clay after years of neglect. The Erharts relied on two different men for such tasks, natives who had phased out of farming but still had the equipment. I thought that if the Erharts' approach took hold in Maine it would certainly give a lift to those many ex-farmers with old machines, men who need to make money wherever they can.

Close to the house, to discourage woodchucks and rabbits, they laid out "the greens garden" and planted cucumbers, two rows of lettuce, a row of two different mustard greens and a row of kale. Back in Connecticut, in a plot on family land, they had started many of their vegetables, counting on the use of compost to be able to adapt them to different soil conditions depending on where they went. Now they planted these seedlings by hand, using a hoe and digging down to ten inches for the deep-rooted vegetables.

Broccoli, Chinese cabbage, regular cabbage, beets, Swiss chard, Japanese white radishes, regular radishes and four kinds of beans all grew well. In a big field they put down half an acre of buckwheat, half an acre of millet and another half acre in varieties of corn and squash.

A winter garden went down in August: vegetables that could survive in the frozen ground, like carrots, rutabagas, and some daikons (the Japanese radish). They hoped to return to a traditional diet based largely on grains, a diet patterned after ancient agrarian societies. "Wholegrains were the staples for these cultures," Shep said, "and in the frontier settlements it was whole wheat bread."

With hard work and vigilance, they did well in the new ground. Yet there were some failures. The cauliflower didn't make it and 350 feet of onion transplants failed to grow. The buckwheat and corn were planted too late, so Shep decided to let the immature wheat stand and turn into "green manure" (as the farmer refer to mulch crops). The corn was nipped by fall frost.

Their new neighbors helped out in these and other dilemmas. One gave the Erharts much of his sweet corn crop. Another donated onion plants. Still another man gave Shep a chance to earn money. For helping to harvest and prune Christmas trees on a sixty-acre woodlot, Shep collected enough evergreen clippings to go into the Christmas wreath business. The man also let Shep cut firewood, vitally needed for the Ashley stove that was the Erharts' main house heating unit.

"If you come into any rural community with long hair, with a car painted funny colors, if you are arrogant and you say, 'I'm going to do it my way,' you create bad feeling," Linnette said. "But you meet your neighbors, ask them for help and they respond. They know how to make it here and most can remember how it used to be done."

As the Erharts saw it, the rural natives may have abandoned the traditional ways but they still respected hard work. And there was another element, closer to heart; a deep-seated sentiment about the Erharts' determination. "They sense that they've lost something in the old way of life," Shep said. "There is almost a nostalgic twinge when they find out that what we're doing is what their mothers and fathers did."

At Thanksgiving, the Erharts drove to Connecticut, harvested carrots that they'd left behind, and sold $75 in Christmas wreaths. They were also in the seaweed business. At extremely low tide they had discovered two very tasty and healthful varieties on a coastal promontory. According to the Erharts, seaweed is a curative that helps the body get rid of dangerous trace metals, cadmium and radium. We had it both times I visited. Regardless of what it does for you, I thought it was delicious sautéed with carrots and daikon, served along with brown rice, baked buttercup squash, chick-peas, onions and celery.

After they read *Living the Good Life*, the Erharts were impressed by the Nearings' insistence on keeping an exact daily schedule. "Those people are together, that's the way we want to be," Shep said.

So the Erharts tried it too. But it didn't suit their bodily or psychic chemistry. Their happy notions about the rising with the sun, eating meals at regular hours, and going to bed early went unfulfilled. Shep found he had to use an alarm clock to awaken anywhere near sunrise. "It wasn't spontaneous at all," he said. "It was a conception of the way things should be, that's all. And it turned out that that wasn't what we came here for."

Instead he did what came naturally, getting up most of the time around eight, then doing exercises, sitting and meditating for a while. There was lots to think about. Some days they didn't get outside until eleven. "What we are trying to establish," Shep said, "is a sensitivity to rhythms. There is a difference between rhythms and routine. Rhythms are both the product of what's happening inside of you and what's happening outside of you, how the cat is, how the weather is, who drops in."

Sometimes it was hard to muster the effort to go out and dig more trenches in the gardens. And sometimes whole days were spent just casting around, feeling muddled about priorities and being indecisive, even as they began to feel the pressure of winter coming. "We have an awful lot to learn," Shep said. "After all, we bring twenty-eight years of habits that are very strange to this environment. And I don't want to kid you. We have our fair share of goofing off. Sometimes we sit and just do nothing. Or maybe we'll binge, as we say, and and we'll just sit around and eat waffles all morning, and get so absolutely stuffed we don't want to move."

Expenses for the first year in Franklin would be over $3,500, Shep figured, on account of starting costs and some unavoidable capital expenses. "We'd like to get the budget down to $3,000 or less by next year and then way down after we've finished with such expenditures as a Rototiller, truck, building materials for a new grain shed, tools, shingles, et cetera, and are growing more of our own food." Until then, they would have to dip into the savings account, sell home productions, take on odd jobs, and maybe turn to Shep's talent in cabinetry for outside income.

The first time I went to Franklin, Shep was obviously apprehensive about winter. As we stood on the tide flat below his place, the wind funneled up the inlet with an ominous relentlessness that made me think of Napoleon trapped in Russia. Shep felt it too and shivered slightly. "It's coming up on us fast," he said.

There was not nearly enough firewood cut and stacked, not nearly enough vegetables in storage, and the house was in no shape to withstand a winter like the one just before. I thought of the time I stood high upon one of the Camden hills and looked with amazement out over the deep Penobscot Bay, its entire surface a vast frozen whiteness, mottled and streaked where the sea had welled up through cracks.

Back inside the house, in the kitchen where the stove was lit, it still felt raw. Shep burned his slipper without even knowing it as he rested his feet up on the stove's edge. "Come January, you may not find us here," he said as I was about to leave. Though he smiled, it was more than a jest.

But his mood had changed when I returned nearly a month later. The enemy had been met in the form of a biting northerly that froze the pipes in the cellar. Even though Shep had banked the foundation walls with evergreen boughs after the native fashion, the wind still found openings in the uncemented granite blocks. To thaw out the pipes, Shep installed heat lamps where the radiating low heat would do the most good. He counted on this tactic to ride out future cold winds.

"The seasons don't wait for you to plan. They make their own demands. Winter has been like a final exam, the big test," he said.

And so far I could see they would pass it. Their bodies had adjusted to the cold. As Shep had insisted, "The natural rhythms will become our rhythms and we won't have to worry about winter, for winter will become us."

On that second visit it was snowing again, this time more steadily as befitted the fortnight before Christmas. They hoped it would fall deeply and blanket the ground until the spring thaw. Shep led me through the house to show exactly how they were prepared.

Just through the kitchen was a dining room. In the corner, the newly installed Ashley wood stove gave off a smooth velvety wave of warmth that was having a good effect on the seaweed hung to dry on a laundry rack. In the next room, Linnette had set up an office where she was keeping track of seaweed orders and apparently was making Christmas presents. One of these was a needlework illustration of the Maine sunrise. Turning the corner of the house, we entered a small sitting room with a fireplace that Shep said they would sit close to at night sometimes. Indian rugs decorated the wall and a wooden pitchfork from Spain hung over the mantel.

Upstairs the air was bitter cold. There was a guest room with a double bed covered by a fine patchwork quilt. In Shep's and Linnette's room, the double mattress lay on the floor, with another handsome patchwork quilt covering the sleeping bags they had bought at L. L. Bean and used as a comforter. Through a small room, child-sized, we entered the attic. As it was above the warm kitchen and was penetrated by the stove chimney, Shep felt this attic would not freeze. He had piled squashes on the floor. Ears of sweet corn hung from a diagonal corner beam. He planned to get a small wood or briquette stove up here, since the rising chimney had a place to attach a stove-pipe. Linnette's clothes, a modest quantity, were visible in an open wardrobe under the north beams. Shep's tools, including a scythe, hung on the south wall.

We went downstairs and farther down in the cellar that rose above the ground levels, its walls the huge blocks of granite through which the northerly had shrieked. The floor was wet in places and it smelled pleasantly enough of vegetables packed in leaves in boxes: beets, onions and a variety of tubers. I saw the heat lamps shining off the pipes that went into the bathroom next to the kitchen and the kitchen sink. The pipes were exposed where the cellar became a low crawl space. In this area I saw a collection of absolutely round stones, like gigantic bowling balls or curling stones. Shep said they heated some of these and used them very effectively as bedwarmers. There was a big wood-burning furnace in the center, but Shep said it needed a lot of work, was missing some pipe sections, and that it wouldn't be used, since the Ashley stove had been a success.

All the same, I was thinking about February as I drove away. Shep disappeared around the corner of the house wearing a knit wool cap, carrying a "buck" saw to make firewood. My old feelings of November came back. It would be a tough winter for these people. The elation of weathering the opening blasts, the sharp cold mornings and the first deep snowfalls might give way to boredom and discomfort as winter progressed. Then what would life here lead to? They talked about wanting to form a community where participants had their own homesteads but worked land in common, sharing equipment and tools, in the manner of early New England towns. They hoped to lessen their dependence on modern paraphernalia, although once Shep said with a helpless look, "I'm afraid we're destined to remain strung out between the machine age and the horse and buggy days."

They were thinking about having children and of setting up a school where the emphasis would be on human values as opposed to the sheer development of intellect, where children would be encouraged to play as much as work. "Kids should be taught in a way that allows them to retain their natural sense of wonder," Linnette said, "taught about nature and gardening for example, and allowed to naturally link physical and symbolic aspects of life."

Shep said he would not feel fulfilled until he could build his own house, from the ground up. He wanted to grow rice and wheat crops. Maybe they could meet their cash needs by growing goods for the increasingly busy organic food market. Hope and enthusiasm were unbounded, although the Erharts were not shortsighted about the obstacles.

I was genuinely relieved when I heard they came happily through the first winter. At least that is what I asuumed when I got a card from Shep in April telling me where I could acquire patchwork quilts I had expressed an interest in when I saw theirs.

The last three lines made me especially happy: "Spring still in birth pangs here — but we've planted in greenhouse. Going to Nova Scotia Apr. 25–29 for aquacultural conf[erence] — see about seaweed — think things are beginning to develop on larger scale."

SIX

Community

VILLAGES AND SMALL TOWNS

DRIVING SOUTH near Sherman Station late one September afternoon, I pulled off the road to stop for a rest. The shoulder looked grassy and firm but, under the spell of the countryside, I was dreaming. Both right wheels dropped suddenly: the shoulder, in reality, was the edge of a swamp.

The first motorist I flagged for help stopped. He had a thick hemp rope that we used to hitch the cars together, and with one slow tug he pulled me out.

Since I felt foolish about my stupidity, I was effusive in expressing my sense of relief. It was turning dusk and I was late to meet a friend in Orono, nearly an hour away. At first I couldn't believe that I had broken my own imperative for Maine drivers: always carry a tow-line and shovel. Where had I put them? Was the chain hooked up to the tractor at home?

My Good Samaritan, though, seemed prepared to cope with most situations. And since he wore work boots and green twill trousers, I guessed correctly that he was in the forestry business. He said he managed a plywood mill nearby and was also headed for Orono, where he lived.

"These are such lovely towns out here," I said. "Why do you bother to commute?"

He thought for a moment and still didn't answer me right away, but explained instead how he and his family used to live in the mill town, how the relationship between plant and community was uncommonly good, and how it was an ideal location for doing things outdoors. Then he got to the point.

"The small town life has its appeal," he said. "But there are three big drawbacks that you've got to keep in mind. Medical facilities generally are not available. The schools are awfully provincial. The teachers are good people but they live in a small world with no exposure to outside thought, so education falls into a rut. The third problem is lack of outside recreation and culture, activities that get people out and doing things. There is no culture to speak of, so that leaves recreation. Conservationists are upset about the snowmobile, but truly it has a place in this region, because it has gotten a lot of people who used to sit all winter, stewing in a hot kitchen, outdoors and feeling the elements."

He had to move on; so did I. But before we parted, I promised I'd visit his mill someday and we'd resume the talk about rural life.

I haven't kept my word, at least not yet. But in the course of my travels I have met with many people living in small towns and I have formed my own views. There were those who felt trapped, just like many people in the city. There was economic and intellectual stagnation. There was rural poverty. There was inadequate health care. Old-timers were left to fend for themselves in derelict farms far out of town. All too often the sugar maples planted by a forefather were cut down to obtain money for food, if not to make a down payment on a snowmobile or television set.

Yet as often as rural people were victims of cruel circumstance, because their way of life or the community's traditional economy existed no longer, they were the victims of their own delusions about their aspirations and needs. In their present state of mind, misled by false expectations and done in by failing institutions, many of these people would probably not make peace with themselves in any environment.

Was I being unfair? There were moments of distress when I began to wonder if the only people who could be idealistic about the future of rural towns were outsiders like me, brought up comfortably in the exciting atmosphere of an urban cultural center while enjoying the best features of country life on a "gentleman's" farm.

If this were true, then one of my strongest hopes was dimmed. From reading history and from observing the present dissolution of the American city, I'd come to believe in the potential of the small town, where I thought most families developed a strong sense of community and assumed a moral obligation to take part in local affairs because they had been there a long time, planned to stay and wanted to secure a good environment for their children and children's children. Yet if these rural Americans really didn't appreciate what they had and were displaced by exurbanites who had learned what was wrong with society while making enough money to escape it, what happened to my thesis?

No clear answer ever took shape because the generalizations of the mill manager were no more correct than my own. The only general truth was that small town life was undergoing a reevaluation at the same time that it had become a focal point for philosophic and institutional redirection in a way that could not be dismissed and in a way that justified my optimism far more than the mill manager's pessimism.

In the late sixties, English philosopher and historian Arnold Toynbee observed that the hippie movement was important not so much because it was an affirmation of a new life style, as because it was a red light to warn Americans that their social and economic structure — really their entire value system — was coming apart. Lewis Mumford, in *The Myth of the Machine,* traced the dehumanization of society through a misunderstanding and misapplication of technology. But he was optimistic, at least in part.

> When the moment comes to replace power with plenitude, compulsive external rituals with internal self-imposed discipline, depersonalization with individuation, automation with autonomy, we shall find that the necessary change of attitude has been going on beneath the surface during the last century, and the long buried seeds of a richer human culture are now ready to strike root and grow, as soon as the ice breaks up and the sun reaches them.

Lewis Mumford and Arnold Toynbee are great original thinkers and I'm not certain that their complex patterns of thought are entirely within my range of comprehension. Yet simplistically, at least, I could relate to their observations by thinking about Maine's small towns. I was hopeful that someday, maybe much to the surprise of the mill manager, small town life would blend the best of both worlds — rural and urban — as far as human values were concerned. Then there would be a future for both old-timers and newcomers.

Indications that this would happen did not abound, but they clearly did exist. It was still probably true that more people wanted to get out of rural towns than wanted to come to them. Among those who stayed there was generally no pronounced feeling that theirs was the best of all possible worlds. To read the *Maine Times* and features in national publications, and to hear in conversation about some people's euphoric plans, it was far too easy to imagine that the twin migrations "back to the land" and back to the country towns had swollen to immense proportions. This had not happened. But eventually it might, and already acreage values for inland Maine were soaring upward, just as coastal land values began to fly out of sight a decade ago.

Among the rural figures and families that I met there were some views held in common, although I never found my composite rural town. The prevailing state of mind was that in the small town you had time to get to know yourself and then conduct your life in a way that positioned you where you wanted to stand in this world as a whole. There was plenty of time and usually the opportunity.

In urban society you became strangely emboldened within your shell of anonymity. It appeared not to matter how you acted publicly, because there were so many people on stage that nobody really paid much attention. It was quite different in a small town, and in a way that might detract from a sense of security. Yet the situation also had certain advantages, as described by the wife of a young country doctor.

"The great thing here is that you can't just walk out of your house and go and observe what people are doing, the way you can in the city," she said. "If you're going to be occupied, you have to do it yourself. You really have to fall back on your own resources and your resources have room to expand. Whatever you want to do, you can make waves."

With her husband she helped open a rural health care clinic in inland Maine. Newcomers, they were openly excited about the prospects. For doctors the rural environment certainly offers many challenges. Conditions are crude, complex, and inconvenient. I found that Maine seemed to be attracting young doctors, newly in practice, and the reasons were twofold: people had been neglected medically, by comparison with other places, and the natural environment was immensely appealing.

Maine is a good place for people of universal skills, like doctors, who can apply their energies and talent *anywhere* and who do not depend on the urban environment. Artists, writers and all kinds of craftsmen and creators are among these. In the small town, they can obtain the privacy and freedom from distraction that their work demands, while still being able to take part in community affairs.

Then there are those activists who not only are committed to the revitalization of local government but who find a special excitement in becoming big fishes in small ponds. Many of those presently in the swim of things are migrants from other localities or cities.

Harrison Richardson was fed up with the commute to his Chicago law office and the split existence he was living between city and suburb. He came to Maine, immediately got involved in politics, and before he was forty rose to majority leadership of the Maine senate. He was the man most responsible for leading to passage the Site Location Act. While he did not move to a small, rural town, he cut his commute — to Portland, now — down to fifteen minutes and was able to live in comparative country. His children were horseback riders. Harry was an outdoorsman, and whenever I ran into him on my travels he was enthusiastic about the quality of Maine life and the prospects here for the citizen to reach his government.

Another migrant like Richardson was Marc Nault. Tired of promoting aerospace in Washington, D.C., he moved to Machias, the home of his wife, Marie. He bought the small printing shop there and, until he was slowed by a heart attack, he put out a first-rate weekly newspaper. Both Marc and Marie were deeply embroiled in local educational and public affairs. They agonized when the oilmen promised to alleviate severe economic hardships in Washington County. Whenever I argued with Marc that recreation, wildlife management, summer colonists, and the existing ways of life like fishing, clamming, and blueberry picking would not destroy the matchless coastal environment, he agreed in principle. But he had spent far more time than I in discovering that the realities were something else. The activities that I envisioned were distant possibilities whereas the oilmen were knocking on the door. Whenever I passed through town I stopped by the printing shop, and I saw Marc's position evolve until finally we were in fundamental agreement, only he was really off and running and doing something about it, in spite of his heart attack. Maine was his place.

Marc's boys played in a creek across the field below his house, and on weekends the Naults combed the beach in front of the land they acquired not far from where the oilmen wanted to put a refinery.

Not all the "big fish" are migrants, however, although those who are active in environmental preservation and protection invariably turn out to be newcomers. Rob Page, my host in Aroostook County, a Yale man, was a native of Caribou, where his father was a respected doctor. Peter Kelley, Page's close friend and contemporary, a Harvard man and a rising state legislator, was the son of a successful Caribou potato dealer. Both were excited by the challenge of practicing law there.

"I get every damn thing you can imagine," Kelley told me. "Divorce, bankruptcy, personal injury, assault and collection cases." Kelley missed the symphony and other urban cultural institutions, but he and his wife enjoyed gathering with the Pages and other young couples for dinner at somebody's house where the conversation was apt to be concerned with the future of Maine and its environment. Caribou most certainly was not a backwater as far as human challenges and human relationships were concerned.

Rob and Jane Page found an old farm outside Caribou in New Sweden, one of several settlements in the vicinity still populated by the descendants of Swedish immigrants. Two languages were spoken there and the customs and culture of the old world were still observed. The houses and churches were simple, trim and elegant. Rob Page had a fine vegetable garden and rolling fields that he let a farmer make hay from, although Rob liked to work around the place, too, on an ancient Farmall H tractor. Jane fixed up the old barn as an arts and crafts center to sell cottage industry products made by neighbors, particularly the old people who did needlework, knit clothing, and made lovely quilts.

A generation older than Page and Kelley, John Merrill chose to stay in Skowhegan to practice law. His father had been a trial lawyer of substantial reputation in Maine and his uncle had been chief justice of the state supreme court. "There's nothing like the outdoors: the people who are really worth something are on the land," was what Merrill's father had told him, and he took the advice to heart, leaving Skowhegan only to camp, fish, and hunt on wilderness land he owned in the north.

"I get my vacation from day to day," Merrill told me, explaining how he'd copied his father's habit of keeping a golf bag, fishing rod or shotgun in the trunk of his car, depending on the season. But Merrill was soured on the trend of the times toward conglomeration and homogeneity. He recalled when every rural center had its local mill, a woolen factory, a leather or forest products operation, owned by Maine men, employing Maine people, and keeping Maine money in the state. These old operations had abused the environment and sometimes the people, said Merrill, but they had not degraded the state nearly as much as the giants, the companies managed by out-of-state interests that now owned most of the land.

Merrill was simplistic about moral and social changes. "Television has set the hearts to yearning for things that aren't really important," he would say, "and as people around here have become less self-sufficient they have lost a lot of individuality and become more materialistic. The horizons used to be closer and smaller, and I think people were happier."

Yet I couldn't help but think that maybe Merrill had a point — although probably that state of bygone happiness was not nearly as much appreciated by those of past generations as by a nostalgic man like him, musing in retrospect.

Then, too, there is the danger of becoming so insulated that a small town loses its vitality. As Captain Littlepage put it in *The Country of the Pointed Firs,* "a community narrows down and grows dreadful ignorant when it is shut up to its own affairs, and gets no knowledge of the outside world except from a cheap, unprincipled newspaper." Somewhere a line was to be drawn between localism and worldliness, between emphasis on the family unit and the needs of mankind, between local and national institutional imperatives, so that the best of both sides could be blended and understood. I never did decide where to draw the line. No sooner would I envy life in a small town than I would clearly see where a few newcomers were needed to stir things up and inspire a sense of appreciation.

Many of the migrants were not ready to make the plunge to a place as remote as New Sweden. Instead, they moved tentatively, going to busy coastal towns like Wiscasset, Camden or Rockport and places just inland within the orbit of such "cities" as Bath, Brunswick, Lewiston, Augusta, Portland and Bangor. One housewife referred to life in a place like Rockport as being village life, different from the rural environment in its emphasis on community, not self-reliance, and where the cooperative instincts of close neighbors are more dominant than the forces and moods of the land.

She and her family left a Massachusetts suburb, where every morning husbands took part in the commuter exodus and where all the time families tended to withdraw within the shells of material conveniences and comforts that they had carefully created for themselves. "We wanted a place where we could live with integrity, in a nonexploitive way," she said. In Rockport she thought they'd found it.

A CITY TO LIVE IN

I WORKED for a while in San Francisco. It is one of the only two cities in the United States where I would like to live. Portland, Maine, is the other. "Often I think of the beautiful town / That is seated by the sea," wrote Henry Wadsworth Longfellow, who was born in Portland. And that, even now, is the picture. Nestled between two hills on a peninsula, Portland looks out across ocean waters to a full score of islands that are counted within city limits. It is a grand view. It is a good feeling.

At this point in time, though, in order to conceive of Portland as an East Coast San Francisco, one must talk about potential and not the facts of recent history. Because Maine's largest city has fallen into a difficult condition, reflecting the demise of many other East Coast fishing and shipping centers.

Yet on the bright side, supporting my own feelings, the renowned Philadelphia city planner Edmund N. Bacon has said, "Portland has many things going for it in the long run." Bacon was thinking about Portland's waterfront when he made this comment. There is no question but that this is the city's most important asset. The port can be revived to suit new kinds of requirements, it can be treated in a way that will enhance the whole urban environment and, above all, it can take on a new dimension as a place for people.

But there are other factors to back the contentions and hopes of Portland's boosters. The city's 1970 population of 65,116 (a drop of 7,450 in a decade) hardly qualifies it as a big city. (It is an eighth the size of San Francisco.) Thus, understandably, it has not become as congested and generally unmanageable as many other urban settlements in the United States. Even though it is geographically confined to a peninsula, Portland is not densely developed or populated. In fact, more than 52 percent of the land remains vacant, there are 38 parks and playgrounds comprising 460 acres, and the city government owns another 303 acres, *excluding* parks, public building lots, school grounds, the airport and street rights-of-way. This is the sort of situation that excites a man like Edmund Bacon. And it gives Portland a golden opportunity to do the kind of innovative planning that could establish models for both public and private urban land usage throughout Maine and elsewhere.

What is more, the existing town has a good feeling to it, expressed through its architecture and the way the city stands by itself, as yet uncompromised and swallowed up by suburbs that have lost their way. It strikes you coming in from the north, having driven over the Turkey Bridge that spans Back Cove. To be sure, there are old houses, rundown commercial buildings, tenements, and truck lots, all mixed together in an overall state of rot and ugliness on this side. But up on the crest of the ridge, where Portland rides the saddle between the humps of Munjoy and Bramhall's hills, you smell the damp salty air coming off the bay, and the old city spreading out before you looks a lot more fine and handsome than the sterile, homogenous city centers that proliferated during the urban construction boom of the sixties. While many of Portland's early and finest edifices were destroyed by the great fire of 1866, and some old houses, such as Longfellow's birthplace, have been torn down, many remain, waiting for a new surge of love and care.

You approach the waterfront, where great piers have been reduced to rows of piling that march out into the harbor. Overlooking this scene is the abandoned grain elevator of the Grand Trunk Railway, built at the turn of the century. A massive, straight-edged, cement cathedral without the spire or ornamental relief, it is handsome now because it is a relic that speaks of Portland's past as an important shipping terminus. Down in the narrow, cobbled approaches to the harborside, there is a restoration aborning. Boutiques, two restaurants, new law and insurance offices and a candlemaker's shop are among the signs that Exchange Street is making a stand. And I know that the small group of souls who have argued and toiled to bring this about are on the right track. And that Portland will remain true to its Latin motto, inscribed on the city seal: *Resurgam.*

234

It means, "I will arise."

It is not a romantic notion, nor is it a literary touch, to say that from its settlement by white men in 1632, Portland has been doing just that.

George Cleeve and Richard Tucker came to the peninsula (known to the Indians as *Mach Chegun,* a literal description in the Algonquin dialect meaning "Great Elbow") after they were driven out of Cape Elizabeth by John Winter. The king of England had granted him all of Casco Bay, Winter claimed. By 1675, there were forty families in the town, then considered part of Falmouth. But that was the year the Indian sachem King Philip declared war on the New England colonists, and in 1676, Falmouth was wiped out.

In the next hundred years, there were only a few intervals of peace, and Portland was true to its Phoenix image and motto. A fort was built to become the center of a compact village, but this entire community was also annihilated, and by the end of the seventeenth century there was reportedly not a white settler living anywhere in Maine east of Wells, thirty miles southwest of "The Great Elbow."

As an historical simplification, it can be said that during the next 272 years Portland enjoyed four periods of great prosperity (as this word is applied to a whole city), interrupted by three disasters, before falling into the slow decline that brings us to the present. From around 1750 until the Revolution, the town was the supply center for pine masts for the British Navy. According to the excellent new history, *Portland,* published in 1972 by Greater Portland Landmarks, Inc., 1,046 masts, averaging three tons each, were shipped from Falmouth between 1768 and 1772. In addition, trade flourished in other wood products — lumber, barrel staves, cordwood and planks. This period came to a fiery and destructive end when a British fleet shelled Falmouth in 1775, then landed and put to the torch most of the buildings that still stood.

The next boom followed national independence. Again Portland was a center of maritime commerce and was perhaps really frequented by the "Spanish sailors with bearded lips" that Longfellow remembered in his poem "My Lost Youth." But when President Jefferson pushed the Embargo Act through Congress in 1807, curtailing trade from U.S. ports, Portland died again, with import duties alone dropping from over a third of a million dollars to practically nothing.

After the abortive War of 1812 with England (or between 1820 and

1866, the year of the Great Fire), Portland was more than a market junction for Maine and a busy New England harbor. Not only was the city used as a winter ice-free port for the Canadian Maritime provinces, with goods flowing to Montreal over the Grand Trunk Railway; wood products also went down to and molasses came back from the West Indies, to be converted into both sugar and rum. Portland was reported to be one of the nation's meccas for serious drinking — a place where even the workingman's day was broken up by rum breaks, referred to as the time to "take some support." Thus the city was the predictable birthplace of the temperance movement, led by Longfellow's contemporary, Neal Dow.

While the 1866 conflagration did not cripple Portland's maritime posture for long, it came at a time when one probably could have predicted that Boston and New York would prevail as the most important cultural and commercial centers of the northeastern coastal region. The blaze occurred during the Fourth of July celebration. It spread in a northwesterly direction from a small boat shop on Commercial Street, not far from the present International Ferry Terminal, and left a gaping hole in the center of town all the way to Munjoy Hill. Destroyed were the customs house, the post office, city hall, the most important commercial, retail and wholesale facilities, and many fine old residences. "Desolation! Desolation! Desolation!" wrote Longfellow when he saw the ruins.

To be sure, Portland rose off the floor once again, and at the turn of the century was still a bustling rail center and harbor. James Phinney Baxter, father of Percival, made a fortune with the Portland Packing Company. He also became mayor and is credited with the foresight of establishing the city's impressive park system. But in reading back through historical accounts, it seems to me that something was lost in that 1866 fire, if only the chance to keep up the competitive pace. Maybe when a city is destroyed three times (counting continual devastation during the Indian hostilities as one blow) it has no more energy left or is so sapped of its drive for eminence that really only a few extraordinary souls, like Mayor Baxter, have the fierce determination and pride to devote themselves to their community.

In any event, bringing history quickly up to date, Portland lost certain advantages for reasons having nothing to do with the fire. The wonderful rail connections were less and less a premium in a market transportation system that was blatantly and shortsightedly structured to favor trucking interests and highway connections. Shipments of raw materials, notably wood products, declined. The fishing front became a disaster area. With more room to expand and start from scratch, South Portland made an aggressive move to become the oil port. The old city watched its waterfront decay, and by 1972 was putting far more raw sewage into its harbor (20 million gallons a day) than tons of cargo into ships.

As if this were not dismal enough, it seems that only a handful of businessmen and civic-minded people really cared. A contemporary of mine told me many times that it was not a question of capability but, rather, an unexplained drainage of the spirit and will that affected Portland. "There were fortunes made here in the good old days," he would say. "Many of those families are still here. So is the money, multiplied through investments and trusts. And do you know where it is invested? Not in Portland or even in Maine. But in Standard Oil and IBM. It would be nice if the descendants of our leading people would commit themselves to Portland. When *they* don't, who else will?"

Judging from news clippings, the Portland City Council has been antediluvian in its thinking. Like too many others, it is entrenched, tired, afraid of change, guided by all the traditional concepts of economic growth and social improvement that have too often backfired and dashed our high hopes. This might have been the natural inclination, considering that Portland was founded on the basis of its potential as a commercial and industrial settlement. And I can see how there are still opportunities in industries such as metal fabricating and assembling parts, and jobs where the steady dependability of the Maine worker, rated high in this regard nationwide, is an advantage. With rail ties still very much intact (for the nation must turn again to rail transportation — it is only a matter of time), Portland still can be a very important channel for shipments into and through Canada.

Scott Hutchison, executive vice president of Portland's Canal Bank, an institution that financed much of the recovery from the 1866 fire, sees Portland not only recapturing its position as an ice-free port for Montreal but becoming a center for the flow of goods into the midwestern United States via Montreal and the Grand Trunk. Already, he has told me, Halifax sends two-thirds of its cargo to Chicago, yet it is *800 miles* shorter to send it overland from Portland.

Essentially, however, Portland holds the most promise by expanding its present position as a financial and retail center for northern New England, while at the same time attracting new and *different* kinds of activities, such as printing and publishing. (Close to the source of paper, Portland should be one of the nation's busiest printing centers — or so it seems to my way of thinking.)

Then there are several generators of economic activity that have hardly featured at all in shaping Portland's future, although important first steps have been taken.

With so much of its intrinsic and original picturesque quality and architectural beauty still intact, Portland should hold great appeal as an academic and medical center. In short, it should base its future on activities that cannot adversely affect the environment but that attract people who have a fair amount of money to spend on goods and services. I refer specifically to a medical center, because Portland already has a good new one that shows promise of becoming a significant part of the future of the city. As I write this, plans are taking shape to create a University of Maine Medical School tied to the Maine Medical Center in Portland. The University of Maine already has an undergraduate branch, as well as its law school, in Portland.

The other activity I am thinking about is tourism. There are all those islands out in Casco Bay, a waterfront with the potential of vying with San Francisco's Ghirardelli Square, and a natural jumping-off place for coastal cruising — by pleasure yacht or passenger ferry. As Edmund Bacon told a Greater Portland Landmarks, Inc., lecture audience, "Your waterfront could become world-famous."

These last observations of mine are already supported by the success of Portland's brand-new International Ferry Terminal, from which a ship departs each night for Yarmouth, Nova Scotia. Getting the ferry service in the long run may well be as big a deal as winning the rail line to Montreal over a century ago.

The key negotiator in obtaining the ferry service was John Menario, Portland's able young city manager. The ferry people demanded a million dollar guarantee from which they could draw up to $200,-000 a year to cover operating deficits. It would be repaid from the revenues in profitable years. Menario had only three weeks in which to obtain pledges from a hundred leading businesses, telling them to be prepared to lose up to $2,500 a year. Eventually it cost the city $2 million to launch the operation, but it has generated a revival of interest in the waterfront. The hope is that passengers will linger there before and after trips. At its present rate of use, the ferry terminal will have paid for its investment within ten years, aside from serving as a catalyst for tourism. In fact, the ferry has been such a success that a second ship was to go into service in the spring of 1973, more than doubling its present capacity.

At about the same time as the ferry terminal went in, a movement began on the order of New York's South Street Seaport Museum, a project involving an eleven-block area on the Manhattan waterfront, backed by a membership of 15,000 and a several million dollar line of credit from a banking consortium. In Portland, the Mariner's Church, a handsome survivor of the 1866 fire, was restored by young artists and craftsmen. It led to the establishment of the Old Port Exchange District and buttressed the existing effort to restore other historic landmarks. A first-rate restaurant, the Gaslight, opened in one of the handsome brick buildings on Exchange Street.

What is needed now is a good marine complex tied in with restaurants and a maritime museum. Here is what I have in mind — a pier from which replicas of coastal schooners set forth with charter passengers. A docking area for yachtsmen. A boat repair facility that in wintertime does annual overhaul jobs and has a crew of carpenters busy "finishing off" bare fiber glass hulls mass-molded in California and Florida where fine joiner work simply is not a tradition. Ship chandleries and model shops, selling equipment in the boat season and nautical books and gifts during the winter. A bakery and various shops carrying gourmet items, from food to cooking ware. A cabinetmaker's and furniture shop, whose craftsmen work on boats in the summer and make desks, chairs, and tables in the winter. A fish market (where better?). These are all places that attract people, spenders and browsers. There should be lots of walking space, benches outdoors to sit on, and eating places with a warm and sunny vantage for taking in the view during the winter.

There is no question in my mind but that Portland is a city where there should be lots of gathering and exploring and meeting. That is because, along the waterfront, such human excitement has always been a natural thing. It also fits in naturally with Portland's history.

No sooner do these notions flash through my head, however, than they are tempered by other observations. Men like Charlton Smith, president of Greater Landmarks, Inc., have campaigned steadily to maintain a living, livable Portland, based on a balance between historic preservation and new development. His view is reflected in a comment, made in the book *Portland,* that "Portland's particular richness derives both from the juxtaposition of many building styles and from the continual uses and associations of its structures."

And yet this view runs counter to the trend of the times. There are considerable pressures working to redevelop Portland as a place where people commute to and work in at the expense of urban livability. There is talk of new road arteries to relieve traffic congestion, when it seems to me it would be far more foresighted to talk about improving *public* transportation *within* the city and making convenient connections to parking terminals on the fringes where commuters stop. This way, Portland's narrow streets and handsome old buildings will not have to be destroyed to make way for wider streets and new highway corridors. This way there is an incentive to live as well as work in the city. For it is sad to say that the American city today has been reshaped to conform to the needs and conveniences of suburbanites. In a sense, the outermost ring of residential settlement is where the usual city's fate is determined. The man who lives out there wants little more than a fast route to town, a place to park, an air-conditioned office building and a convenient luncheon spot. And then, on top of this, he balks at the prospect of putting any of his tax dollars into the city.

If Portland can break away from this kind of suburban polarization, everyone will benefit.

One day I returned to ask Portland City Manager John Menario some questions. He was tied up. Portland's latest renewal project, called "The Maineway," interested me. It emphasizes the preservation of many fine old structures, returning streets to the pedestrians and creating new plazas. I wanted to learn more. The only person who had time was the assistant planner, Gerald A. Holtenhoff. Our meeting turned out well. We never really got around to the Maineway. But like so many junior men on the totem pole, Holtenhoff was bursting with enthusiasm and good ideas.

A young transplant from Iowa who finds pioneering challenges in

Portland, Holtenhoff has high hopes about the Portland of the future. As he sees it, the population eventually will nearly double. It can well afford to, better here than in the suburbs, and, as I have said, Portland has a low population density. Highways will provide convenient access to the city but will not be allowed to overwhelm it. "Increasingly, we are planning for people on foot," Holtenhoff said. Portland will consolidate its present position as the number one office, financial, retail and convention center in northern New England (all of the region north of Boston). The port area (South Portland) will continue as a major oil transfer station, but the oil will be refined somewhere far inland where its environmental side-effects can be minimized. In this regard, Portland and outlying suburbs within the metropolitan circle will cooperate increasingly to work out problems common to all the jurisdictions: transportation, waste disposal, air and water quality control and economic development. This is to be done through the Council of Governments, which has already made progress on a voluntary basis. The suburbs will finally recognize that they are not just places where commuters hole up for the night. Rather, they are functioning subsystems of the city. Even South Portland. All are dynamically dependent on Portland proper.

That is Holtenhoff's vision. It is not yet a reality. But Holtenhoff made an observation that intrigued me. When I stop to think about it, it applies nationally, even to the suburbs where I live outside Washington, D.C. "Maine is cursed, or blessed, depending how you see it, with generally poor soils for septic systems," he said. In the Portland suburb of Scarborough, 95 percent of the soil is environmentally incapable of supporting residential development unless it is accompanied by construction of sewer lines and adequate waste treatment facilities. Scarborough installed the first sewage plant in the area, back in 1963, but it was not enough to accommodate a fantastic growth rate, tripling to 8,000 people in the decade and expected to mushroom to 15,000 people by 1975. The Maine Environmental Improvement Commission had just cracked down with an order requiring Scarborough to install an additional $10 million sewer plant by the fall of 1974. And until then, no more building permits were to be issued unless the soil was suitable. Already, according to Holtenhoff, this had resulted in new interest in city housing developments.

"The romance of the small town atmosphere and the car have left the cities high and dry," he said. "And there definitely has been an antiurban feeling in our culture. So what have we done but made the country less country and the cities less cities."

However, this trend can be reversed with situations like Scarborough's preventing urban decentralization and sprawl. The city would become attractive again, at first because it was the only place where sewer systems were economically feasible (with enough people to support construction bonds) or environmentally efficient. Future outlying developments would be forced to cluster, as they should, with large tracts of wildland being preserved: open space communities, open space planning. Or as Holtenhoff put it, "The planned, controlled density of human settlements, changes in property tax laws, and the recycling of worn-out sections of the urban core should be the most critical imperatives of the environmental movement."

"But surely a temporary lack of environmental facilities is not the only way to bring this about. There has got to be something less crisis-motivated, something deliberate happening, hasn't there?" I asked.

"Yes. Definitely," Holtenhoff answered. Then he made a second observation. "There has got to be some kind of regional or even state zoning authority to make sure that all catalytic land uses do not encourage urban sprawl."

"Catalytic?" I didn't follow his term.

"Any development that brings a lot of people together, like a shopping center, campus, high-rise apartment, convention hall, theater, office complex. The proper location of such facilities should foster massive reinvestment in urban centers," Holtenhoff explained.

"How do you prevent developers of catalysts from going to where they find cheap land, thereby creating transportation problems and a host of new environmental side-effects?" I asked.

"That's the whole point. The existing patterns are perverse. Instead we should say that these catalytic developments must be located within a certain radius of the urban core," he went on.

Put a dot on the city map to define the center point. It may be geographic. It may be the business center. It may be the city hall. In most U.S. cities there is no visible central focus, so this point will be arbitrary. Then place concentric rings moving outward to the very extremities of the metropolitan environs, a circular limit best determined by the commuting range or environmental characteristics such as land and water features. Next devise a formula to reflect the impact of different and presumed catalytic land uses. How big is the project in terms of space to be taken, square feet? How many people will it hold? How does it enhance people? Clearly a cultural center or a new college has quite a different value than a shopping center. Planning authorities will also have to relate catalytic impacts to existing development and land availability. But, as a starting point, Holtenhoff's idea is loaded with good sense. It is one of the best ways I've come across to put an end to urban design fragmentation and the rule of the car. As we talked about it, he put down on a piece of scratch paper the way such planning would restrict a shopping center. It looked like this.

POPULATION	SIZE IN SQUARE FEET	DISTANCE FROM CITY CENTER
50,000–100,000	250,000+	within 1 mile
25,000–50,000	100,000+	within ½ mile
10,000–25,000	50,000+	within ¼ mile
10,000 and less	any	⅛ to ¼ mile

I was excited. So was Holtenhoff. We were both smiling and gesturing as we talked on about the prospects for Portland.

It was late in the afternoon and outside the ice storm raged on. I had been in the city hall nearly two hours. I left feeling a lot better about the planning of Portland.

YOU CAN'T GET THERE

"THEY GOT A LOT OF SEASHELLS UP THERE," said a fat lady as she parted from her girlfriend and stepped down from the bus. Moments later, air brakes hissing, gears grinding, we were off: past the Statler-Hilton and the Boston Common, through the North End, and over the Mystic Bridge, headed "downeast."

I thought back to the last time I took public transportation to Maine. It was on the Boston & Maine Railroad, at least twenty years before. There are two moments that I remember clearly from that train ride.

First was crossing the Kennebec River at Bath. Here I began to taste coastal Maine. On the west bank of the river destroyers were being built or overhauled at the Bath Iron Works, their gray superstructures, as tall as the town steeples, seeming far more menacing here than when appearing as specks on the high sea. The shoreline of the east bank of the Kennebec was well defined, just as it should have been: granite-hewn, rimmed by evergreens, and indented by tidal flats and marsh grass. As the train picked up speed again, leaving Bath behind, the conductor announced the coming stops: Wiscasset, Damariscotta, Waldoboro, Thomaston and Rockland. His voice was nasal-flat and the words rolled forth sonorously, the emphasis heavy on the first syllable. "*Wis*-casset; *Dam*-riscotta; *Wall*-daburra; *Thom*-aston, and *Rock-land*." The last town became two separate words. The rockbound coast of Maine was here at last.

The second moment came not long after crossing the Kennebec and the conductor's call. It also featured ships, only these were three coastal schooners long since abandoned on the mudflat waterfront of

Wiscasset. Even today I slow down and cast a glance at those rotting relics. They are all too real — reminders that, yes, indeed, there *was* an Age of Sail, and Maine was a proud part of it. The ships leaned over in different directions, topmasts dangling in the slack rigging, hulls hogged and sagged out of shape. Once these ships had carried lumber, granite, ice and other cargoes. Now their holds were most likely full of rats, living the good life just above the rise and fall of the tides. When the train pulled into Rockland station, where we were to disembark, I remember that I was still thinking about those ships.

It wasn't the same by bus. I felt cramped and stifled. The blast from air-conditioning vents chilled my left side while my right was still congealing in sweat from the hot air of Boston. The roadside was terribly dreary, serving up the worst in American commercial design: flimsy food stands, garish restaurants faced with neon signs, cabin courts in all colors, used car lots, gas station after gas station. Somewhere on the North Shore of Massachusetts we passed a big highway project, what appeared to be an interchange in the making. It drew comment from the foreign woman behind me. "They seem to be tearing up all America as fast as they build it," she said.

But Bath was the same as ever. So was the Kennebec east bank, all seamed and creviced and surmounted in thick blue-green. So were the Wiscasset hulks, even to the dead-eye suspended against the sky on one, an artifact that my cousin and I once had thought of going after. But I missed the conductor's song and the outrageously expensive ham sandwiches. And where the railroad by its very nature offered a view of a rich and diverse landscape, mostly unspoiled by development between the stations, the highway was devastating in its effect on the countryside. It was a sterile strip, and every form of manmade creation along it was without distinction. If I had been set down in this bus from the midst of my sleep, in most roadside places, when I woke up I would think I was in Virginia just as soon as Maine.

It is indisputable that transportation — the desire for mobility and the way we attain it — is the single most important factor today in the way human environments are shaped, and in the way the future preservation or transformation of any community is planned. The tragedy is that, while various forms of transportation have determined the way the nation was explored and opened up, transportation has by and large been an afterthought in community land use planning.

It was the automobile that unleashed the indiscriminate plunder of the Maine coast, and now it is the arrival of supertanker oil transport that threatens to complete the destruction (if the vacationland developers don't do it first). The most enlightened land use planning in the world will be to no avail if the state Highway Commission continues to run roughshod over people by establishing new routes without giving due consideration to local views and by making the interstate channels wider and faster, seemingly for little reason other than to keep a hand in the federal highway till.

The bridge just opened across the Piscataqua River will bring only short-term relief to the congestion that has beset motorists entering and leaving Kittery during the summer months. History has shown that new roads and road improvements only create a vicious cycle by generating still more traffic. The money for the Piscataqua River bridge, for example, would have been far better spent in beefing up public transportation within Maine and in promoting tourist travel to less congested sections of the state, notably the wild and beautiful interior, instead of the overcrowded coast.

Back in the nineteenth century, Maine had a transportation system equal to the finest anywhere in the world. It served Maine people first, visitors second. At one point there were thirty-one different railroads, including branch lines, running throughout Maine, and they boasted not only first-rate service to Boston, Montreal and other outside cities, but a busy network of interurban lines serving such cities as Portland, Rockland, Lewiston, Biddeford, Waterville, Norway and Fryeburg. Horse-drawn stagecoaches coursed the state and coastal steam packets moved up and down the coast.

The tragic demise of good transportation systems comes to our attention so often, as we find an inordinate amount of our time wasted in motion. For example, when Thoreau took canoe trips in Maine he had far less trouble arranging his travel to and from the river than I did when I set up a trip over the same route 125 years later. Thoreau spent an enjoyable night coming down the coast from Boston to Bangor by boat. From Bangor he took a stage to Greenville, at the foot of Moosehead Lake, having an eventful trip and a memorable meal on the way. A paddlewheeler took him, his companion and their Indian guide up Moosehead Lake to the Northeast Carry. There all the gear and the canoe were loaded onto a handcar and ferried a short distance over a rail spur to the West Branch of the Penobscot. When the party arrived by canoe at Oldtown on the Penobscot, there was yet another stage to begin the trip back to Boston. Travel was convenient. It was inexpensive. It was full of fun and unexpected surprises. You were in good hands; and there was no sense in looking at your watch, for there was nothing you could do about matters if you were running late.

By car, with stops to obtain supplies, it took us just about as long as Thoreau to get to the West Branch. Only we had to make arrangements for others to shuttle one of the vehicles, while we left another car parked in the woods. At the end of the trip on the Penobscot, arrangements again had to be made for cars to come and pick us all up, along with the canoes. Then I spent a day getting back to pick up the car by the West Branch and driving us home from Bangor. It would have taken part of another day, too, had I not been able to get a "bush" seaplane flight to the Northeast Carry. None of these travel hitches, except maybe the plane trip, was very enjoyable in itself, yet all told we spent most of two days in a car while putting in five on the river. For Thoreau, the trips by ferryboat and stage provided nearly as much adventure as the canoeing.

Back in the 1830s, a redoubtable and eloquent man named John Poor aroused Maine people, particularly the community of Portland, to a fever pitch over the possibilities of expanding rail service within and without the state. Naturally, Poor saw rail service as a lever for economic development, although he took pains to see that transportation was a *forethought*, a means of directing growth, and carefully planned in the people's interest. He traveled far and wide, by horse and by buggy, to determine where routes should go. He interviewed farmers, foresters and fishermen before coming up with plans for two major routes. The first would be a line between Portland and Montreal that would give a considerable boost to Portland's trading position and would in effect provide the Canadians with a deep, ice-free port. He conceived of a second line from Portland to Halifax as a connection for transatlantic passenger service.

Despite the counterefforts of well-organized and powerful Boston figures, Poor landed for Portland what became the Grand Trunk Railway. It took passengers to Montreal until 1968, and it still is a busy freight line. Poor's second route was never put through, even though he founded a weekly newspaper expressly to publicize the proposal.

There are some two thousand miles of rail still making convenient connections throughout Maine, although all that is carried over them is freight. The Boston & Maine stopped taking passengers as far as Rockland over a decade ago, and abbreviated service to Portland was dropped in 1965.

Like most of the other railroads in the nation, Maine's have been mismanaged, while economic and political mechanisms have been built up to encourage even more car and truck movement. Moreover, the railroad structure is badly fragmented so that the three main freight carriers, the Maine Central, the Bangor and Aroostock, and the Boston & Maine, suffer from inefficiency and inability to compete with larger lines. However, Maine citizens don't have to look far to see that their Canadian brethren still support train service. Every day, the Canadian National train between Montreal and St. John passes through the North Woods. You can board it at Greenville, Maine.

While there are almost half as many cars and trucks (400,000) in Maine as there are people, 30 percent of the state's households have neither a motor vehicle nor public transportation available. For both rich and poor a car represents the worst possible investment under almost any circumstances, considering its depreciation in value, operating costs, and contribution to environmental pollution. Cars cost on the average about $1,500 a year. Peter Sandberg, chairman of a group calling themselves "People against the East-West Highway," put the automobile in perspective when he argued against the road that would have run from upstate New York to Calais, Maine, roaring right through the Maine woods and shooting spurs southward to Portland and Bar Harbor. The highwaymen tried to sell this one as an economic development windfall for hard-pressed rural areas, but the people who learned about it were not fooled one bit. Sandberg, a New Hampshireman, led the opposition.

As I write these words, the east-west highway has for the moment been dropped for environmental reasons. Here is what Sandberg said, however, in an exchange with a highway proponent:

As for paving over the country, we build each year over 20,000 miles of new highways, and in doing so we consume annually as much as 200,000 acres of our real estate. We already have one linear mile of road for every square mile of land in this country, have already paved over 4 million square miles, have already put down enough concrete in the Interstate system alone to build six sidewalks to the moon. What is more, if we continue at our present rate, we will add some 30 million automobiles to our current traffic jams by 1980. There is nothing "sensational" about any of this. It is the way things are, and it is extremely depressing, and it accounts in part for our strong opposition to this road you are studying.

Sandberg's comparisons are not concocted. They are based on the sort of figures and statistical hoopla that is regularly put out by the highway interests themselves, from the automakers to the cement and asphalt men.

As the people began to question proposals like the east-west highway, there were also some good ideas coming to the surface. The Bath Iron Works looked into the feasibility of building a large ferry to transport people, their vehicles, trucks, and cargo between New York and Portland. Richard L. Robbins, a lawyer from Gray, suggested in the Natural Resources Council newsletter that 150,000 of Maine's cars be replaced by 5,000 buses serving the entire state and passing through communities at ten-minute intervals. To create such a bus system would cost between $700 and $1,000 per household. The idea is not farfetched but it needs practical attention, and it may be unworkable within the existing institutional framework.

Stuart A. Cunningham of the Androscoggin Valley Regional Planning Commission drew up a plan for a statewide mass transit system called "Mainetrain." It would use existing rail lines to send fast turboelectric trains to modern stations with parking facilities throughout Maine. Cunningham projected operating costs no higher than seven cents a mile, a lot less than it costs to run your car.

Ocean Research Corporation, a Kennebunk marine engineering firm, recommended that ferry service be inaugurated between Portland and Lubec, with seven stops between. A twenty-knot vessel could make the 180-mile trip during the daytime. The most efficient system would employ containerized cargo methods with feeder vessels coming out to the ferry from each stop so that valuable time would not be wasted negotiating tricky channels and docking. The intervening stops would be in sheltered bays or thoroughfares convenient to the towns of Boothbay, Port Clyde, North Haven, Stonington, Southwest Harbor and Jonesport.

Putting all the practicalities and impracticalities, as well as the political considerations, to one side, I formed my own vision of a Maine where Maine people could get around, where travel would be enjoyable, convenient and comparatively inexpensive, where the environmental damage from roads, vehicle noise and pollution, and the satellite commercialism spawned by car would be kept to an absolute minimum.

First, the state Highway Commission would be reduced to becoming an office with a state Department of Transportation that included desks for rail transit, air transport, water-borne commerce, public bus travel and interurban services. Money from the Federal Highway Trust fund, from state gas and automotive taxes, would not be restricted to roadwork but instead would be siphoned into alternative forms of transportation (including roads) as determined by the state DOT under a master plan for balanced transportation.

Having access to state transportation funds and given favorable borrowing terms, a quasi-public corporation would be empowered to create and administer a multiform transportation system *within* Maine. There is ample precedent for this, inasmuch as regional transit systems throughout the nation are financed by public bond issues and run with a public say. It is obvious that private railways and bus companies have neglected the people, so let the people be given the advantages in their own corporation — a ComSat with an earth focus.

The Maine Authority for Transport (MAT, we'll call it), in negotiation with the private companies or on its own, immediately would launch different pilot projects: a coastal ferry, intertown/city bus or rail service, and a scheme for moving tourists and vacationers without disrupting regular travel patterns. Call this last creation Maine Tours. It would encompass rail, bus, ferry and small plane services tailored to suit fishermen, canoeists, campers, boating enthusiasts, hunters and skiers. Thus it would have to be geared to seasonal loads. Maine Tours would be an invaluable tool for land use planners of all state agencies, particularly for parks and recreation people because it could emphasize travel to areas that are presently less congested, like inland Maine. Maine Tours would also negotiate with the pulp and paper industry in order to provide select and limited service over private wilderness roads to scenic areas where recreation is environmentally acceptable.

The quasi-public (or quasi-private) corporation (MAT) would also test out an automobile leasing service with the objective of reducing the need for the "second" car, even the one and only car, when in so many instances the use can never really justify the investment. Most important, such a system would encourage visitors from out of state to come by public transportation, renting a car for use within the state when MAT facilities would not do. (How pleasant it would be to have the boat service to Portland, from Boston and New York, revived, with coastal ferries continuing the trip.) The leasing service would maintain cars at all public terminals, setting rates deliberately to encourage public transport except when additional mobility was desired within a locality. I have felt for a long time that on the whole it would be more of a benefit than an inconvenience if all interstate motor travel was subjected to competition from such a leasing operation so that auto ownership would create far less havoc than at the present. One way to encourage this would be to boost highway and bridge tolls for cars with out-of-state plates. Another way would be to grant family discounts for out-of-state visiting parties who travel exclusively by MAT.

These ideas may seem farfetched. Yet I can't help but think, when I read about public travel a century ago, when I hear my father tell about the night boat down the coast, and when I recall my own trips on the Boston & Maine, that there are glorious possibilities.

There are a lot of places, too, that should stay off limits to travel. Off-road vehicles, notably the snowmobile and the tote-goat type scooter, are a menace to the beauty and the solitude of Maine's open spaces. I don't care if they are responsible for getting many more people out of doors. Already there are well over 50,000 snowmobiles in Maine, more per capita than in any other state, and there have been few restrictions enacted against their assault on the countryside. Wilderness thoroughfares like the Allagash teem with machines in midwinter when the waters are frozen solid. A Maine DOT would establish regulations for the off-road vehicles, allowing them *some* open space but leaving plenty of room for the cross-country hikers and skiers. These noiseless travelers go into the woods and fields for the diversified effects of nature, to spot wildlife, or to be in peace. The snowmobilists I've talked to are mostly enthralled by the narcotic effect of their machines, their noise and their power. Give them a circular track or a course near town.

One of the best "Burt and I" stories concerns the man who is asked the way to Millinocket. First he tries to direct the traveler to the toll road. But on thinking it through, he suggests instead that the motorist keep on the country road, until it turns to dirt, and then . . . That won't do, either. Try the scenic, coastal route. The countryman ponders, then finally says, "Come to think of it, you can't get there from here."

It may be a case of rural pride. It may be a bit of pointed advice. It might just be true. And if it is, I happen to think that, often as not, it is a good thing.

252

SEVEN

Vacationland

TOURISTS, VACATIONERS,
AND RUSTICATORS

LONG BEFORE its 1936 license plate proclaimed that the state was "Vacationland," Maine's woods, lakes, rivers and coastal haunts were sought out for peace and quiet, hunting, fishing and outdoor exercise. The people of Maine have had ample time and reason to cultivate a love-hate sort of relationship with vacationers. The natives have taken their rural backyard and wilderness pretty much for granted, enjoying it any old time without necessarily looking at it as something special. They have been quite content to make a killing on coastal property sold to "rusticators," and to run wilderness camps, serve as guides and work in resorts.* That is, up to a point.

Inevitably there was that moment when it dawned on many a Mainesman that he had been dispossessed of his finest land and that he was in a pretty demeaning position waiting on a horde of visitors who put on superior airs, had money to spend, and took the worldly pleasures in stride. As proud as they are durable, the Maine people for many years have drawn a line between themselves and the "outsiders." It's as much of a defense mechanism as a matter of pride. And they too have superior attributes. On top of this has come the invasion — it can be termed nothing less — by car-borne tourists during the postwar years. They don't leave as much cash behind in Maine as it was hoped they would. They are a nuisance besides, causing monumental traffic jams that get worse as the myopic highway planners add and "improve" roads crowding the Mainers right out of their old home ground. It is thus to be believed that a newly formed

*Webster: *rustic*: an unsophisticated rural person. *rusticate*: to go into or reside in the country.

group, known as KPOOM (Keep People out of Maine), reportedly went underground because it could not handle the volume of requests for membership and bumper stickers. But I'm getting ahead of myself, vacationer that I am. First some history, some terms.

Tourists are transients, travelers. They want to see as much as they can, hit the high spots, swim at the beaches, picnic in the parks, take the easiest trail to the mountaintop, catch a fish, get the one deer. Primarily, they are not interested in developing a relationship with a place or its people. *Vacationers* are a degree different. They spend a week or more in one place and often come back to it season after season. The *rusticators* are nonresident householders, vacationers who like Maine so much that they buy a piece of it. Many of them spend enough of the year (six months or more) in Maine to become legal residents.

Saco's exquisite four miles of beach, Old Orchard, was ceremoniously dedicated to tourists in 1840. Undoubtedly the first Maine vacationer of note was Henry David Thoreau. He came straight from Walden Pond on August 31, 1846, to climb Mount Ktaadn (his spelling). He wanted mostly to see how Concord (certainly not a suburb at that time) had looked before it was cleared and settled by white men. He struck the forest at Mattawamkeag and it was pure rhapsody. "The evergreen woods had a decidedly sweet and bracing fragrance, the air was a sort of diet drink, and we walked on buoyantly in Indian file, stretching our legs," wrote the man of Concord.

Seven years later, James Russell Lowell, poet, essayist and diplomat, watched the moon rise and the sun set simultaneously over the West Branch of the Penobscot. He too was euphoric, as he wrote, "Adam had no more in Eden — except the head of Eve upon his shoulder."

Both Thoreau and Lowell published journals about their trips. For detail and enthusiasm, they are better than any brochures put out since by the state boosters. These and verbal accounts drew increasing numbers of outdoor lovers, hunters, fishermen and artists. Winslow Homer moved to Prout's Neck in 1884 and liked it so much he seldom left thereafter, except to go south in the bitter winter months. Robert Henri, founder of the "Ashcan School," Rockwell Kent and George Bellows led the parade to Monhegan, John Singer Sargent to Mount Desert, and there were others with famous names, such as John

Marin, Childe Hassam and Edward Hopper, whose *Lighthouse Hill* became the statehood commemorative stamp in 1970. Georgia O'Keeffe departed at least once from her stark New Mexico desert to study the waves striking a Maine beach. The artists' ranks hold firm today. Undoubtedly the most famous is Andrew Wyeth, who summers in Cushing. These visitors were and remain the recorders, certainly not the mainstream of vacationers. But they are vital in capturing the mood that ought to be — but alas, seldom is — the essence of Vacationland.

The Maine coastal resort began to bloom in the wake of the Civil War. "Roughing it" was no longer an escape from the greens of Concord. It was flight from the increasing madness of the Industrial Revolution. Thomas Bailey Aldrich, editor of the *Atlantic Monthly*, built a house in Tenants Harbor. "I am as happy and dirty as a clam," he wrote. But the best-known summer spot became Bar Harbor. Artists, scientists and hunters discovered it first. They were free spirits who liked to canoe, hunt rock specimens, and find scenic outlooks where they would sit down and sketch. During the 1890s, families from Boston, New York and Philadelphia built enormous mansions called "cottages," which of course they were not. But the characterization helped to define the attitude taken toward the rugged and beautiful place. As Richard W. Hale, Jr., wrote in *The Story of Bar Harbor* (1949): "The old free-and-easy spirit of the first summer visitors still hung over its life — and for that matter, it still does." Hale also described one celebrated incident that holds meaning for Vacationland in the 1970s.

A few years before the century turned, he recalled, Bar Harbor's summer residents rose up in wrath against the automobile. The first one, in 1896, was a homemade machine. Naturally it inspired more similar contraptions that made such a racket in town and were such a nuisance on the peaceful horse tracks and carriage paths that a law was passed banning cars from the entire island, except on the road coming from the mainland. This didn't last long because some summer people found cars a convenient luxury; year-round residents decided they would like more of the predicted auto-tourist trade, and doctors complained they would be hindered in getting to patients.

George Dorr, who later was one of the benefactors of Acadia National Park, proposed a compromise. Previously he had obtained a route for an electric train to the town. Why not use it instead as the sole access road for cars, he proposed. Agreed. Through excellent contacts in Augusta, the new bill was passed. But it only stayed on the books one year before the car finally was allowed open competition with the horse and buggy.

Consider how much better off all the people on Mount Desert, at all times of year, would be today if George Dorr had developed a train system. Let's say it had expanded to embrace the entire island, a network of tracks connecting the other towns. Instead of roads, rail lines would now snake through the gorges and along the mountainsides, set back from the sea far enough to give the beach to artists, strollers and nature lovers, but not so far that the passengers wouldn't have spectacular views now and then. The resident fishermen, boatbuilders and others living off the sea would not be hurt. On the contrary, roads and parking cars would not blight the waterfront and the boat business perhaps would have boomed.

Visitors would leave their cars on the mainland, in Trenton. So would residents, if they bothered to own a car, at special year-round rates. They would all board trains that ran out to the island. The people of Trenton would benefit greatly by providing food and rooms at the junction and marine services for those who went back and forth to the island by boat. The tourists would have the thrill, the sense of history, of riding the train. Maybe the train would take them to where they could walk to their lodging. More interesting still, they might be met by the horse and buggy and sped over the many miles of carriage paths that exist yet throughout Mount Desert.

I just know that if such an arrangement were ever tried, if the cars could be put down for just a moment or two, it would be a smashing success. But instead, the politicians and government planners keep conspiring to widen the roads and build new bridges, overwhelming the vacationlands of America. Every new highway project is counterproductive because it only generates or invites new motorists to try it out for size. Or it deludes the vacationer into thinking his vacation will be much more enjoyable if he can increase his speed and expand his driving range. Damn the car! I have to use one because they won't let it be otherwise. It is a plague on vacationland.

An all-consuming locust.

MYTHS AND REALITIES

I WENT TO SEE Lawrence Stuart, Maine's commissioner of Parks and Recreation, and planner Thomas Cieslinski, who I had been told was hard at work on a Recreation Master Plan. Surely these would be the men to tell me about Vacationland.

We sat around a table in Stuart's overheated office. He was a pleasant man in his fifties who'd been around the state government a while. In fact, I realized soon that he was one of those men I'd met before in the hierarchy of a federal government agency. He had the right instincts, the best of intentions and a backlog of experience. But he was compelled by power blocs and political impasses to make compromises in order to obtain any results. Along the way the original fires of hope had waned, while resignation and skepticism had become pronounced. Short, dark-haired and much younger, Cieslinski was a recent arrival from New Jersey where he had earned a degree in forest recreation and had worked on the state outdoors plan.

"How can we help you?" Stuart asked.

I went into my prepared preamble. In general, I explained, I wanted to know what priority the state gave to recreation, since in dollar volume I understood it was second only to pulp and paper. I wanted to hear about the tourists that come every year: what do they expect, where do they go, what do they contribute? That sort of thing. What did the master plan encompass? I said I hoped that it would consider ways of protecting open space aside from buying parkland and that it would contain an expression on transportation systems insofar as the various means and routes of travel are the key factors shaping outdoor recreation trends.

259

"I guess I'm obsessed with the destructive influence of the car," I said.

Cieslinski looked forlornly across the table to Stuart, who shifted in his chair and began to speak. "I'm afraid we're going to waste your time. I wish we had the answers to these questions of yours. But there is no data available, no data anywhere in the state."

"That's right," Cieslinski broke in. "There has never been a study of the recreation industry; nobody knows the impact of tourism in Maine."

What now? I should have known better. Stuart's department had a narrow assignment. To acquire land for parks, then develop and maintain it to make sure the campsites were well manicured, the picnic tables ample, the toilets cleaned out regularly, the litter barrels emptied and the roads and parking lots in smooth shape. Moreover, Parks and Recreation had nothing to do with the biggest state park, the 200,000-acre Baxter Wilderness deeded in trust to the state by the former governor.

Baxter had been a wise old man. Right up until his death his occasional pronouncements revealed a true understanding of what was happening to the Maine environment. He also knew that people were too often misguided when it came to enjoying wilderness, and he understood just as well the nature of a parks bureaucracy. The Baxter gifts were to be administrated by three trustees who would hold right to the letter and spirit of the deed. The American version of a responsible aristocrat, Percival Baxter was not unmindful of the needs of the public and the less privileged. On the contrary, he wanted them to have a park that was the real thing. He did not want an overdeveloped playground.

The other big park in Maine is Acadia, the 30,000-acre federal sanctuary. All told, throughout Maine, Stuart and Cieslinski have some 80,000 acres to to worry about, not counting land set aside for parks but not yet opened. The Allagash Wilderness Waterway is the most famous. In 1970, some 37,000 visitor days were logged along the 85-mile waterway. Assume it takes five days to canoe it, that the season lasts about a hundred days, and this means that 74 people each night are putting up at 50 campsites.

"On a windy day, when the going gets tough, there are enough places along the Allagash to absorb all the people and retain the wilderness experience," Stuart said. At the 1970 visitor rate, he was probably right. Only he and I both knew that the Allagash crowd was growing fast and getting out of hand.

The master plan, Stuart explained, would spell out how much parkland the state would need to cope with future pressures, what parcels it would like to acquire, how much it would cost, and how it would be managed. If approved by the legislature, the plan would next be submitted to the Federal Bureau of Outdoor Recreation in hopes of obtaining 50 percent matching grants from the Land and Water Acquisition fund. Already in 1968, Maine voters had approved a $4 million bond issue for parks. But that referendum contained one hitch. It specified that the state could not employ the power of eminent domain, even after it was determined through public hearings or the master plan that a particular piece of wilderness was desirable for a park. This provision was the achievement of the pulp and paper lobby. The industries were bitter about the threat of eminent domain that had been applied in the Allagash corridor, even though they were more than adequately compensated to the tune of $3 million.

"Is there no overall authority for recreation policy in Maine?" I asked.

"No," Stuart answered. "You can ask the people at the Department of Economic Development about tourism. They're doing all those studies. I don't know what I'd be able to do with more data now or how I would use the answers to your questions anyway," he added. "There's so much study talk going on around here that I can't bother with it when I have to make a decision. I use my own judgment based on twenty-three years of experience and the advice of my men in the field when I buy land for the state. An attorney comes in here with a deed and if the price is right and the land is suitably located or of wilderness value, I buy it. What *does* bother me is to read in the papers that there are going to be ten commercial centers in this state and that the Department of Economic Development already knows where three of them are going to be. Here I am spending $8 million on land and I want the parks to be near the people so they can enjoy them, and yet I'm not told where they plan to put these centers."

I went over to the Department of Economic Development and left more confused than ever. Commissioner James Keefe had recently returned from the new Disney World in Florida. It was the model of a concentrated, homogenized and mass vacation complex, as Keefe saw it. He thought it would go well in Maine.

"Whereabouts?" I asked.

"At Sebago, at Evergreen Valley. Around Moosehead Lake there are three hundred miles of shoreline," Keefe replied. "If it were well operated it would be a lot better than hit-or-miss development, tar-paper shacks and hot dog stands."

I agreed with that observation, but I also felt that these were not the only alternatives. To me, Moosehead was still the obvious base camp for wilderness trips.

But Keefe didn't think that many people were really anxious to savor the unspoiled outdoors.

"I've talked to a lot of recreational consultants," he said. "When you get right down to it people only want to *imagine* they're 'roughing it,' then come in at four o'clock, take a shower, have a martini and a good dinner."

If Maine's outdoor recreation planners emphasized that viewpoint, then Vacationland was in trouble, I thought to myself. I was not edified any further when I went through the written material that Keefe gave me, reports prepared by his staff assistants.

First, I looked at Chapter 12 of the 1971 *Maine Pocket Data Book*. "There is, as yet, no accurate data concerning visitors and the dollar value of Maine's recreation industry," the chapter opens, "though a great deal of research is currently underway to gather this information." The chapter then lists five "indicators" that at least recreation counts for a lot.

— A high concentration of boats — one for every 22.46 people compared to the national average of 1/34.97.
— A staggering number of snowmobiles; 42,933 registered in 1971, a 48 percent jump in one year (and one for every 23 men, women or children in Maine).
— Over two million fish stocked by the Inland Fish and Game Department in 1970.
— In the past five years, 170,000 deer killed.
— Public recreation areas logged 5,040,000 visitor days in 1970.

So much for figures that in fact prove little. What do they mean in the context of Maine? What do they portend? What's to be done?

One DED report placed the value of the vacation business at $540 million. The figure was based largely on sales taxes paid by motels, restaurants, camps and outfitters, etc., even though many of those customers could not possibly have been spending vacation money. Another study was proposed, an in-depth look at vacation travel, to find out where the tourist goes, what he wants in Maine, where and how long he stays, what he spends and what new jobs he creates.

The term "vacation travel" is unfortunate. It clearly expresses the concept of mobility, and this implies that the tourist is most concerned with superficial attractions rather than with the universal qualities of the Maine environment. This in turn leads to policies that are geared to comfort and convenience rather than to creating ways for vacationers to develop a communion with the land. And yet, all the state officials I talked with, including Keefe, said unequivocally that the reasons so many people came to Maine were already well known. These visitors were attracted by scenic beauty and the sense of peace and solitude gained from being in the midst of it.

Without a doubt, mobile tourists and vacationers must be dealt with in a positive manner. It will take imagination and a stunning plan to redirect the flow of summer visitors who mostly crowd the coast, to somehow mute the effect of cars, to inspire these people to abandon their mechanized trappings and conveniences and get out into the open air, and then regulate their numbers once they are willing to take that step.

It can be done. But not when the DED is thinking only mobility and Disney World. Not when the parks and recreation staff is in a fit of despair because it needs $5.5 million to develop over three thousand acres in eleven new parks that cannot be opened until this money is spent on roads, parking lots, picnic tables, fireplaces, toilets, athletic facilities, nature centers and trash cans. Nature centers are worthwhile when they are manned by rangers who truly take pleasure in interpreting the unimproved natural phenomena of a place. However, other developmental outlays should be put off and the money used instead to acquire more parkland and to purchase scenic easements that will protect open spaces from ever being developed, even if they don't become parks. Open space needs open space as much as the public does. I have said this, explicitly and implicitly, more than once in the preceding chapters.

If Maine opened the eleven parks with minimal development (e.g., access roads), and if they were patrolled by no more than a few rangers who also manned a check-in point and stressed certain rules of wilderness etiquette, I am certain the state would be pleasantly surprised. Having, for a change, not been led to expect conveniences better suited to New York City's Central Park, the visitors would probably enjoy the trust as well as the chance to test themselves.

What are the realities in Vacationland? There is one big one. Over 60 percent of the revenues coming from vacationers is accounted for by seasonal households — summer cottages, wilderness cabins and ski chalets. These are the nonresident propertyowners who create jobs and pay for public services and education without being around enough of the year to put a heavy burden on tax-supported facilities.

The best data I saw was contained in a report for the Allagash Group by Tufts University professor Hossein Askari. (At the time the state hadn't paid any attention to it.) Askari gleaned information from a host of sources and from many previous assessments of single aspects of Vacationland. Here are some figures that tell a story.

— In 1970, personal property values in Maine totaled $761,412,938, of which a whopping $333,389,380 worth belonged to nonresidents, presumably vacationers of one sort or another.
— In the decade of the sixties, the number of seasonal houses rose from 74,413 to 84,232. And in 1968, taxes paid by these householders amounted to $79,022,646 — 43.8 percent of the entire collection.
— Vacation colonists spend an average of $2,046 a year. Multiply this by the number of seasonal houses occupied in 1970 and you get expenditures of $123,091,452.
— Add to this the costs of 1,745 new vacation houses valued at $30,230,380, and you see that $153 million was generated by seasonal householders in 1970.
— Through direct employment and what the economists call "linkages," over 150 new jobs are generated for every $2,500,000 in new construction. As part of this formula, one new job results from every $25,000 spent in construction.

Askari noted that it would take one camper 511½ days to equal the economic impact of one seasonal resident family. Based on a University of Maine study of the state's Lily Bay campground, which showed that the average family spent only $3.10 a day on site and $1.46 a day outside, the professor computed that campers using public sites spent only $5,193,538 in 1969. Those that used private campgrounds spent three times as much because private owners charge rental or user fees. But even private campground users are outspent six times by the vacation colonists with "second homes."

These facts would not be particularly helpful to Lawrence Stuart. For he is cast in the special role of dealing with people who flock to public places. But they should tell James Keefe something very important. Without a policy, without a plan for the mobile tourists, it is utter madness to keep putting out all that literature about the many places in Maine that can accommodate campers.

What are my own conclusions? I agree with Askari that the state can do much more to support vacation colonies. To be sure, seasonal jobs that result from these developments are always uncertain and are often menial. And yet the ultimate impact is obviously huge when compared with other forms of recreation. In my travels, I found that many more people with summer houses were spending more time in Maine. Many hired carpenters to winterize these places. In many resorts, there was year-round activity in the construction trades. There were also countless unexploited opportunities to be given a boost by the state, by town governments and by the colonists themselves. On the coast, for example, it seemed to me that most people with yachts were unable to find a local boatyard for winter storage, overhaul, or the modifications that every yachtsman indulges in. Inland, it struck me that there were untapped possibilities to attract the exploding number of semipsychotics, daily additions to the ranks of those who are frustrated and gone batty from the stresses and strains of our ruinous civilization. In my reveries, I was certain that a lot of people would come to Maine any old time of year if they could settle for a week on a farm where crops were harvested or maple sugar was made, at an inn in undeveloped countryside or forest with terrain suitable for cross-country skiing, or at a lodge deep in the woods where the ice was about to break up on the rivers and streams and the coming of spring could be tasted.

Reveries? Not really. Hopes? Yes. Based soundly on what could be seen happening around the country. An explosion of backpackers; not just young people or hippies, but older folk like the couple in their seventies who end-to-ended the entire 2,025-mile Appalachian Trail. I sensed on the part of many people a desire, hidden and expressed, to catch a glimpse of "the way it used to be."

Mainesmen must face the facts. Maine is indeed Vacationland. There should be nothing commercial or servile about it. It is a state of mind as well as a state of business. Both aspects — psychological and economic — must be assessed and weighed ever so carefully by state planners and the public at large. Only then will Vacationland begin to be managed on Maine's terms. Only then will the motto reflect real pride and not, instead, provoke cynicism.

ONE WAY TO ENJOY A PARK

A SOLITARY PATCH OF CLOUDS was all that remained of the storm that had dumped three inches of snow on Mount Desert the night before. These remnants broke up above the plunging cliffs of Norumbega Mountain off to my left, dissipating like wisps of smoke over artillery. The early morning sun already was brilliant. Accompanied by warmer weather, it brought on a sudden melt that in turn was responsible for the dominant sound in the woods — the sound of water. It roared down two big brooks, a quarter of a mile apart, that came off Parkman and Sargent mountains and fed Upper Hadlock Pond, the snow-covered opening four hundred feet below me. It trickled out of crevices and seeped down the moss and lichen coatings of the dark rocks that dropped to the inside of the trail. And it dripped from branches and boughs. As shafts of sunlight finally hurdled the granite ridges that blocked the view southeast, dazzling, blinding crystals danced out of the snow in front of me. A soft whoosh followed by an abrupt thump signaled that the snow had lost its grip on a spruce tree and, for the moment, on winter.

I thought about the advice John Good had given me the day before, when he spotted the cross-country skis in my car. "The best way to get the feel of this park," he said, "would be to put those on and walk into it alone."

Good was the superintendent of Acadia National Park. Bright, intense and extremely likable, he had made himself a reputation for going to extra lengths to understand the confusion and hostility existing in the minds of so many people, particularly those who crowded into Acadia in the summer months. Not much over forty, he had made a dramatic switch in careers. After studying geology at Washington University in St. Louis, he was an exploration geologist for Standard Oil of Texas. But when he had to move nine times in one year, he and his wife Mary got fed up with the oil business and they came back to St. Louis where he worked briefly with his father as a coffee broker. Then they went on a trip through some of the western parks — Grand Canyon, Zion, Bryce and the Petrified Forest — and Good knew right then that he wanted most to be a park ranger. First he went to Carlsbad Caverns as a guide and began to educate himself about animals and plants. Then, before coming to Acadia in 1968, he was naturalist and ranger at Lake Mead and chief naturalist at Yellowstone. Over this stretch, his views about industry had changed radically and now he was at the forefront of well-organized opposition to the oil refineries proposed along the Maine coast.

"What sort of a person is the average visitor?" I asked Good as we sat in his office. "Why does he come to the park?"

"People don't really know why they come," he answered. "They're looking for something, but it's hard to tell what it is. We have people coming a long way, from cities like New York and Newark, and we suggest things to them that they would never buy on their own turf. If they take the nature cruise, the naturalist will point out the eagle on the Porcupine Island, and there's a chance to talk about DDT and how it affects birds high on the food chains. We can tell them about the oxygen cycle in the sea and how it affects our life support. By showing them how life functions in a tidepool, maybe we can get across the idea that the world is a closed system. But the best thing we can give them is a rock or the soft ground underneath a tree by the shore where they can sit down and think, about themselves, about their life in Newark. It doesn't matter. People don't have much of a chance to do that anymore."

On an impulse, one Sunday night during the previous summer Good showed an experimental film to nearly a hundred people who were gathered in the Acadia Visitors' Center. Titled *Man, Buddhism and Nature*, the film was acquired to train new rangers. But with its strong emphasis on Buddhist philosophy it bothered the general public. They remained silent and perplexed when it was over and Good tried to get a discussion going. So he stood up before the group and in his words repeated what he felt was the main message of the film. Man has a covenant with nature, not a mission to master it, nor even to understand it. Nature is like music, he said, it does not have a destination. It just unfolds, replete with mystery, and we should let it act upon our senses without necessarily trying to analyze it or without trying to visualize a perfect symmetry in its ways and works. So many people, Good told the visitors, came to the park with their *Golden Guides*, frantic to identify every sprig of vegetation, every bird, and every rock, without finding real pleasure in the spell of wild and unspoiled things that are just as complex and unexplainable as we are.

"It is certainly better to try and understand the park than to stay in your car," Good said, "but there is nothing wrong either with just coming here and being passive, sitting down somewhere in peace."

A woman raised her hand. "You've made me feel wonderful," she said. "When my family played on the beach today, I went off and sat on a rock for two and a half hours. I've forgotten what I thought about but I've felt guilty ever since. Now I don't feel guilty any more."

Neither did I, as I continued cross-country on skis. The carriage road, deep in snow as it climbed the mountainside, opened to a new vista at each bend. It rose gently so that I made good progress by just sliding one narrow ski ahead of the other. I could not help but wonder, though, how there was going to be room in Maine for people to continue to find a spot to take pleasure in the way that both Good and myself felt meant so much.

At 30,000 acres, Acadia is not a very big park. Yellowstone, the sanctuary that most Americans equate with the wilderness, is seventy times as big. Yet in the summer of 1970, Yellowstone was many times less crowded than Acadia. The Maine coast refuge logged some 2.8 million visitor days (i.e., one visitor for one day). Since over 57 million people lived within a twelve-hour drive of Mount Desert, park reservations would soon become necessary. Some sort of an early warning system, maybe radio and newspaper messages and bulletins posted at turnpike plazas, could alert families driving east from New Jersey or New York that Acadia had reached the bursting point. If they did not have reservations they would have to head somewhere else.

All this was hard to envision when earlier Good and I had walked over sections of the park. Most of the roads were not plowed in winter; many were carriage trails like the one I skied on. There were more than 125 miles of these carriage paths, many of them built by land donor John D. Rockefeller, Jr. They were beautifully engineered, done with picturesqueness in mind. The Hadlock Trail, which I followed, was chopped right out of the rock cliffs in many places. The outside edge was guarded by blocks of granite three feet high and spaced apart like the teeth on a Halloween pumpkin.

Most of the carriage roads were restricted to hikers and horse-drawn conveyances, except that in winter some were marked with orange disks set on poles to signify that these were also snowmobile routes. I was disturbed by this concession but Good, with his refreshingly open mind, tried to put me at ease.

"People are hung up on stereotypes," he said. In summer they had visions of the park being invaded by hippies playing rock music and smoking pot. In winter they saw the park being terrorized by snowmobilers whose narcotic, then, was the noise and power of their machines.

"The kids really appreciate this place," Good said. "They litter a lot less than their elders, and if they smoke pot, at least it doesn't make a mess. They seem to be able to control themselves. It's the kids on the beach with beer who get belligerent with the rangers, and in the condition they are in, you hate to tell them to leave in their cars. The snowmobilers don't use as many roads as the cars do in summer, although they have 85 miles of their own trails over some of the carriage routes and unplowed roads. It might surprise you, but most of these guys understand the woods better than the summer hiker."

When Good arrived at Acadia, already hordes of people were ruining the most secluded and unusual spots. For example, off the Ocean Drive winding southwest from Bar Harbor was a sign directing tourists to the Anemone Cave. It was an enormous rock cavern that was exposed at low tide. The anemones clung to the walls of a shallow basin, just under the water's surface. When Good and I climbed down icy rocks to inspect the cave, the low winter sun brightened the clear, shallow water to reveal a vivid abstraction of reds, greens and yellows, the colors of the seaweeds and other growth, and of the small pebbles, shells and tiny organisms on the shore bottom.

"People were fighting to get in," Good said. "They drove away the swallow that nested here."

One of his first acts was to remove the many signs leading tourists to natural landmarks, like the Anemone Cave — signs that used to be placed along the roads in the park like advertising reminders strung out beside a highway. Good had the cave marked only on a map of the park. "It makes the impact so much greater," Good said. "One day I watched a little boy just stumble onto the cave. When he scrambled back up the rocks to tell his mother and father what he'd found, he was gobbling like a turkey. I'm sure that moment will stay with him."

On the Hadlock Trail, alone on the skis, I envied Good's simple and unaffected outlook. There were many ways and many levels of appreciation in these woods. You could just go your own way and let the pleasant surroundings work unconsciously on your soul, or you could deliberately play the naturalist, scanning the woods for revealing signs — the passage of a fox, rabbit, porcupine or deer. These were ample and always afforded an opportunity to ponder about the course and mission of the animal in question. Did the tight, frantic circles at the end of a rabbit's trail mean he had been attacked by a fox? No, because there were no other tracks approaching. But then maybe a hawk or an owl struck from the air. Okay, but if so, the rabbit got away unscathed because there were no signs of blood or fur and his tracks emerged from the mad circles, going off in a new direction. Twice the aroma of skunk hung over the trail. Another signal of a recent confrontation?

Getting bogged down in speculations like this is a tendency that Edward Abbey criticized in himself when he did seasonal stints as a ranger at the Arches National Monument in Utah, and he wrote a superb book about his experience, *Desert Solitaire.* Our characteristic trait as nature lovers, Abbey wrote, is to become anthropomorphic, always looking in the behavior of wildlife for actions and interactions that can be translated in human terms. Making love, making war, looking for food, digging a shelter — these are all tendencies we can relate to ourselves. But maybe the animals have a different code, their own rites, that cannot be compared to anything we do, notwithstanding the delightful fantasies and child's stories written by authors like Thornton Burgess and Beatrix Potter.

Perhaps my own feelings of exultation came from the realization that I was just another element in a piece of natural country of extraordinary and diverse beauty, of myriad and fascinating goings-on. But it seemed much more likely, still sensing John Good's words, that the good feeling and the sense of excitement came mostly from being out alone, cutting tracks in virgin snow, being challenged by the exercise, sweating and turning red-cheeked — all in a setting that provided, for that moment, absolute and total privacy.

As the carriage road veered left and west, I crossed the first of two handsome stone bridges several hundred yards apart. These were skillfully joined together, the stones carefully selected for texture and uniformity, simple arches on stone piers fording wooded gullies twenty feet or so deep. The first bridge crossed the Hadlock Brook, the second an unnamed stream that converged with the brook about a quarter of a mile below me, half the distance to the pond. On the slopes above and below, marching right down to the stream banks, were hemlock and balsam fir. The great fire of 1947 never reached this corner of Acadia. The trees grew thick and tall so that the undergrowth had given way to primary forest and there was plenty of maneuvering room underneath and among the evergreens.

A modest sign pointed the way left, down through those trees to the Hadlock Brook Trail. I imagined that in the spring this would be a good walk. All the small water courses that I had seen frozen over or reduced to a thin trickle would be active freshets then, joining these larger brooks so that the slopes would come alive to the orchestration of many streams of different size, speed and volume, all racing for Hadlock Pond and thence emptying into Somes Sound.

The path ran west for three quarters of a mile after the second bridge. At last I could look out to the ocean, which was barely ruffled by a light westerly. It was clear enough to see Swan's Island, the last thin green strip on the horizon. There was a commotion ahead. I had startled two deer. They took the hard escape route, plunging upward toward Parkman Mountain, their white rumps flashing conspicuously through the evergreen cover. No wonder the hunters call them flags.

On the ascending two miles, in the sun, the snow had become sticky and my wax failed. In order to avoid dragging heavy clumps along the bottoms of my skis, I simply traveled in the shadows. But the moment the path ran downhill again, on the back stretch of the loop

John Good had marked for me, out in the open the skis tracked cleanly. I simply moved one foot and then the other, going faster and faster without any effort, like a toy wood penguin that falls into a metronomic step when placed on a tilted surface. Exhilaration came entirely from the feeling of speed. I could barely see where I was going because the light changed so — from dark shadows cast by trees to blinding patches of sunlight.

I slowed down along the edge of Hadlock Pond, a final half mile on the level, and the Victorian stone gatehouse appeared at the end. A park ranger had the enviable assignment of living here. His children's toys stuck up through the snow in the garden behind the house. Long ago, this sturdy stone structure must have been just an outbuilding for one of the houses of the several hundred people who had such strong feelings for this land that eventually they gave it to the park to be preserved.

The snow on the roof of my car had begun to slide over the rear window. I pulled out the hand choke and started her up, changing my boots inside and consuming a box of raisins as the sweat on my back turned cold. It had taken three hours to complete the trip, including a whole hour in the beginning when I didn't follow Good's directions, and had gone off a different trail and then had to cut back through the woods.

I drove three miles to Northeast Harbor to make a phone call and did not notice until I was out of the car that without warning the sky had turned to a cloudless slate gray. The sun was gone, the air was turning chill again. All the signs of another snowfall coming. The day had brightened only briefly and I had been lucky to savor the interval, the breakup of one storm before the onslaught of another. "There is no serenity so fair as that which is established in a tearful eye," Henry Thoreau wrote, when the sun followed a squall in the Maine woods. A fine observation where Maine weather is concerned.

Such moments come rarely enough so that they are a treat, but they also come often enough during the Maine winter so that you are forever in a state of expectation for the blessed event. I drove off the island, intending to be back at my temporary retreat in Friendship before the snow, which indeed had begun to fall, became heavy. I thought about the interviews I had missed and when I would come back. But I didn't feel guilty. Not one bit.

BOBCATS, DEER, AND MOOSE

YOU TURN OVER the tail of a bobcat to a Maine game warden and the state pays you $15. On the fur market you can get an equal sum, maybe more, for the pelt. It is of course assumed that if you have the tail, the animal is dead. Each year, the state pays out around $10,000 in bobcat bounties. Since the reward has been offered, persecution of the bobcat has cost Maine taxpayers nearly half a million dollars.

This information was provided by Marshall Burk, executive director of the Maine Natural Resources Council, just after he'd asked me if I'd like to accompany him to hearings on a proposal to end the bounty. In recent years, repeal had become an annual consideration, yet the Legislative Committee on Inland Fisheries and Game had never come close to recommending any of the proposals in spite of mounting evidence that the taxpayers were not being well served.

Burk himself felt that the bounty was wrong from both the moral and the biological standpoint. "It represents a mercenary attitude toward fish and game management," he later testified. But he explained to me that it was also a matter of basic misunderstanding, that he had good friends on both sides, and that I really should come along because the hearings would offer some new insights into Maine. He was right.

One of the first to testify at the meeting was a fine-looking, white-haired, straight-backed man who told the legislators he'd spent much of his seventy-two years as a hunter and guide. "This bobcat bounty," he said, "continues to be a ridiculous issue because no one has come up with scientific facts as to what damage the bobcat does in the woods." Since the bounties came out of hunting license revenues, he said, it hardly made sense to "pay one man to hunt at another's expense."

Another man stood up and said that if the bobcat's depredations of deer were the reason for the bounty, then the state should also offer rewards for dogs, because they annually attacked many, many times as many deer as the bobcat. Moreover, explained this witness, packs of dogs were merciless, as reports from all over the state had indicated. The dogs would snap and tear at a deer, exposing the animal's entrails before killing it, whereas a bobcat, with his own life needs in mind, was well known to kill with surgical precision and speed, always going for the victim's jugular vein.

This was an appropriate commentary, it seemed to me, on the evolution of human behavior in America. Maybe once, when there was still a wilderness to reckon with, a man could not afford the luxury of a dog, unless the animal was a trained hound who would earn his keep by helping to track down food. Then, as the survival crisis of frontier experience became a dim memory, dogs became household pets whose instincts in the natural environment were just as dulled as their master's. Deep down, they still lusted to kill, and that's why they attacked deer and even the neighbor's sheep. But they no longer knew how to do it.

The men of Maine, it appeared, were both emotional and unreasonable when the subject was deer. The reason must be that deer hunting is said to account each fall for about $25 million in license fees, ammunition, clothing, gas, lodging, food and other expenses that are incurred mostly by out-of-state hunters. Each year, about 30,000 deer and about ten hunters are killed. The notion that the bobcat is a significant enemy of those cash-generating deer incites the hunters to shoot the cat too. Besides, it means even more hunting parties and, instead of paying a license fee, you get a reward.

What is more, those who favored the bounty on bobcat were the local people, the men of the back country and the lumber and the farm towns, who lived on the deer's trail. One of them was a genial brute of a man with an enormous stomach who represented the Rangeley guides, three hundred strong. When he said in an impassioned voice, "It doesn't make economic sense to let cats kill deer; the only thing we need a bounty on is people," the committee room resounded with applause and the legislators all smiled approval.

Then another guide spoke in urgent, high-pitched tones. He had a kind of boyish sincerity stamped all over him, from his tousled white hair and clear blue eyes to his proud posture and faded, checkered flannel shirt. He confessed that he didn't know the full extent of the bobcat's predation, but he had seen evidence of bobcat kills many times. The deer herd was in trouble down his way. And he ended each of his last three sentences with the same utterance: "Gentlemen, we've just got to give the poor deer all the help we can."

Except for the two men who suggested early that there was no evidence to denounce the bobcat compared to, say, the house dog, conservationist opposition to the bounty appeared to be ineffective and irrelevant. Richard Anderson, a biologist and the executive director of the Maine Audubon Society, read excerpts from a magazine article about the failure of bounties in other states. But he did not address himself to Maine's bounty or to the life history of the native bobcat. The repeal proposal didn't come any closer to being accepted by the committee this time than it had in previous years.

Not long afterward, while passing through Orono, I looked up Fred Gilbert, a University of Maine professor and a wildlife biologist whom I had heard was contracted to the state as an adviser on wildlife management policies. His rather grand title, in fact, was "Big Game Project Director." He was qualified to talk about deer, bobcat, moose, bear, and all of the larger animals that live in the Maine woods.

Much to my surprise, Gilbert told me that the state had collected ample evidence over the years to show that bobcats were hardly a menace to the deer herd — that climatological and land use patterns were the main population influences. Even in a severe winter when the deer were vulnerable prey, the number killed by bobcat would only be around a thousand, many times less than the number killed by cars and dogs and *eighteen times less* than the number killed illegally by poachers. Moreover, said Gilbert, the men who hunted bobcats did it mainly for sheer sport and the exhilaration of being out in the woods, not because of the bounty. It was an arduous exercise, often lasting all day, and requiring a well-trained pack of hounds and a man able to keep up the pace on snowshoes, although recently snowmobiles had entered the picture.

Gilbert gave me a study done back in 1964 by a University of

276

Maine predecessor, Chester Banasiak. Prepared for the state game people and financed in part by federal funds, the 163-page report, *Deer in Maine,* concluded that "removal of deer by bobcats does not represent serious competition to hunters." In fact, it showed that bobcat actually helped stabilize deer herds in northern Maine just as the wolves are fundamental to the health of northern Alaska's caribou range. In both instances the predator kills weak animals who would contribute to a food shortage, if left alive, through overbrowsing.

When Maine was first settled by white men, there were plenty of deer along the coast but hardly any inland, where the heavy canopy of the climax forest prevented the growth of deer fodder — herbaceous plants in summer, tender apple, cedar and red maple tips in winter. As the woods were cleared, the successional scrub growth attracted the deer. The animal population exploded. But by 1865, the first lumbered land had grown up again beyond the ideal condition for browsing and the deer had to struggle again to find food. Overpopulated, the Maine herd died off in staggering numbers. They came back in the 1890s when the introduction of pulp operations made heavy demands on the northern spruce forests. In addition, cleared farm acreage — which had reached a peak of six million acres in 1880 — slowly reverted back to brush land, ideal deer habitat. Up to 1920, one million acres of farms, an area the size of Washington County, went to scrub. And up to 1950, another million and a quarter acres, the size of Franklin County, went back to the deer. So that in recent years, with close hunting regulation and with sustained yield forest management producing a stable habitat, the deer herd has held its own at around 200,000.

In the same period, the bounty system everywhere has turned out to be ineffective as a tool of game management. Out west, livestock farmers have mercilessly hunted down the coyote as a predator. But then biologists have discovered, if the ranchers haven't already, that coyotes are important agents in the control of rodents that cause untold crop damage yearly. In the Southwest, the U.S. Wildlife Service has led the attack on coyotes only to discover that the result was a porcupine explosion which in turn threatened to wipe out the pinyon pine. Competing for food, unmenaced by coyotes, the porcupines turned to the pine bark for nourishment.

In Maine, the deer explosion has wrought a disruptive change in wildlife patterns, and the bobcat would be well encouraged to increase its depredations. The deer introduced meningal worms to the North Woods region formerly frequented by moose and caribou. Since infestation by the parasitic meningal worm is fatal, there are no more caribou in Maine, in spite of an abortive attempt to restock them in Baxter Park two decades ago. The moose herd had dropped to a population of 3,000 in 1935, when hunting them became illegal.

Big Game Project Director Gilbert was in charge of an official census, and he told me that the moose had come back in the north country. As of 1971 they numbered nearly 15,000. Possibly the comeback was based on changes in the forest character, possibly it was because of the hunting ban. Moose like to browse on fir and spruce whereas the deer like cedar. Since the pulp and paper operations encouraged fir and spruce, they may also have helped bring back the moose. Not all the answers are clear.

Gilbert felt, though, that conditions warranted reopening the moose system on a carefully regulated basis, by creating seven different northern wildlife management districts. Each area would be treated according to its specific biology, so that hunting limits and the open seasons might vary greatly. Gilbert also hoped that the forest companies would go a step further in order to make the moose *the* hoofed animal of the north region by clearing out the so-called "deer yards," where hundreds of deer congregate to browse during the period of deep snowfall.

As Gilbert explained matters, I could envision a very different scheme of things for the hunter. The common denominator would be the experience in the woods, the best reason anyway for being there with a gun. The prey would vary. In some places, you might even be able to hunt bobcat.

Carrying this vision a step further, I could see how a sensitively structured wildlife management system would encourage hunting on a far more selective, qualitative basis. And it might encompass other wildlife interests besides killing. The managers in these districts would know their animal populations and would be able to enlighten those who come to the woods with a camera or those who quite simply enjoy seeking out natural habitats in an unobtrusive way for the sheer pleasure of studying other forms of life.

I don't know whether Gilbert intended my thoughts to go in that

278

direction. But they did, inevitably, as I thought how much more Maine would benefit from wildlife than in the present scheme of things, which is based entirely on the fall slaughter of the white-tailed deer. To be sure, the motels and the forest deer camps do a brisk business with out-of-state hunters, but it doesn't last long and these visitors don't leave all that much money in the till. How much better it would be to have a wildlife recreation plan that provided *year-round* interest in animals and birds, and not just for meat or trophies.

EIGHT

The Inland Waters

WATER, WATER EVERYWHERE...

TRAVELING AROUND MAINE, there are few intervals when you can't see water somewhere. This is to be expected within ten miles of the coast, because it is so punctuated by tidal inlets, bays and river estuaries. But driving far inland, your eyes wander constantly down streams that emerge from the woods next to the road and across ponds bordered by farmland. I spent some of the best moments of my boyhood exploring the marshes and woods along the Charles River in Massachusetts, which ran past the farm where we lived. In the spring, these marshes came alive with color and excitement. In the fall we would stalk through them in hopes of getting a pheasant or a stray black duck. Sometimes it was cold enough in winter to allow us to take shortcuts across the ice. Having such a strong feeling for rivers and brooks, it never ceased to amaze me when countless times in Maine I would drive across waters that were bigger and faster than my native Charles, and yet when I pulled over and studied the map I was not always sure I had found the right stream. There were so many. The map was striated by them. Quite frequently, the one I was looking at was undesignated — at least on the official highway map of Maine.

Many of these river crossings were so appealing I would find myself wishing that I was carrying my canoe. The water would be whispering and sparkling as it ran out of sight around a bend, passing through boulders or turning abruptly around a gravelly bar. I was always reminded that these waterways had been the key to the opening and development of the Maine frontier. Going against the current, the boatman would use a long pole with a steel pike fitted over

283

the end to prevent splintering on the rocky bottom. Headed inland, he could, if he was fortunate, make good mileage on a long lake or chain of ponds connected by brooks or close enough so that portages were no great inconvenience.

Maine's inland lakes and flowing streams comprise over one and a half million acres, 7 percent of the state's total area. This of course includes only the inland waters that can be surveyed with any precision. It does not count the thousands of acres of marshes and bogs that are flooded much of the time, or the small, winding brooks and freshets that rush through farm and forest during the spring thaw and persist as trickles all year. The value of Maine's inland waters is beyond the scope of official comprehension. To arrive at their real valuation, you would have to put into the equation the waterways' worth in economic, aesthetic, biological, social and psychological terms. But, of course, nobody would agree as to the relative importance of these various factors.

For example, if you were merely talking economics, would the water be more valuable as an essential element in a manufacturing process, or as a sewer to carry away manufacturing wastes? To just what extent is a town enhanced by a stream whose banks have not been usurped by factories or housing developments? How important is the stream as a source of drinking water? What does it count to be able to fish and swim in it on a warm Saturday morning or after sneaking away from school on a spring afternoon?

If I were working out the equation, the most heavily weighted factor would be psychological — what it means to your soul to know that there is an unspoiled pond or stream in your community, which at any time can be all yours to enjoy. Or maybe its psychological worth is more symbolic. If it has been protected, you know that people have been foresighted and that mechanisms for group cooperation have functioned well. Conversely, if it has been ruined you are depressed. You know that mistakes have been made that will be difficult to turn around, that one or another selfish set of interests has taken advantage of the public environment.

Long ago, a fisherman, or perhaps someone else who simply loved nature, said that this law ought to be passed: anyone who used the river water should be made to place his intake pipe downstream of his outfall. Then he would be forced to reuse the water that he had just dumped out. Such a law would enforce recognition of the river's natural life-supporting qualities.

Unfortunately, the suggestion has never been taken seriously.

Maine's waterways, like those elsewhere in the country, have been terribly abused. Without ever considering the nonsense of it, river industries have accepted the necessity of purifying the water they consumed to the degree acceptable for using it in manufacturing, e.g., papermaking, before they poured the water back into the river, contaminated by chemicals and loaded with organic substances.

That the industries have never stopped to consider the illogic of their practices was demonstrated in classic fashion during a recent exchange in Bucksport, on the Penobscot River. The St. Regis Paper Company quietly raised objections to the state Environmental Improvement Commission when a developer wanted to put up housing on a lake behind the town. St. Regis has a big mill on the river in Bucksport, but it has to have the lake as a source of *clean* water, not tainted by septic runoff from house lots. If St. Regis and other mills on the Penobscot had faced realities in the past, they might have agreed to keep the *river* clean.

As I moved around Maine in 1970 and 1971, I found that a great many people were demonstrating a new concern for the natural and humanistic values of the inland waters. The industries also began to face up to the reemphasis in values. Moreover, environmental studies showed that the economic and conservation needs for the rivers were frequently quite compatible and sometimes coincided.

Under prodding by the Environmental Improvement Commission, the paper companies professed that they were doing what they could to meet water quality standards. Deadlines have been set for 1976 on the Kennebec and Penobscot rivers. Public pressure is a necessary ingredient. Without it, the state alone will never be able to make its point with industry.

A biologist named Howard Trotzky initiated a suit against five companies who used the Kennebec for log drives. He demanded a stop to the log drives so that he and the public at large could enjoy the common rights and privileges of the river. He bought a house on the river in Caratunk and then helped organize the Kennebec Valley Conservation Association. He contended that by using the Kennebec above the Wyman Dam for running and storing logs, the paper companies had violated the state's classification of the river as B-1. Water that is so rated must be "acceptable for recreational purposes including bathing." It must not adversely affect "fish and wildlife habitat." These phrases are lifted from the Water Quality Code. The sentence that Trotzky emphasized the most seemed pretty strict as far as logs were concerned: "These waters shall be free from sludge deposits, solid refuse and floating solids."

Trotzky got support in the courts from Maine attorney general James Erwin, who filed a friendly suit on behalf of the people. And Everett Dam, an inappropriately named representative from Skowhegan, introduced legislation to end the river drives.

With such an abundance of fresh water visible throughout the state, there should have been plenty to drink. But by 1971, so much of it had been polluted that many communities' water needed extensive doses of chlorine. Nothing can get the malodor from potato wastes out of the drinking water in Caribou even though it is heavily treated to be healthy. Portland's drinking supply is Sebago, a lake whose 28,672 acres have become so attractive for recreation that camp and cottage developments pose a threat to the water quality.

As I looked into Maine's freshwater situation, overdevelopment of lakes and riverfront in the name of public recreation seemed to me to be as potentially harmful as all the previous pollution. The roads that I took ran past many lakes that had already lost their scenic value because houses and docks had been strung around the shore. It would not be long before seepage from septic fields choked the waters with algae. Heading north on Route 27, I would see the houses lining the east shore of Long Pond, one of the Belgrade Lakes, and I always thought how foolish and self-defeating the towns around here had been not to insist that all building be done back a distance from the lake so that the spruce and hardwoods around it would remain unspoiled and the natural beaches would be unpenetrated by private piers and boat arrangements.

The Belgrade Lakes are a prime example of an inland water system that could provide tangible economic benefits if well managed and protected through public spiritedness and minimal local laws. There are five main ponds, scooped out like sinks by the glaciers millennia ago and dropping down one by one from an altitude of around 250 feet to where the last pond, Messalonskee Lake, empties via a stream of the same name into the Kennebec. During the seventeenth century, the Abenaki Indians were active in this region trapping beaver and other animals whose fur they traded in Augusta (then known as Cushnoc) ten miles south. Next the woods were opened for rich farmland. Then, before the turn of the last century, the area became a favorite of fishermen. The lakes were particularly known for big, active bass, and the fishing is still considered good compared to other lake regions. The summer population is around 36,000, 25 percent higher than in winter. The lakes' coverage, an area of 210 square miles, is within an hour's drive of over 150,000 people.

And the pressures of people have begun to tell. In the spring of 1971, James Putnam, a Colby College student, reported on the changes as an ecology assignment. He found serious decay in the lake water from organic overenrichment (what the biologists call eutrophication). Cottages had become a visual blight, particularly around the lake shores, and the water levels were changed willy-nilly by whichever blocs of residents prevailed in controlling the dams on the brooks joining the ponds. None of the communities in the region had passed land use codes to prevent overcrowding on the lakes, pollution from septic seepage, construction on flood plains and the filling in of marsh habitats. Seasonal enjoyment of the lakes' environment provided a strong economic base for the towns in the area, but the recreation business was in danger of overexploitation. Putnam reported to his professor, Donaldson Koons, who also happened to be chairman of the Maine Environmental Improvement Commission, that "the area cannot support much more development."

FOR WANT OF A FISHWAY

IT CAN BE ARGUED that Maine lost its chance to obtain the maximum benefit from riverine recreation and freshwater fisheries when the first dam was constructed on the Kennebec River, in 1837. Why? Because it was not provided with a fishway. Serving like a ladder, with each rung consisting of a pool of water for the fish to jump up to, the fishway would have cost very little, a mere fraction of the expense of the dam. It would have allowed Atlantic salmon and other migratory fish to travel freely upstream to spawn in the headwaters and lakes of the wilderness.

More dams were built on the Kennebec, the Androscoggin and the Penobscot, as well as on all the smaller rivers that run to the sea. Rarely, if ever, was a fishway installed, in spite of a longstanding doctrine that the people of Maine were entitled to the protection of their fishing rights and free access on the river. So the dams, always the keynoters of industrial development, signaled the end of Maine's rivers — and lakes — as unspoiled aquatic habitats.

The basic principle, cited earlier — protecting both the fish and the people — remains intact, upheld by the courts. It was stated in an ordinance that clarified general public rights and was adopted in 1641, and amended in 1647, by the general court of the Massachusetts Bay Colony:

> Every Inhabitant that is an howse holder shall have free fishing and fowling in any great ponds and Bayes, Coves and Rivers, so farre as the sea ebbes and flowes within the presincts of the towne where they dwell, unlesse the free men of the same Towne or the Generall Court have otherwise appropriated them, provided that this shall not be extended to give leave to any man to come upon others propertie without there leave.

As is the case today, people in the Colony were probably so engrossed in making new laws to cope with changing times and situations that they never bothered to implement or enforce the laws that were already on the books.

In any case, Maine's industrial growth depended heavily on dams that were built to generate power and to regulate flowing water so there was always an ample supply for use in manufacturing processes and carrying wood to the mills. The private utilities and the forest products companies came to dominate the rivers and lakes.

I would love to have a scale model of their network. You could open a dam on a small brook way up north and watch the water raise the level of a small pond downstream. When the pond was high, you could open another dam and watch the water keep on going, into a larger lake or maybe down a bigger brook. It might go through a series of passages before rising up behind one of the big dams like those far up on the Penobscot branches or on the Kennebec. When you opened them, you'd see a big wave of water run right down the river toward Bangor or Augusta, where it was needed to move the blades of a hydroelectric turbine, or maybe the dam was opened for a few hours to flush some more logs downstream. What fun it would be to play with the thousands of dams on that model and see the water surge in all directions, through all of Maine.

However, what happened with the full-scale dams has not been any fun at all for the citizens of Maine. What happened was that the companies opened and shut the dams solely to satisfy their own momentary needs. To be sure, the public wanted electricity, but the evidence shows that the power companies gave little or no attention to alternatives in providing it, and they disregarded entirely the biological importance of allowing the rivers and lakes to maintain natural characteristics. For example, the fish would always spawn in shoal water. Later, when the dams were opened, lake levels would drop enough to expose and doom the fish eggs. I saw the evidence of this myself. On lakes where the natural level was clearly marked by scum and wearing action on the rocks, the surface had dropped ten feet or more late in the summer after the dams had been opened to obtain water supplies far down on the slope of the watershed.

Of course it probably didn't matter by the time I came along. The dams without fish ladders had already prevented the spawners from getting there and the only fish came from stocking. I would be reminded of this when I saw signs pointing to fish hatcheries. They were costly installations, some running into millions of dollars. I knew that they were needed because mismanagement of the rivers interrupted normal life cycles. But the hatcheries could never replace the fishways.

Nobody paid much attention to these sad events until a few years ago. The polluters were not deliberately immoral, even if their deeds were bad. They behaved entirely in accordance with the apathetic public climate that allowed the industries to gain control over the state government and stifle competitive interests.

In 1958, a few years before Ralph Nader attacked Detroit, a Maine lawyer named Jerome G. Daviau launched a bitter case against what he termed the "industrial bloc" in Maine. The results of his investigation were published in a small gray book of 139 pages, *Maine's Life Blood*. As a work that might influence people, the book failed. It was too vitriolic and full of damnation toward everyone, including those who were in a position to do something constructive. But the book remains a striking example of advocacy writing, scathing, sharp-edged — an avowedly one-sided "hatchet job." Like Nader's documentary attacks against General Motors — and eventually the entire auto industry — for designing dangerous cars and causing air pollution, Daviau's presentation was meant to drive you to flaming indignation.

It is hard to find *Maine's Life Blood* in the state today. It is said — and not in jest — that the remaining supply and much of the first printing have been salted away or destroyed by the menacing "industrial bloc."

The lifeblood Daviau spoke of consists of Maine's 5,000 rivers and streams; he traced their bit-by-bit destruction and described the alternatives. His main points were backed by impressive detail. Here is a sampling.

• Maine could look to the achievements of Washington State to see how a multimillion dollar freshwater fishery, as well as countless benefits to sportsmen, similarly might have been developed in Maine, but had been lost instead through self-interested stupidity.

• The utilities, supported by their friends in paper, lobbied successfully for a law that prohibited the sale of *public* hydroelectric power, outside of Maine, to states like Massachusetts and New Hampshire who needed it. Thus public power was effectively prevented from gaining a foothold in Maine, since the larger public companies could not afford to sell power only to small rural communities. While the Fernald Law was eventually repealed, the private utilities were by then well established and they kept their rates among the highest in the nation.

• For years, the paper companies sold the legislature on the line that, if the industries were forced to abate pollution, they would have to leave Maine, thus denying communities the property tax revenues essential to finance treatment of *municipal* sewage. This argument persisted, Daviau wrote, even after biological assessment revealed that municipal wastes were only a fraction of paper company discharges. Pulp and paper effluent had created oxygenless barriers on the rivers, through which fish could not pass alive.

• When the Central Maine Power Company built the Wyman Dam on the Kennebec River, it said a fish hatchery would be built above the dam to avoid the need of a fishway. The public and the legislature were taken in by this gesture, unaware that CMP was prevented by law from making that type of an expenditure. Neither fishway nor hatchery was built.

• Maine's first water quality laws should have been directed toward the control of *existing* pollution. Instead, and rather than becoming the basis of an *abatement* program, the laws were weakened gradually to allow the "industrial bloc" to keep their old licenses to discharge pollutants. One law said it was illegal to dump potato wastes into waterways, but it granted an exception to the pulp that results from the manufacture of potato starch. This happened despite the fact that potato parts themselves did negligible damage. It was the sticky pulp that coated rivers in slime and used up the oxygen.

• Had the dams been provided with fishways and the rivers kept clean, the inland lakes would be thriving fishing grounds, both commercially and recreationally. Freshwater canneries, boatbuilding, fishing resorts and dock maintenance would have been additional contributors to the state economy.

• Senator Edmund Muskie, known later as a pollution fighter, backed away from strong action against the "industrial bloc" when he was governor of Maine in the late fifties, Daviau charged. In his campaigns and in office, Muskie promised a cleanup as well as the creation of "Maine Rivers Authority" to administer pollution abatement, regulations regarding water levels and the construction of fishways. The agency was eventually the subject of a legislative proposal, but it lost its bite when the fishways provision was stricken and it died, largely because the governor suddenly withdrew his support. In Muskie's second term, Maine suffered economically as the last textile industries moved to the South. Muskie helped launch a campaign to attract new industries to Maine and cooled the war against pollution. He reappointed as commissioner of Inland Fisheries and Game a man named Roland Cobb, who, Daviau contended, had refused at every opportunity to fight for fishways and proper water levels and who had never protested against river pollution.

"Our recreational income is almost equal to our industrial income and climbing steadily," Daviau concluded. "If we combine our recreational with our saltwater commercial fisheries, we outstrip the industrial payroll. Most important of all, however, is the fact that recreational facilities and freshwater commercial fisheries are the only two assets that we can possibly hope to expand and increase."

Twelve years after Daviau's book was published, I found that both the public and its representatives had paid little heed to his words of warning. (Indeed, a doctoral dissertation entitled *Politics of Pollution: The Case of Maine*, written by James Wilson at Syracuse University in 1963, had continued Daviau's theme. "Maine residents have never been very interested in their rivers," Wilson wrote, "although a few people do get fired up occasionally.") At the same time a new and complex question arose that the old crusader had not considered. If the water is cleaned up and managed properly, what do you do to prevent despoliation of the waterfront?

The debate thus moved up to a more sophisticated plateau. The citizens protested the befouled and choked-up rivers, although nobody had figured out how to take on the utilities. The "industrial bloc" agreed that past abuses must be corrected. But the talk usually exceeded the action. Moreover, even if the 1976 deadlines were met by polluters, the danger would remain that an increased volume of effluence would still damage the waterways. The paper companies, for example, were told they had to reduce the Biochemical Oxygen Demand of their wastes per ton. But in a growing economy, what if the companies enlarged their plants, built new facilities, and doubled or tripled their outflow? The BOD would have to be decreased four or six times, a step that had apparently not been contemplated by those to whom I asked questions about such problems.

Daviau was far ahead of his time when he told what had happened to Maine's inland waters and deplored trends toward increased industrial development. But then when conservationists became known as environmentalists, and everyone seemed agreed that pollution must go, the industrial trends were not the only threat. Even recreational use of rivers and lakes was proceeding with indiscriminate ugliness, and in many places it didn't seem to matter whether the water had fish or not.

In other words, as odd as it may seem to say so, perhaps the pollution of Maine's rivers delayed the ruination of the land along their banks, because when the water was filthy, nobody wanted to build beside it. Yet it is a sad statement to have to make. Daviau was right to demand a cleanup. Now it is up to others to see that proper land use controls are developed at the same pace.

A DAY ON THE KENNEBEC

WE DROVE DOWN Arnold's Highway on a misty early October morning with a long green canoe on top of the station wagon and a golden Labrador retriever named Chum anxious for freedom in his wire cage behind us. My escort was Clinton Townsend, a lanky man with graying hair in his late forties. He wore wool trousers and a heavy canvas olive-drab hunting jacket. Lately he had been chairman of Maine's active and respected Natural Resources Council. Now, as a practicing lawyer in Skowhegan, he was leading the battle to develop a plan for the Kennebec Valley before the river's pollution was cleaned up by the state-set deadline of 1976 and its banks had become attractive to the land speculators. We had left my car on a dirt road beside the river, opposite Savage Island in North Anson, where we would end up, and we were headed about six miles upstream on a route named for Benedict Arnold. Arnold had come this way in 1775 in a vain attempt to capture Quebec, leading eleven hundred men who were described in the title of Kenneth Roberts's book about the expedition as a *Rabble in Arms*.

We parked the station wagon on the shoulder, just before the road turned east to cross the river a mile below Solon. Townsend pointed to picnic tables standing in a grove of trees on a slope on the other side where the river swept west to make a bend. "That's Bill Perry's Evergreen Vacation Center," he said. "They've found artifacts there showing that it was an old Indian campsite and there is evidence Arnold stopped there too. They dug up a pewter powder horn with the initial A on it, like the ones his men carried."

Townsend put on boots, laid the canvas case holding his shotgun in the canoe and rigged a light fishing rod to a gunwale clamp. He'd told me we might get a shot at some woodcock and that the season was still open on the river for fly fishing, so I'd brought along my own gun. I'd also brought lunch for both of us in a waterproof pack. I eased myself onto the bow seat, Chum found a place amidships, and Townsend shoved us away from the bank. We were quickly caught in the current, which was fast and powerful, although there were no rapids in sight or to be heard around the bend.

For the next ten miles there were few ways of getting onto the river; the roads on both sides ran well back except in a few places. Townsend's plan, presented in a detailed public letter, was to protect such stretches of the river through agreements with private owners and the big landowners like the Scott Paper Company and Central Maine Power. If access to the river remained difficult, this section would hold its diverse abundance of waterfowl, its pretty and varied countryside of fields and forests, and outdoorsmen like Townsend would continue to earn the right to appreciate it, paddling in canoes and slogging on foot.

Other sections on the Kennebec that were already more developed would be planned for residential or recreational development, but the river must be allowed — as much as possible — to keep its natural and historic character. Small cottage lots, heavy residential construction and additional industrial development right along its banks would send the Kennebec to the fate of all too many great New England rivers, such as the Connecticut and the Merrimack. This was Townsend's thinking. But when he first broached these thoughts, the winter before, he was the object of snide comments on the part of many conservationists. Howard Trotzky had just sued for the injunction to stop five paper companies from driving logs down the Kennebec. Townsend wondered aloud whether Trotzky was not moving too fast. And there were dark hints that Townsend was, after all, a friend of the paper companies.

Yet what he had really been thinking was that, while the log drives hurt his enjoyment too, if the river became clear and clean for boatsmen, fishermen and eventually swimmers and water skiers, and there were no plans for controlling development alongside the river, chaos and degradation of the Kennebec Valley would inevitably occur. His detractors began to realize that Townsend was foresighted

295

when he produced the plan that he had worked on for so long —
a plan that, by painstaking use of topographical maps and other data,
analyzes the river's environmental prospects, mile by mile, from its
headwaters all the way to Skowhegan.

"I've personally covered almost every inch of this part of the
river," Townsend said. And he liked to tell people about his plans by
taking them out where he could illustrate some of his points and
where they could get the feel for the possibilities. This was one of
those trips.

We hadn't gone a hundred yards before we met up with history —
to be precise, prehistory. Townsend pointed to a slate ledge that entered the river from the west bank to our right. "On the back of it are
Indian pictographs," he said. "When they cleared this section for
logs to pass, they must have blasted out a lot more of these drawings.
Let's take a look."

We nosed the canoe around the tip of the ledge, bow first, and I
saw a row of figures etched on the rock face. I could clearly discern
dancing men and a bear. "Has anybody figured this out?" I asked.

"Not that I know of," Townsend said.

Just fifty yards ahead, the main river continued south, but we cut
to the left up a narrow logan. This particular diversion circumscribed
Gray's Island, which was at least a mile long and was owned by Central Maine Power. Townsend got out his fishing rod, and for a moment the soft rippling of the water was interrupted only by the whir-
ring of his reel.

"What can you catch here?" I asked.

"Oh, native salmon, some brown and brook trout, small-mouth
bass," he said. "I haven't caught anything on the river for years. The
fishing has declined terribly, the old-timers say. I don't know exactly
why, but I'm sure that that has a lot to do with it." He pointed to the
banks where four-foot pulp logs, matted strips of bark and other bits
of wood debris had been deposited by higher water. You could also
see waterlogged pulpwood lying everywhere on the bottom where the
tea-colored river was shallow.

"They always tell you that the winter cleans it all up and that the
spring grows back over all signs of the drive," Townsend said. "But
that's nonsense."

"Haven't the biologists been able to show yet that this decaying wood uses up oxygen and releases chemicals that affect the fish population?" I asked.

"Not precisely, and that's one of the big problems," Townsend said. "It's obvious that the mass of logs coming down here has to prevent the breeding and hatching of fish, and the fishermen say that the small organisms on the bottom that the fish feed on are no longer there, but nobody has proven that this has resulted from the logs. The paper companies know darn well that the river is a cheap way of debarking the wood. But so far we've been speaking as citizens, not scientists."

There was a sudden slapping on the water ahead and we both turned in time to see six or more wood duck get up and scoot downstream. They landed a hundred yards ahead and kept on rising and moving the same distance whenever we got close. We also surprised some sheldrakes and one black duck. Fortunately for them, the season was not yet open.

We were being carried along without effort through low brush and oak and maple. The sun had begun to burn through the overcast and the foliage was brightening in the promise of a warm Indian summer day. Occasionally we'd pass a lone white pine or clumps of spruce and hemlock, overlooked by the loggers when they cleared this valley maybe the second or third time since it was first cut heavily in the beginning of the last century.

"My interest in this river began with duck hunting back in 1963," Townsend said, as he pointed out a backwater favored by black duck. "About once or twice a year two of us float down here in a canoe. The rule is that only one man at a time, the bow man, can shoot. For safety. Sometimes you get a headwind and it can really be rough in the open. I've had some close calls. We take an outboard in order to make the run back. One time we ran out of gas. It was in December. We dragged the boat upriver right past Gray's Island here, stumbling into holes, up to our chests in water."

At the south end of Gray's Island, Townsend kept to the left and pointed to two islands dead ahead that were divided by a narrow slough.

"Those are Fowl Meadow and Indian islands," he said. "I used to own them. Now they're the Nature Conservancy's, but I've reserved the right to camp and hunt here during my lifetime."

We floated past the east side of Indian Island, then turned around the end, paddling hard to get back up the slough on the other side.

"Now *there's* a big beaver house," Townsend said excitedly, as he broke the cadence and pointed to a mound of sticks at the head of a swampy inlet. We grated to a stop on a gravel bar a ways above the house. Restrained thus far, the dog leaped out and began to sniff around furiously in the brush for signs of wildlife. Townsend and I shed our jackets and uncased our guns. The sun was now beating down from a clear blue sky.

We plunged into the thick hardwood forest, brushing through waist-high fiddlehead ferns and climbing over fallen trunks. Our objective was the beaver house. It was well worth our efforts to see. We found an extraordinary set of canals dug in the mud, as if men had dragged a scoop through it. The earth was piled up in neat ridges on either side of the channels. The beavers had shoveled it in their small paws, and it reminded me of excavations performed at the beach by my children.

"They sure have been at it," Townsend said. "Do you suppose they made those canals to float pieces of wood down to the house site? They hadn't begun when I was here six weeks ago."

There was an old beaver house set back a ways from the new one. Built of freshly cut sticks, the new one commanded a superior view of the Kennebec, just as Fort Popham guarded the river's entrance to the sea nearly a hundred miles downstream. And I thought, as I had every time I'd seen a beaver operation in the Maine woods, that these fellows are the smartest engineers in the whole country.

We picked our way back up the island, carrying our guns and changing position so that one of us would have a safe shot if a woodcock suddenly got up out of the brush. The growth was heavy and varied. Wild grapes climbed with abandon through the woods behind the beaver works. Twice we stopped to gauge the biggest white birches I'd ever seen. When I hugged one of them the tips of my fingers were still a foot apart. The one woodcock we flushed was long gone before Townsend fired, but the dog took off, expecting a hit, and thrashed around by the shore in the direction of the bird's escape until his master called him back.

We came to a slight opening, facing west across the slough to Fowl Meadow, and Townsend found the campfire remains from an outing with his family the previous spring. He had come to inspect the damage done by a big clutch of pulp logs that had piled up on the island. Bulldozers had been sent to push them back into the river. Townsend found that they had made an awful mess, churning up the ground and battering down small trees and the brush screen along the river.

He'd bought the island from a Mr. Piper, who used to drive over in his tractor when the river was low to chop and haul firewood. We encountered a big oak that Mr. Piper had cut and sectioned and never returned to pick up. It lay strung out like sausage links rotting on the forest floor. Years back, farmers in the valley found that the river islands made superior hayfields. It pleased me to think of it; horses being exhorted through the shallow fords, hauling wagons to a place like this for a farmer taking care of his own needs and for whom this supply of hay was very important.

Back on the river and just beyond Indian Island, a stone's throw from the beaver house, Townsend pointed out a tiny islet where each year he set up a crude blind and waited for black duck. Still keeping to the left of the main channel we passed another island.

Then *it* appeared, just as I had been alerted by a friend of Townsend's — a vivid apparition, a terrible chink in nature's order. Townsend didn't say a word. But there it was, sure enough, just upstream of a grove of hemlock beside a brook that gurgled into the river, on a bluff looking down on us — a pink house trailer. Against the cool green forest it looked like a giant stick of bubble gum.

"My God, it exists," I said.

"Well, you know, I can live with *one* like that," Townsend said quietly. "And it happens that the people who own it are the salt of the earth. But it *is* a symbol of all that could happen along the banks of this river."

He looked back to the right where a deep cove indented the island we were passing. "That is a great haunt for black ducks," he said. "But you can't hunt there anymore because you sit on the shore and shoot toward the trailer."

The river opened up. During the spring freshet it must have been even wider, because the trees had been scarred by pulp logs ten feet above the ground. A blue station wagon was pulled up next to Dunphy's gravel pit on the west shore, the only place where you could get down to the river in this eight-mile stretch. A man in business clothes stood looking into the water and taking in our approach. He waved and Townsend hailed him. The man started to take off his jacket and rummage in the car. "Well," he shouted, "I'm going to change my clothes and do some fly fishing."

Townsend was reminded he'd brought along his own gear. "A friend told me there were some salmon in this rip," he said, as he fastened his favorite fly ("the thief") to the fishing line and cast where the two channels of the river converged. He had no luck.

We stopped for lunch on another gravel slope with a good southern exposure. It was on the tip of an island belonging to a friend of Townsend's named Bob Butler. In 1969, it had been devastated by rampaging logs. The northern, exposed end of the island was low, and it was easy to see how high water would have brought an avalanche of pulpwood across the fields and into the woods, crushing everything in sight and causing just as much damage being moved back into the river.

"Why couldn't Butler sue the Kennebec Log Driving Company for trespass?" I asked.

"He could, if he wanted to take all the trouble to go to court," Townsend said. "But these operators have always taken the river for granted and felt they could fill up people's fields with logs any time. The ethic was different then. But that's changing."

We soaked up the good sun and ate our sandwiches of pastrami with mayonnaise on Russian rye, followed by crisp "Maine Delicious" apples and coffee, hot from a thermos. Townsend talked about the Kennebec and his plan. He felt strongly that the big landholders, like Scott and Central Maine Power, should take the lead and show a public responsibility to protect the wildland they owned from uncontrolled and unsuitable development. Along this stretch they should keep it undeveloped as a scenic easement. There were places like Wyman Lake, behind Wyman Dam fifteen miles upstream, where there was a good opportunity to provide public recreation and creative shorefront facilities. But not here.

"Heavy horsepower boats for water skiing or joyriding have no place here," Townsend said. "The only people who come down here now are a few hunters and fishermen and those who want to enjoy one of the finest three-hour canoe trips anywhere."

As we conversed, we collected rocks along the gravel beach. It was good picking. I pocketed a sandstone specimen that had been rounded by the river's action into a smooth, perfectly symmetrical sphere. Townsend was absorbed in a hard, dark, shiny stone that had been shaped into an oval and was striated by rust-brown veins.

I told him about my trip down the East Branch of the Penobscot a few months before and how I could not get out of my mind the natural similarities between the two rivers, except that the mood here was very different. The East Branch had been just that much more narrow than the Kennebec so that the afternoon sun lit up only a thin strip on one side. You sensed that once you were ashore, you would be enveloped by a vast no man's wilderness. Here, the river was brighter and the same kind of country — deciduous trees, broken up by meadows and logans, with patches of pine — seemed friendlier somehow. Maybe it was because the margins of this river held back civilization instead of the deep forest.

"All the rivers have different moods; you are right," Townsend said. "Some are very spooky. Others are light and open."

There was not much farther to go and I slacked off in my paddling and looked around to savor to the fullest the last half hour. We passed an island where whistlers liked to congregate, and Townsend explained how he had learned in New Brunswick to build a blind that looked like a flat-bottomed pram that you would lie down in until the ducks came in. We passed pure green grassland next to a recently harvested cornfield. And then it was clear we were leaving the open river behind.

Over a ridge to our right had been dumped refuse of every description — cans, bottles, paper, old appliances, cloth scraps and rubber tires. Black smoke rose from somewhere in the midst of this mess and there was a stink in the air.

"That's the North Anson dump," Townsend said. "A real beauty spot, isn't it? In the plan I've relocated intrusions like that."

There was one final scenic reprieve before we spotted my car. We passed the remains of a bridge, a pier standing alone out in the river, made from huge blocks of granite fitted together without cement. Then we turned a sharp bend and paddled down a narrow channel with an island on our left. It was bordered by big swamp maples that screened wide open meadows. "That's Savage Island," Townsend said. "They pasture cattle there."

Another mile and a half and we would have turned south around the island and run into the Carrabassett River where it enters the Kennebec at Anson. The water was shallow opposite Savage Island and the bottom was packed thick with sunken pulp logs. The current had slowed perceptibly as the heavy volume of water from both rivers was gradually backed up by a dam at Madison six miles below us.

We tied the canoe by its painter to a tree branch and drove to pick up the station wagon. I followed Townsend back to help him load the canoe. It was four-thirty and still warm. The sun dropping low made the river sparkle. Chum took a final sniff along the edge of the river. We joined him and looked up and down the Kennebec.

"That's a fine exhibit of river," I said.

"It makes a good day's run," Townsend said.

NINE

The True Heritage

Anyone who has studied the history of the conduct of "the white man" toward the Indian must feel, together or in succession, emotions of indignation, disgust and bewilderment. Over a period of three and a half centuries, acts of injustice have been so blatant and common that the attitude of bewilderment follows quite naturally. One assumes that if the extreme and insensitive cruelty of official policy, let alone unofficial behavior, is real, then this inhumanity is justified because of contemporary historical perspective in the early periods when, as they say, America was being forged.

However, the problem with this trick of self-justification (and I have to assume that some of my ancestors diligently persecuted Indians) is that the inhumanity has in fact *not yet* been dislodged from our present policy or even from our present thinking. It is all too easy, still, for us whites to slide into a subtle, racist stereotype, for example, when we admire the Indian for *instinctively, unconsciously* being a good ecologist.

All my life I had read about the plight of the true native Americans, but only recently have I come to understand how bad it is. The turning point for me was the fall of 1969, when I traveled through Oklahoma, reporting for *Time* magazine's first cover story on the Indian. It had been a standing inside joke for years that the magazine would never do it. Somebody — maybe it was Henry Luce, I don't know — had a thing about Indians. Only when the hippies took us back to the land of the commune and the tipi, when Indianwear and jewelry enjoyed a revival in the late sixties, was there any chance. A tiny group of us had to fight to get him on the cover. Then for two months it didn't run. Once the story was displaced by a cover on Raquel Welch — that was Thanksgiving week, historically a most apt moment to feature the Indian, not Hollywood.

"Why don't the Indians do anything for themselves? Rise up like the blacks? Where do they fit in, anyway? What do they have to tell us, now?" These were questions asked verbatim, or in similar words, by the top editors. I felt sort of sheepish answering "Read your history." I gradually got so mad that I was incapable of rationally explaining why the Indian fit in. But I was sure that he did fit in, and that we were the ones who perhaps still had not made it.

Back in Oklahoma, representatives of the U.S. Bureau of Indian Affairs looked the other way or unashamedly transacted Indian grazing rights and agricultural land holdings into the hands of white ranchers. A white said to me, "Just look at the land around here and you'll see why. The Indians take good care of theirs. We've overgrazed ours." Farther to the southwest, along the Rio Grande and the Colorado, the U.S. Bureau of Reclamation promised white farmers and white-run cities like Phoenix and Albuquerque that there would always be enough water to keep on growing and planting in the desert. With whose water? The Navajos' or the Pueblos'.

Bill Veeder was a dedicated Interior Department lawyer who had worked for years to build a case for the Indians, documenting step by step the disintegration of their treaty rights to water throughout the West. The upper echelon in the agency succeeded in squashing Veeder from time to time, but he always surfaced, carrying briefcases bulging with data to prove his points. Eventually he was instrumental in generating publicity about the Paiutes' rights to Pyramid Lake, Nevada. The tribe had literally been dried out. They depended upon their lake for fish, and upon fishing to provide recreational revenues. But the fish were gone. The lake had become too saline to support life, as it was drained away for state and federal reclamation projects that depended on continuing subsidies to avoid bankruptcy.

The Paiute tragedy was only one of many nearly identical cases. Along the Colorado River, arable Indian bottomland was seized by the government for agricultural development. On the Fort Yuma Reservation, back in 1893, the Quechans were "persuaded" to let the feds sell lands classified as nonirrigable, for which the tribe would be paid. In 1970, the government was still holding the land on its books as "nonirrigable" while actively leasing it for irrigated farm-land. And the Indians had not yet received a cent.

All along the Rio Grande, the U.S. Government encouraged and facilitated irrigation projects by white men. The Bureau of Reclamation's Middle Rio Grande District was consuming millions of gallons of water a day that belonged to the Pueblo nation. The San Ildefonso, Santa Clara, Santo Domingo, Sandia and Isleta tribes could not have stepped up their own agricultural efforts if they'd wanted to. Their streams were drying up and their tributaries were being diverted, under the auspices of the U.S. Government.

All the time the Indian, out of pride and a traditional sense of politeness, took it in silence. One day I had a chance to reflect on this as I stood on a hillside in eastern Oklahoma, watching the shadows cast by the falling sun deepen on the floor of the valley three hundred feet below. A well-tended wood shack stood behind me, surrounded by the small scrub oaks that prevailed in this flint-rock, hard-earth country, the foothills of the Ozarks. This was the Rocky Ford Chero-kee Community, one of many small back-hollow settlements where the families converse and carry on in their native tongue, castaways ever since they were first driven there from their ancestral home in North Carolina, down the terrible Trail of Tears, herded by Andrew Jackson's cavalry back in 1838. Up the hill a boy came running. His name was Tommie Belt. He was eighteen, a senior in high school, handsome, bright and outspoken, and he hid the bitterness that must have festered deep inside with an enthusiasm and humor that surprised me. He carried a pair of spurs.

"What do you use those for?" I asked.

"I've been riding bulls," he said. "I've got to do something to get out my frustrations." And then he laughed so I wouldn't take him seriously.

Bilingually fluent, I learned he was instructed more by his fine, proud parents than by white schoolteachers. He hoped a good college would accept him. He seemed intelligent and perceptive beyond his years during the hour of conversation we held there on the hill. But for him it was still a long way out of Rocky Ford, I thought. I never have found out whether Tommie made it. Or if he did, whether he used his college experience to help his people.

The feelings I had stored up from Oklahoma and my conversations with Bill Veeder came to mind again as I visited the Indian settlements of eastern Maine. It was winter and the weather report said forty-four inches of snow had fallen in the previous fortnight, not counting another four inches the night before. I was driving north along Route 1, through the forest of the Indian Township, just out of Princeton. That's what it's called on the official state map, but you don't see any boundaries drawn for it or the Pleasant Point Reservation to the south, near Eastport. Maybe the state Highway Commission doesn't dare. And no wonder. It is well recognized, though arrogantly ignored, that the Indians own all the land in this region — not just the 15,000 or so acres onto which they have been cornered by the state, but at least another 8,000 or more acres stolen from them by white settlers, forest products companies, town settlements and commercial developers ever since the Passamaquoddy tribe was given treaty rights five times: in 1777, 1789, 1790, 1794 and finally in 1820, when Maine broke away from Massachusetts to become a separate state.

The forest on either side of this road is strikingly pristine, unlike so many other wooded corridors in Maine where the lumberjacks have had easy access. Big hemlocks, spruce and pine looked down on me, their tops shivering slightly in the bitter northwest wind; snow lay piled beneath them. The road was in a hellish condition, heaved and contracted by seasonal extremes, snow removal equipment and the monstrous logging trucks that pass this way to and from the Georgia Pacific pulp mill in Woodland and a local sawmill.

The Passamaquoddys have managed their woods well — that is, what timberlands they've been able to hang on to. The forest companies have taken the rest and overcut it. There have been instances of trespass when white logging crews have been discovered by the Indians out in reservation trees, and the Passamaquoddys have negotiated to get the whites off, but not until more acres of Indian trees were harvested with no compensation. It was on this route that in 1969 the tribe struck a blow in a manner to which they were totally unaccustomed, but which had become necessary in order to attract attention and to show that they meant business.

Even early historians of Indian-white relations concede that the native was a peaceful, acquiescent, noncompetitive individual who *fought back* only when his territorial rights were openly violated. It was not until 1675, after mounting encroachments, that the Indian's resentment erupted. This was King Philip's War, the beginning of six wars that ravaged Maine for thirty-five years, on and off, until the last fight at Meduncook (now Friendship) in 1758. William Williamson in his official (and excellent) history of Maine (1832) wrote:

> the English were the aggressors. The generous treatment and welcome they first received from the natives had been repaid, as accusers say, by kidnapping their benefactors, by disturbing their hunting grounds and fisheries, and by "a shameful mismanagement of the fur and peltry trade." In the gradual encroachments of the white people, the Indians foresaw the danger of being totally exiled from their native country.

What happened in July 1969 was the culmination of broken faith stemming from the last agreement in 1820. This time, the state inexplicably cut off monies used to pay for doctors' visits, prescription drugs, milk supplies and repair of old homes. The Passamaquoddy people appealed in vain over a long period before they took matters into their own hands. Then, as state officials and police watched in helpless amazement, they barricaded Route 1 and started to charge passage through *their* lands — one dollar for each car, two dollars for each truck. The motorists were actually happy to oblige, being either sympathetic to the Indian cause or delighted at the opportunity to abet a scheme aimed at the unresponsive bureaucracy. Some got out of their cars and mingled with the Indians and a traffic jam ensued. It was all over forty-five minutes and $59 later. Passamaquoddy governor John Stevens had been dragged along on the bumper of a truck waved through by state cops. But the state gave in, admitting that somewhere along the line the Indians' money had got hung up.

During the past day, Stevens had been my escort in the Indian territory. Now, momentarily, I had left him off at the Basket Cooperative in Princeton where he was to discuss how a large donation from a private trust could best be put to work in the arts and crafts project that he had encouraged. He was Maine's first *native* Commissioner of Indian Affairs, from which vantage I sought his knowledge and interpretation of Maine history.

I was about to turn left onto the road to Grand Lake Stream and the Peter Dana Point Reservation (named after a kindly early Indian homesteader) to talk with Fred Tomah, a "medicine man." And I was reminded of one of Stevens's complaints as I entered the turn. At the corner stood a handsome house with a sign indicating that it was the residence and headquarters of the area forest ranger. Since the forests hereabouts are Indian-owned, Stevens has tried hard to have a native assigned to this station, and in fact there is a well-qualified and experienced Indian available. But the present ranger, notwithstanding his friendliness toward the tribe, was a white man. "This is the Indian township. We have special hunting and fishing laws. We have 27 miles of roads here and the three other towns have only 14 miles," Stevens had told me. "And yet there is not a single Indian employed full time here as a forester, warden or highway construction worker."

As I looked back at the ranger's house and up at the tall, barely swaying trees, I thought to myself that the situation was so outrageous that most people wouldn't believe it. The degradation of the Maine Indian was far more extreme than the conditions I encountered in Oklahoma.

Let's go back to the first treaty, the first recorded in legal accounts, overlooking the various compacts made during the early wars. This is a treaty between the Passamaquoddys and Colonel John Allan, U.S. commander of the Eastern Indian Outpost. The Quoddys fought hard and bravely as a rebel unit against the British redcoats under King George III. In fact, all the Maine Indians under the so-called Wabanaki Confederacy made sweep after sweep — successfully — through the part of Maine north of the Kennebec River (two-thirds of the present state) and even into Canada in order to keep the British out. (It was Francis Joseph Neptune, son of the governor of Pleasant Point, who fired the shot that killed the captain of a warship sent to assert British authority. He later became Indian governor himself and lived to the age of one hundred and thirteen.) During a meeting with the tribe, Allan promised that "they should be forever viewed as brothers and children under the protection and fatherly care of the United States. . . ." Not only did he verify the marksmanship of the Indian leader and repeatedly credit Indian support, but he wrote to

George Washington and the U.S. Congress to put on record the Indians' rights to protection. Typically, the "treaty" was never ratified.

But let's go back even further than that and see what happened to the 35,000 or more natives (estimated by a 1615 census) who were living in Maine when the first settlers came. According to the historian Williamson, troubles started with Captain George Weymouth, who explored Muscongus and Penobscot bays in 1605. After friendly exchanges — knives, glasses, combs and toys for the furs of beaver, otter and sable — Weymouth turned nasty and seized five captives whom he took back to England. This event implanted a long-lasting Indian antipathy toward the English. It is clear from looking at the historical record of the next century and a half that the English never held the Indians' trust the way the French did. Some historians — revealing a Protestant bias — say that the Indians were not comfortable with Calvinism and its abstract doctrine of moral restraint, whereas they could easily respond to Catholicism with its greater emphasis on mystery and ritual.

Actually, it is more likely that the Indians were willing to see similarities between their spiritual men and the Jesuit priests because the French came first and followed a more humane policy than the English.

Susan Stevens, wife of the commissioner and a Ph.D. historian of Indian culture, told me that the Jesuits not only were more tolerant toward Indian life but that they had a far better record for keeping a bargain. The French feasted and intermarried with the Indians, she explained, while the English only dined with Indian chiefs to conduct diplomacy, and they passed miscegenation laws that stayed on Maine books until the 1930s. So, if the Indians did not fully accept Jesuit dogma, then at least political considerations and traditional rules of behavior dictated politeness on the part of the natives.

English animosities were given full vent during the period following King Philip's War, a period of outbreaks known in the English language as the French and Indian Wars. In fact, the Indians were only pawns in a monumental struggle between the nations of England and France, whose stakes included supremacy in North America.

By this time, embroiled in alliances over the fur trade, given different promises regarding land rights, and having taken up firearms, the Indians were tied inescapably to the white man's world and had no choice but to take sides. Since it was the English who encroached on their lands and who already had broken promises granted before the inevitable expansion of the frontier, and because the French were closer to begin with, the Indians sided mostly with the French.

Yet throughout the French-English conflict, the Indians never really did know the nature of the game. Alas, they seldom got the word as to when the war between the white nations was on or off — that is to say, if the fighting was not simply the result of another instance of the white man's greed for land.

The Indian sagamores (chiefs) didn't know what to do. Some of them guided their tribes clear of conflict. One of them, Passaconaway of the Pennacooks, old and near his end, held a great feast in 1660 at which, according to Williamson, he delivered this sermon: "The white men are the sons of the morning. The Great Spirit is their father. His sun shines bright about them. Never make war with them. Sure as you light the fires, the breath of heaven will turn the flames upon you and destroy you."

He was right. But succeeding sagamores of every tribe had little choice as their lands were taken and settled, forests cut down, and their hunting regime replaced by white agrarian methods, the harnessing of water, and the use of timber for profit. Williamson recorded these events at a time when the natives were openly regarded as the due victims of frontier expansion, the unavoidable consequences of pursuing the American dream. Even so, he felt that the natives were badly abused. When a sagamore granted white settlers land holdings, Williamson observed, the Indian assumed that the property rights did not extend beyond his lifetime, and even then were not exclusive but, instead, allowed mutual use of the land. The free enterprise system was befuddling because it seemed designed to remove freedoms. The Indian was content to live and let live, if only he was allowed to. His laws did not cope with property rights, only personal honor and injury. "The fires of avarice and ambition — the passions for riches and affluence, which are the great disturbers of the civilized world, lie comparatively dormant in the savage breast," Williamson wrote. Back in 1832, such sentiments were rarely expressed.

Vine Deloria, Jr., a current Indian spokesman and author, has written, "Indians traditionally rejected any notion that a society had a right to impose upon its members pre-determined patterns of ac-

312

tion." In the native way of life, there was no need for rigid behavioral codes and, according to Deloria, common rules were adopted only during the period when a tribe faced an outside crisis. The normal pattern was "a rule of custom in which religion, law, politics, economics and other familiar academic and vocational fields merged into one living tradition of tribal life."

Yet while they were unprepared to deal with the white man's laws, the natives did a fine job of managing their environment, as they do today. They cut only as much timber as was necessary to provide wood for shelter and warmth. (Now, they would like to sell only enough wood to support a reasonable modern life style.) They knew that to pollute their lakes and streams with wastes would destroy the fisheries they depended upon for *food, not cash income*. The native didn't need a job when all he wanted was food to eat, clean water to drink, and a shelter to live in. Hard labor, in the Indian context, was not only unnecessary, it was undignified.

All this was shattered, although it didn't need to be, when the white men broke the treaties. These treaties would have given the Passamaquoddys and the Penobscots plenty of room to perpetuate their cultural heritage and native ways, with some modifications for the times.*

When the U.S. Constitution was adopted in 1789, all native populations became the responsibility of the federal government. A year later in 1790, and then in 1793, successive Non-Intercourse acts stated that it was *illegal* for any government but the federal government to negotiate with Indians, for lands or anything else. Regardless of these declarations, for reasons never made clear, the Commonwealth of Massachusetts signed a treaty with the Passamaquoddy tribe in 1794 that reserved for the tribe fifteen islands in the St. Croix River and the Indian Township and Pleasant Point tracts — today's reservations — over 23,000 acres of land, while Massachusetts took some 1.5 million acres of Indian territory. Later on, under the Act of Separation agreement in 1820, Maine agreed to assume Massachusetts's treaty obligations.

*The treaties did not specifically cover the Micmac and Maliseet. Yet invariably they were worded to extend to "those connected with" the named tribes, so that certainly the Maliseet and to some extent the Micmac ought to have been protected. Susan Stevens pointed out to me that the 1794 Jay Treaty guaranteed free access between Indians (notably Maliseet and Micmac) on both sides of the U.S.-Canadian border. "I never met a border guard who ever heard of the Jay Treaty," she said.

What happened instead is both shameful and extraordinary (putting aside for the moment what already had taken place to the benefit of the parent state). It is the subject of litigation and Indian suits involving Massachusetts, Maine and the federal government. But the record speaks clearly even if the courts and their proceedings do not.

To begin with, neither the courts nor the state bothered to recognize the natives as being worthy of equal treatment under the very Constitution that expressly included them under its protection. In 1842, the Maine supreme court said that "imbecility on their part, and the dictates of humanity on ours, have necessarily prescribed to them their subjection to our paternal control; in disregard of some, at least, of the abstract principles of the rights of man." Fifty years later, the same self-righteous body ruled that the Indians did not even have tribal rights (in this case, hunting and fishing) under their original treaties. This was based on the bizarre reasoning that the Passamaquoddys no longer had "a tribal organization in any political sense," that they did not make war and peace, administer justice and so forth, like the American government, which relies on elaborate checks and balances, thrives on confrontation, and at times even seems to need a war somewhere.

At the very beginning, the state legislature allowed white timber interests to commence full-scale harvesting of the Passamaquoddy forests. Thus began the so-called "alienation" of native lands, affecting both the Passamaquoddy and Penobscot tribes. The legislature simply authorized seizure of the lands without any compensation. It is a matter of fact, plain and clear, and nobody in the state today can explain how or why it was justified. Nothing yet has been done about it either. Forest companies built dams and flooded Indian land, farmers openly took Indian hay, one greedy settler appropriated the fifteen islands on the St. Croix (which seizure was upheld by the Maine court). The state granted long-term leases along a mile-wide strip on either side of the present U.S. Highway 1 where it runs through the Indian township. White commercial establishments, including a garage, an auto dealership and a summer resort stand on this ground today. A white Indian agent was also given a mile-wide strip cutting across the township, making it convenient for him to run a road to his farm.

The occupation of Indian lands, over the years, has become such a habit that the federal government, during World War II, knew just where to go to locate a camp for German prisoners. Afterwards, the government routinely "returned" the land to the state, which went ahead and sold subdivisions on it. Today it is a white enclave within Passamaquoddy borders, known locally as Nasonville. On both reservations, the state and a railroad took rights-of-way without paying any compensation. The state finally began to put the proceeds from Indian timber sales into a Trust Fund ($22,500 was deposited in 1856), but the stumpage was sold dirt cheap and the trust was mismanaged by white officials, with the Indians having no say whatsoever as to how the money was invested. To this date, interest from the Trust Fund is siphoned over to the state General Fund. Once the Indian monies were even raided to finance a bridge in Eastport.

This Trust Fund is a source of protest today. The Maine legislature remains unwilling to let the Indians manage their own money. So uncertain is the status of native lands that potential investors or developers will not negotiate with the Indians, and all commercial enterprise by the Indians that involves their land (their only economic base anyway) goes for nought, unless the Trust Fund can be considered as manageable income, and it cannot. Fifteen years ago, the Trust Fund was *charged* $180,000 for a *state* housing project on the Passamaquoddy reservations. The contractor apparently got the better of the state since the houses rapidly deteriorated. Those that lasted at all and were not built on unstable land were, by 1970, assessed at a quarter of their original value.

Once upon a time, in accord with the treaties, the state said that the Indians could hunt and fish in their accustomed way, a condition of just about every treaty ever consummated between white and native Americans. In Maine, as just about anywhere else, it has not been honored. Reduced below a subsistence economy, told he cannot reap the proceeds of managing his lands, stripped of a base for any kind of outside development (i.e., employment opportunity), the Indian is now told he cannot fish and hunt *on his own lands* the way he did for centuries before the Christian settlers arrived, unless he receives special permission from state fish and game people — who rarely grant it.

For two days I visited with the Passamaquoddys. I was impressed by their sincerity, particularly their willingness to talk frankly about their problems. Alcoholism is one. All too often it is their *only* release. And at Pleasant Point, an Indian named Dan Francis entreated with Stevens. "Have you got a good film on alcoholism?" he asked. "We need it *now*. I want to show it this Friday night. You send it and I'll pay the postage."

Unemployment among able-bodied men runs up to 80 percent in the winter and never goes below 30 percent in the summer. This is not because work is disdained, although many men still feel most comfortable under the traditional subsistence regime. What do they want money for when they live in a countryside like this, with lakes, brooks and saltwater coves, great forests and rich flatlands, where survival ought to be easy. Local white-run industries are hurting, and what few Passamaquoddys are employed or are eligible are way at the bottom of the list.

Stevens is the difference between despair and hope. He is an amazing man, one of the most competent and engaging people I have ever met. You can see it in his accomplishments, but it is most obvious in the way he is received and consulted by his people. On our travels, he was back on the reservation as commissioner, not governor, and he was taken aside time and again for advice on personal and reservation problems.

I kept asking Stevens why he bothered, after what he had been through. The question always seemed to puzzle him and he never really answered it but said, instead, that he was hopeful, that he saw the light at the end of the tunnel for his people, that he had started projects that were beginning to bear fruit, that he was winning converts in the government and legislature, and that when everyone realized that his efforts were worthwhile they would all start to pull together for even better results.

When Stevens was three years old, his father was convicted of murder and jailed for ten years. I asked him what happened. "It was a hunting accident," he answered, speaking deliberately and looking me in the eye. "He and another Indian were in a canoe that tipped over in cold water. The other man drowned. The Indian agent (a white man) had my father charged with murder, even though the family of the dead man did not believe it. My father was tribal representative at this time and he showed a lot of aggressiveness. To be aggressive in the thirties was not desired in the state of Maine. I have always thought they were out to get him. But he was not bitter and he never showed resentment to the people who tried him because of the convictions of his religion. He used to tell me, 'Well, Christ was crucified for nothing; he never complained and I'm not complaining either.' So I used to think it was an honor for him to be in jail for something he was not guilty of."

With his brothers and sisters, Stevens worked to support the family and their mother, a woman whose memory makes Stevens's voice thicken when he talks about her. "The whole family was close," he said. "She was the one person who held us together while my father was in jail. She went through a lot of misery. I think she is an angel."

Stevens talked about cutting pulpwood and hauling it across the winter ice, of digging cellars and working summers in the Old Town Canoe works where he went from boatbuilder to being in charge of "quality control." But it was Korea that changed him the most. Until then, he was all set to fend for himself and escape the horrors of the Indian township. But as a U.S. Marine, something stirred within him. As his wife, Susan, explains it, Stevens saw in the faces of the Korean natives, particularly the starving children, the very same expression and suffering he knew too well back in Maine. In a sense, he suddenly realized he was fighting for the wrong cause and in the wrong war. The real struggle was taking place still between the aggrieved natives of the Passamaquoddy and the white-dominated government at home. It is also likely, though Stevens did not elaborate on this subject, that combat action revealed to him his own capacity to lead and organize. He was promoted to sergeant, demoted for drunkenness, and then was offered the higher grade and a big pay hike if he would stay in the service. He turned it down, gave up alcohol forever, and returned to Peter Dana Point. There, only twenty-one, he took on the elderly governor and beat him in a fair election. It was not a bitter contest. "I just said that new blood was needed and that I could do a lot for my people," he said. So for eighteen years, until becoming commissioner, Stevens was sagamore, or "zohgum," as the chief is called. He also had a steady job at the Georgia Pacific pulp mill.

The tribe is badly neglected, as far as state and federal programs are concerned. The state budget for Indians is small and federal relief is nonexistent. Because they were an ally of the Americans and were not defeated tribes like the Sioux or Apache, the Maine Indians were not put under federal trusteeship and thus cannot receive sub-

317

sidies for medical aid, education and housing. Nevertheless, Stevens mastered the book of federal aid programs that apply to the public in general. He secured money from the Office of Economic Opportunity and the Department of Labor for counseling and job training ($100,000). He got the Economic Development Administration and the Department of Housing and Urban Development to contribute a $750,000 grant for new housing. If it is well maintained, this housing becomes the tribe's after twenty-five years. I was impressed by the maintenance of the few Indian homes I visited and I believe the Passamaquoddys will make good on this. Through federal and state programs, the tribe has just built a $1.4 million water treatment plant and sewage system. It is the first in this northeastern region.

But Stevens doesn't want a welfare state. "Developing our own opportunities and getting good education — these are the keys," he has said.

With outside backing, Stevens has started two basket cooperatives. These will enable the Quoddy to cash in on historic skills and preserve an old craft. Already the co-op at Peter Dana has secured a $10,500 contract with the General Services Administration to make baskets for holding laundry, leaves, clippings, anything. Moses Neptune runs it.

Neptune is an impressive, big, articulate man who shows canniness. It had just cost him $150 to modify an old ax-forging machine into a device to pound white ash stakes so they can be peeled easily. The University of Maine, incredibly, spent $35,000 to contract a custom machine for this sort of work; the machine — at the Pleasant Point basket co-op — is a lemon. When I met him Neptune had laid up a year's supply of materials and was in no hurry to develop big markets until he had his operation rolling. An old movie theater had been converted into a shop and it was humming with activity.

When the Passamaquoddys win their land claim, as surely they must, Stevens says the money will be put in a trust fund managed by a tribal corporation. "The trustees will follow the direction of the people," he explained. "The money will be properly invested in some of the things we need and want. We won't need to dip into the principle. The interest alone will be sufficient for spending on the reservation." *

*As this book went to press, the courts had already given the Indians the first round by ruling that the U.S. Justice Department must sue the state of Maine on behalf of the Passamaquoddys and the Penobscots who were victimized when Maine broke the 1794 Massachusetts Treaty.

On existing lands, as well as on lands and lakes obtained through claims, Stevens envisions recreational opportunities of a very select caliber. The present nucleus of Indian guides will be expanded. They will run lodges and provide fishing, canoeing and hunting trips in the proper season, limiting access and the influx of people so that the wilderness will not be violated and native hunting and fishing can be maintained through perpetual conservation management. These are principles well understood by Stevens and his people; they are not so well understood — if at all — by the government game and recreation officials who want to lay asphalt down in the wilderness and open it up for more picnic sites and scenic drives.

I talked with one of these Indian guides, Lola Sockabasin. He was at work in his shop when I met him, hand-hewing canoe paddles from ash and rock maple. From the window he could look out over ice-covered Big Lake, a sensational body of water with sudden inlets and a few islands that feeds the St. Croix River. I arranged with him to order some paddles. I inspected the only one he had on hand, a strong, pliant paddle the likes of which I have never seen. He showed me the "shaving horses" to which he clamps the stick of wood from which he forms the paddle. When it is roughed out, he puts a press on the blade and then hangs it over a kiln, made from an oil drum, where it dries into shape for three or four days.

A beatup cedar canoe sat upside down in Sockabasin's shop, ready to receive a shell of fiber glass. I looked around and was struck by the set of handworking tools, the smell of wood shavings, and Sockabasin himself, a wiry, small man who takes pleasure in explaining his work.

In a few weeks, Sockabasin would be setting out his muskrat traps and then would spend most of April traveling between them in the canoe. In the summer he would disappear upstream to his fishing camp. I thought how I would like to visit him up there, just hang around and watch him fish.

I attended a meeting of the tribal council. It was an occasion at which a white man, Gregory Buesing, presented the tribe with $6,000 from a fund amassed by anonymous donors. English was spoken. Buesing is from the Aroostook Indian Association, a group formed to assist the Maliseets and Micmacs scattered around that county but most concentrated in Houlton. Ordinarily these affairs are conducted in Passamaquoddy, a rhythmic, pleasant-sounding language that has been passed down through generations since there is no written alphabet or primer. Stevens recalls sitting through two years of school listening to the nuns "mumble English" and getting nowhere until one teacher was more understanding than the others. It was a condition of an old treaty that Catholic missions be maintained on the reservations — the "black robe" in residence — and it has been a dubious blessing.

The Church's teachings are out of touch. Large families are encouraged (Stevens's brother George has *seventeen* children), which is disastrous, since the Passamaquoddy no longer lives in a manner by which population control and family planning happen naturally, and the Church is paternalistic, still tending to treat all Indians as children or indolent heathens. Perhaps of necessity, the natives have developed a sort of hybrid religion, blending Christian and Indian testament. "Our hell is here on earth; we believe that we then go to paradise," Stevens once explained.

The Indians also conduct their own funerals, three-day wakes with a feast commencing each new day at midnight. "The prayers are mixed-up things," according to Stevens. "Some are pure Indian translations and some hymns made up by the people themselves. All this time that the dead person lies in the house, nobody will speak badly about him and at no time will anyone insult the family."

Stevens has a fixed plan as commissioner: to end the job. At present, he oversees the affairs of two thousand or more Indians on three reservations. One third of his $400,000 budget is consumed by staff salaries and office expenses. This is utterly foolish, he thinks; he feels the department should be reduced to one accountant, adding, "An adequate budget, probably $500,000, would be turned over to the tribes and administrated through their councils." A United Tribal Council would represent not just the Passamaquoddy and Penobscot (on reservations), but the many Indians off-reservation and the Micmacs and Maliseets as well. "The tribal representatives would prepare their own budget and present it to the legislature. They have very capable and vocal leaders. It's degrading to the community to have someone else speak for them. The accountant would assure the state that the money is being spent well."

If this plan went into effect, Stevens would be free to pursue his current obsession, education: "We had a conference on kids who drop out of high school. Ninety percent drop out and hang around the reservation not doing a thing. The main problem is that the education now is entirely based on the white culture and language. It should be bilingual. There are no Indian texts for language or history. It is only right for us to be inspired by our version as well as the white man's. The English always kept good records, good about themselves. Now we must slant it a bit the Indian way." *

Ecology, environmental sanity, comes inevitably to the Indians. They have lived off the land for generations without destroying it. They dried the meat of porpoise, smoked cod. Blueberries were dehydrated, left in the sun on strips of birch bark. Reconstituted with water in the winter, they were served up with maple syrup. The scoop net, weirs made from stakes driven into the mud in tidewater, burying vegetables in sand to protect them through winter frosts, raising corn and maize, using fish remains as manure, basketry, coursing the white-waters in light birch canoes — these were the Indian ways, ways that permitted them to live in peace with the land. For sickness, nature's chemistry worked wonders. Even today, many still use natural medicines: flagroot, sasparilla, wild parsnip, raspberry bush, checkerberry, fir balsam, spruce gum, witch hazel, pond and horse lily roots.

The first disruption of the traditional way of life came with the white man's urge to clear the land for farms, destroying the Indian's hunting regime, the natural balance that he knew so well. Then came the dictates of the cash economy and the Industrial Revolution. The new technology completed the upheaval. Yet all the Indian wanted was the traditional opportunity to lead his own kind of subsistence life. Now, of course, it is too late to return entirely to that system, although there is evidence that the Indians still have not surrendered to twentieth-century economics based on unlimited growth and technological change.

In 1971, the officers of an oil company came to woo the Passamaquoddys with plans for an oil refinery to be located at Pleasant Point. Indians would be employed and the side benefits would be tremendous, the oilmen said. The Indians listened. Then they dis-

*At present, Wayne Newell, a Passamaquoddy with an M.A. in education from Harvard, is working with the University of Maine and a foundation to assemble Passamaquoddy teaching material.

cussed the assets that meant the most to them from earliest times: their fishing, their water, their forests, their view. Then they voted 175 to 5. No refinery, please.

At one point the Indians sold ash baskets to white fishermen for hauling herring scales, which are used to make fake mother-of-pearl. Pearl essence, it is called. The whites didn't like the Indians' prices. They switched to a plastic material but the baskets wouldn't hold up. Then they tried aluminum, but the metal containers sank if they missed and hit the water when they were thrown from piers back to the boats. After a year, the fishermen came back to the Indians. With his kind of technology the Passamaquoddy won.

But it is his own true heritage that counts most and is so enviable, I think. "The white people are running away from the system they created," Stevens has said, and of course he is right. At least we recognize there is a crisis and we are trying to redefine it. "In the very beginning, the whites adapted to our system, but then they corrupted it," Stevens told me. Now they probably would be happy to have it back, I thought.

Anthropologist Carleton S. Coon put it well and bluntly in his book, *The Hunting Peoples*. According to him, human societies really need a certain amount of primitivism in their makeup. The natural world must to an extent possess its own deities and mysterious inner forces. "When he becomes coldly practical, discards his beliefs and rites, begins measuring things accurately, building efficient machinery, inventing weapons of mass destruction, sending men to the moon, and burning up more of the earth's oxygen than its plant life can replace, he has also begun warming up the wax that will seal his own fate," Coon wrote.

We were driving out of the lands of the Passamaquoddy, past snow-covered East Musquash Lake, heading into the paling red of the dying sun, leaving behind the big hemlocks and pines, and I was thinking about the Passamaquoddy nation and the old way of life. John Stevens braced himself as we crashed into ridges and potholes on the bad roads. But I was absorbed in a vision of winter fires going at Peter Dana Point, where the forest afforded shelter and there was enough wild game and prepared foods to last until spring.

Going with Maine

THIS BOOK began as a look at the problems and possibilities of the state of Maine in an environmental context — or as a look at the problems plaguing the environment generally, as they were dramatized in one state. I had no intention of investigating every problem that Maine has, or even of being investigatory at all. I believe I was right in assuming that events and people would speak for themselves.

From the very outset, I felt that land use was Maine's most critical issue, tied directly to its most pressing economic and social questions. One day in his office at Colby College, Professor Donaldson Koons, chairman of Maine's Environmental Improvement Commission, made two observations that in a way summed up the conditions that already had formed the basis for my fascination with his state.

"Maine is unique in that most of the population — winter and summer — thinks that it owns Maine," he said. "Everybody seems to have a proprietary interest in this state, so if he is convinced that environmental protection is proper he will become actively involved in it."

That is probably true. As I have recounted earlier, it may have been most apparent along the coast when previously apathetic summer residents and fishermen united in 1971 to defy the oilmen.

Koons's second observation came on the heels of the first. "We're very lucky," he said, "that we did not participate in the growth pattern of the United States as a whole during the past several decades. It missed us. But if we're smart, we'll be able to take advantage of this." Another way of putting it would be to note that, almost by default, Maine has become a kind of second frontier, an environment where the tragic mistakes of countless *growing* American communities can be avoided.

Inevitably, my "look" at land use issues in Maine turned into a personal statement — perhaps too personal, considering my background and previous connection with the state, but there was nothing I could do about it. Maine got deeper and deeper inside of my system. My wife and friends were unusually patient as they heard me time and time again extol Maine's people and places and deplore the problems that had to be resolved in "lucky," unindustrialized, unurbanized Maine.

Perhaps I will be criticized for overreaching, as I see in unexceptional events the manifestation of a national tendency. What do Maine's Indians, for example, have to do with today's land use crisis? Personally, I think the Indians are a shameful reminder that the accepted definitions of progress and prosperity are in need of major overhaul. Apart from that, of course, as Gunnar Myrdal once put it, the Indians are the classic protagonists in an American morality play. But I admit that only time and historical perspective will give dimension to these points.

The third stage in writing this book was also inevitable. The personal statement turned into a search for personal fulfillment. In my case it was the search for long-term environmental security and what I came to term the "family place," because that to me is what environmental security is all about. In spite of dense growth, if a community really cares and plans ahead, it will retain its good character and sense of place through succeeding generations. Strong family units, close and abiding community ties, and a strong commitment to the land are the main ingredients of social continuity and stability, I realized. I might not find such a place or, if I did, there might be nothing deliberate and self-willed about it. But that was why Maine had such potential. That was what Koons was talking about. Maine's small settlements were comparatively unspoiled. It was not too late to build upon a foundation of historical accident.

One morning back in 1970, I asked John Cole, the editor of *Maine Times,* to keep an eye out for any attractive saltwater farm that might come up for sale.

"You'll be number two hundred on my list," he answered listlessly. "But it doesn't matter anyway. There aren't any left, to speak of, at least as farms. And in any case, cut up or otherwise, they sell for thousands of dollars an acre."

If the doctrine of public trust prevails along the coast, I thought to myself afterward, insofar as public needs are reconciled with private ownership, then the coastal areas I love so much will be protected for my enjoyment forever. If public trust didn't prevail and, instead, speculative and cottage land development blighted coastal bays and estuaries, I certainly didn't want to have to worry about these encroachments next door to me.

I mulled over considerations like these, couched in purely selfish terms — in other words, thinking primarily how my children and in turn their children would be directly concerned. Regardless of where we went, I vowed I would remain an advocate of coastal conservation and I certainly intend to spend a lot more of my leisure time exploring Champlain's Seaway. Owning a piece of it is something else.

I finally decided that when this book was done I would spend several months looking for that "family place" in Maine. In anticipation, I sounded out several real estate contacts and began to keep a file folder full of listings of rural properties, to get an idea of prices and to find out which agents were selling the sort of place I was interested in. I even composed a memorandum that listed guidelines I would follow in looking for land, as well as criteria that I would apply to any land offerings that came up. Initially, I decided to concentrate on a quadrangle whose corners were Bath, Waterville, Bangor and Winter Harbor, excepting the immediate coastal strip where values were up to ten times those just inland. I wanted enough land to be assured of privacy and seclusion, preferably land with fields, a pond and a brook. One condition was essential: distance enough from the road to be protected from car traffic now and forever (in case the road were widened).

I had various flights of fancy. I would be one of Alphabet Smith's associates, grazing his beef cattle during the summer. I would be a registered tree farmer. (All it takes is a few acres of woods put under deliberate management, planting seedlings and so forth, becoming a sustained-yield operator in miniature.) I yearned to make up for my failure as a partner in our Virginia vegetable garden. (I could claim no part of it except the page-wire fence and clumsy gate to keep the rabbits out.) Above all, I imagined a place where life itself and the process of living would become a never-ending source of pleasure and diversion, a daily drama of small events.

It was a Utopian dream, I confess, without a great deal of shape or certainty beyond my hopes and imaginings. I assumed there would be time enough to collect and combine these ideas in a cohesive way, getting prepared to make a decision based on knowledge of all the options. "If you have built castles in the air, your work need not be lost; that is where they should be," wrote Thoreau. "Now put the foundations under them." There would be time for that.

But then, as is so often the case when one is unprepared, something suddenly came up. It seemed like an ideal place and it met the basic criteria. There was a good deal of land available, all told over three hundred acres, much of it once cleared and tilled but now overgrown, wild and quite lovely, really. The restored brick homestead, made from orange clay dug and fired nearby, was about a mile from the paved road, yet it was within half an hour of the state capital and two handsome coastal towns.

It was an old mill site, the mill now only a granite ruin, dynamited to clear a passage upstream for the May run of alewives. But the place remained firmly in the grip of history, with more granite foundations scattered around and a few crumbling wooden walls, so that it was as yet apparent that half a century ago there had been quite a settlement here. The sound and the sight of running water was dominant, even without a mill to harness it. It rushed out of the lake's winding tip, over a dam of wooden flashboards, tumbling down a set of ledges, and dropping nearly twenty feet in less than a hundred yards through a shallow gorge where the old mill had stood. When my wife scouted the property, she reported that the water in the lake outlet was low (the season had been dry), not much more than a trickle. Its flow was confined to a narrow channel that wound down through the rock ledges, a channel that was created by an early millwright in a most resourceful manner. (The lake had been held back long enough for brushfires to be lit, burning the rocks white hot. Then the cold water was released, dousing the fires and cracking open the ledges. Slabs were easily removed where the channel was wanted.)

But when I saw the place for the first time, it had rained for a week and was still coming down. The water was high and on the rampage, making such a din that you had to shout through it to be heard.

328

Nearly four months went by before we "passed papers" — four months of negotiations, questions, complications, legal details. It was mid-February before I moved in, alone, to give the place a testing and to put in the final fortnight of work on this account. I very soon discovered that our family was plunged more deeply into Maine than ever before. What is more, the notions I had held about rural neighborhoods, about life itself and the Maine environment were put squarely to the test.

I had my most severe misgivings about possible threats to my privacy. Our family likes seclusion. We always have. The new place was so remote that only when I ascended the ridge behind the house and looked across the valley as far as fifteen miles away to the Camden Hills could I see other houses, the nearest building being a church on a knoll a mile off.

Yet woods don't deter the Mainesman, even in winter. The snowmobile has seen to that. I found that the dirt roads that passed through, the trails that had been obstructed by ledges or marshes in the fall, were heaven-sent for the snowmobile. My wife learned this first, before the place was finally ours, when she came upon a battery of trucks parked by the mill site, each one having unloaded several snowmobiles. She was anguished, and I was unhappy too, about this intrusion. Yet I was well aware that the place had not been inhabited for many decades and that the community had come to regard it as a sort of commons. I don't believe in posting land with "No Trespassing" signs, not just because I myself like to walk or ski-tour across other people's property, but because I honestly have come to regard land as an eternal resource whose temporary owner is merely a guardian of a natural trust. Putting up signs seems to me an indiscriminate, inflexible way of asking for privacy, although it may often be necessary as a last resort when the land becomes abused. Moreover, in Maine as well as in other New England states, public access for fishing, hunting and picnicking has been a longstanding tradition, a curious contradiction to the equally longstanding penchant for absolute private property rights that makes Yankees resist the principle of public land use planning, zoning and so forth. It is mostly new settlers from outside, or summer colonists, who put up these signs. In some areas, where absentee ownership is predominant, this has caused understandable resentment.

329

As long as my sense of privacy was not abused, as long as the land itself was treated properly, I decided that I would try to deal with people face to face, as situations developed. A town resident who was a state game warden told me that in the fall I would probably want to put up signs saying "Hunting by Permission Only," because of the masses of deer hunters who would come and present a real hazard. This way I could limit hunting to my friends and neighbors and would know exactly who was on the land with a gun, he counseled.

For the winter season, I conveyed my views to neighbors, because some of them, in subtle and polite ways, revealed a curiosity about my intentions. Every one appeared to own a snowmobile. Occasional passage I would not mind, I said, when the chance came to speak my position. Trucks unloading snowmobiles, turning my land into a parking lot — such visits would stir me to an angry counterresponse. My optimism about people would persist as long as my land was accorded equal respect with other neighborhood private holdings. It would take a while to spread the word, to stem the traffic from out of town, that I knew. But I was going to give it a try.

And in that first fortnight it seemed to work. "How is it down there? Quiet? Nobody bothering you, I hope," one neighbor asked with a broad grin.

"It's a peaceful place, I hope you're getting lots of writing done," said another.

Only once in this period was my tranquility really shattered and my sense of stewardship offended. It was on a glorious Sunday afternoon, the snow sparkling in the bright sun, blue shadows cast by the bare trees; one of those days Henry Beston had in mind when he wrote, "Summer is the season of motion, winter is the season of form." Considering the weather and the weekend, there had been predictable snowmobile traffic, but nothing to get angry about, a few neighbors passing through, that was all.

With my in-laws and mutual friends I went for an afternoon hike up on the ridge. At the crest, we followed deer tracks out onto a brow where we stood and gazed out across the lake and valley to Ragged Mountain and its adjacent hills, which stood between us and Penobscot Bay. What snowmobile traffic we'd encountered or heard had been confined to the trail passing through the middle of the place, an abandoned town road that once bore traffic to the mill.

But suddenly, coming toward us along the narrow, winding path up on the ridge, was the familiar snarl, becoming deafening as it came closer, like a platoon advancing with chain saws instead of machineguns.

"Arctic Cat" read the insignia of the lead driver, who was forced by our passage to come to a stop. I was furious. Had we been farther along, concealed by a bend or hollow, one of us might have been struck.

"This is private land," I shouted to the leader who grinned sheepishly under his helmet.

"It's not posted," he answered.

"I know," I said. "That doesn't make it any more private than it actually is, and I don't want to have to do that. Only I don't expect all the trails to be clogged up with snowmobile expeditions either. Okay?"

He nodded and the group passed on — for the last time on this particular trail, I would see to that. At the tail end of the convoy, an old man with sunken cheeks stared grimly and passively ahead of him, into the next snowmobilist's exhaust, his arms vibrating along with the machine he drove. The snowmobile may have made it possible for this old-timer to get outdoors, this far into the woods, I thought. But I wondered if it made a difference, whether a large oval snow track outside of town somewhere wouldn't have been just as satisfactory.

My father-in-law, at seventy, had moved out ahead of us, on foot, looking for an apple orchard I'd mentioned where he was certain there would be grouse in the fall. This was his way of getting outdoors.

Early next morning, as the sun came up, I returned to the ridge, carrying two signs I'd made that Sunday night: *PLEASE:* SKIERS AND HIKERS *ONLY*. I put one up at each end of this particular trail. Would this stop the snowmobilers? Probably not all the time. But I hoped so. If it didn't I'd just have to fell some trees across all possible routes through.

The confrontation with the snowmobiles was more than offset by the kindly attitudes and actions of my neighbors. One baked me a truly exquisite apple pie. I like apple pies; this one had a proper crust and the filling was juicy, but firm, and not too sweet. Another neighbor invited me to bring my family to the church on the knoll.

Yet another neighbor was the granddaughter of one of the family that had built the mill settlement. In her eighties, she was quick-witted and had a ready sense of humor. I enjoyed hearing her tell about the old days. When I walked into her kitchen the first time, she rose up quickly from a rocking chair and shook my hand with a firm grip, looked me right in the eye, and asked me to sit down for a while.

Throughout her girlhood, particularly on summer days, she said, she had been a fixture at the mill settlement, disappearing from home at sunrise and seldom returning before dark. It was a hectic spot, the lake outlet. There was enough power to saw lumber and clapboards, grind grist, thresh wheat, press cider, and produce barrel staves. She and her childhood friends moved casually around the settlement. "In those days," she recalled, "if you went somewhere, you went in any door in the house."

It was a time of community closeness, enhanced by the aura of excitement created by the mill. The mill was the valley's magnet, drawing long lines of carts and wagons converging from miles around in the summer, and logging sleds crossing the ice of three lakes in the winter. The first electricity in the area was made by a generator driven by one of the mill's turbines. My neighbor remembered the lights glowing in the millowner's "mansion," an enormous edifice behind the mill, now just a granite foundation full of saplings. I wondered whether it would be possible again to generate my own power in the outlet.

As it became increasingly apparent, the people in the valley were quite concerned about our new place. They loved it too, its appealing natural qualities as well as its historical associations. We were offered one of the original grist stones that had been taken away when the old mill was cleaned out. And one day a neighbor invited my wife and me to spend the afternoon with her father, who as a boy had operated the mill with his brothers.

In his nineties, he was ailing. Yet like the old lady, his mind and memory were sharp. He ran through the trade names and details of the mill machinery and described the special fishway he had built to give alewives and other aquatic migrants a clear thoroughfare. He told us where all the old houses, their gardens, outbuildings and wells had been located.

Between him and the old lady, I hoped we could do what was right and sustain the strong community ties to our place.

One day, after one of my sessions with the lady, I told her I wanted to begin using my tape recorder. Her accounts of the past were too valuable, I explained, to be entrusted just to my notebook. Could I come to visit often and start again, right from the beginning of her remembrances?

"Why certainly," she answered. "I'll be here, except when I go out with my daughter on her errands."

She leaned forward, bringing her rocking chair to a standstill. Smiling, looking very alert and happy indeed, she uttered her next remark with particular relish.

"I'm a line tree, you know."

For a few seconds she had me. A line tree? I thought about it. Then suddenly I understood. Line trees, those were the ones that marked the borders and corners of rural properties and were supposed to stand forever. I had already been out to look at a few of my own.

One was a white pine that towered above the rest of the woods and was nearly four feet in diameter at breast height. Previous neighbors had made sure this line tree was honored.

It is an important thing, in this new community of ours, to be in the company of line trees.

ACKNOWLEDGMENTS

IN THE FALL of 1970, before I began writing this book, I drove nearly three thousand miles across the length and breadth of Maine, talking with people whenever the opportunity arose. Some of the people I met then, and subsequently, are mentioned by name in this book. Many are not. For in the end, my list of contacts filled a large looseleaf address book and those first three thousand miles of driving grew fourfold.

Inevitably, there were important gaps in my interviewing. And inevitably, certain individuals gave me far more of their time than I had any right to demand of them: people like John Cole, editor of the *Maine Times*; Marshall Burk, then executive director of the Natural Resources Council; Peter Bradford, an adviser to the governor of Maine on coastal development and on energy problems; Marc Nault, Machias civic leader and printer; and Harold Pachios, a close friend, lawyer, and environmental activist. To these — and to all who helped me — I offer my deepest thanks. And to Polly (Mrs. Samuel D.) Warren of East Sangerville, Maine, who prepared the drawings for chapter heads, I owe a special debt of gratitude.

The *Maine Times* and the Natural Resources Council bulletins were important sources of ideas and information that alerted me to many issues discussed in detail here. I grant that these publications take a strong conservationist position, as I myself do. Yet I have tried to present opposing views of these complex problems fairly.

The list of sources that follow are publications that have been genuinely helpful to me in my writing. Some of the publications are worth reading in their entirety; some contain useful references to

Maine, past and present; and some are concerned with problems of general import that relate to particular problems in Maine. I have relied particularly on government and private reports and documents for the details and supporting data on which I made my own summaries and freely given opinions.

BIBLIOGRAPHY

BOOKS

Abbey, Edward. *Desert Solitaire*. New York, McGraw-Hill, 1968.
Banks, Ronald F., ed. *A History of Maine, A Collection of Readings*. Dubuque, Iowa, Kendall/Hunt Publishing, 1969.
Beston, Henry. *Northern Farm*. New York, Holt, Rinehart & Winston, 1950.
Bousfield, Lillie S. *Our Island Town*. Bar Harbor, Me., Bar Harbor Times Publishing Co.
Clark, Charles E. *The Eastern Frontier*. New York, Alfred A. Knopf, 1970.
Coffin, Robert P. Tristram. *Kennebec*. New York, Farrar & Rinehart, 1937.
Daviau, Jerome G. *Maine's Life Blood*. Portland, Me., House of Falmouth, 1958.
Day, Clarence A. *Farming in Maine, 1860–1940*. Orono, Me., University of Maine Press, 1963.
———. *A History of Maine Agriculture, 1604–1860*. Orono, Me., University of Maine, 1954.
Eckstrom, Fannie Hardy. *The Penobscot Man*. Bangor, Me., Jordan-Frost, 1924; facsimile ed., Portland, Me., Cumberland Press, 1971.
Eliot, Charles W. *John Gilley*. Boston, Beacon Press, 1899.
Hakola, John and Judith. *Greatest Mountain: Katahdin's Wilderness*. Portland, Scrimshaw Press, 1972. Essay by the authors, excerpts from the writings of Percival Baxter, and photographs by his great-grandniece, Constance Baxter.
Hamlin, Helen. *Nine Mile Bridge*. New York, W. W. Norton, 1945.
———. *Pine, Potatoes and People*. New York, W. W. Norton, 1948.
Holbrook, Stewart H. *Holy Old Mackinaw*. New York, Macmillan Co., 1938.
———. *The Story of American Railroads*. New York, Crown Publishers, 1947.
Isaacson, Doris A., ed. *Maine, A Guide Downeast*. Rockland, Me., Courier Gazette, 1970.
Jewett, Sarah Orne. *The Country of the Pointed Firs and Other Stories*. Boston, Houghton Mifflin, 1925.
Lee, W. Storrs, ed. *Maine: A Literary Chronicle*. New York, Funk & Wagnalls, 1968.
Marriner, Ernest. *Kennebec Yesterdays*. Waterville, Me., Colby College, 1954.
Morison, Samuel Eliot. *The European Discovery of America*. New York, Oxford University Press, 1971.
Moulton, Augustus F. *Portland by the Sea*. Augusta, Me., Katahdin Publishing, 1926.
Nash, Roderick. *Wilderness and the American Mind*. New Haven, Conn., Yale University Press, 1967.
Nearing, Helen and Scott. *Living the Good Life*. New York, Schocken Books, 1954.
———. *Maple Sugar Book*. New York, Schocken Books, 1950.
Ogden, Samuel R., ed. *America the Vanishing*. Brattleboro, Vt., Stephen Greene, 1969.
Pinchot, Gifford. *A Primer of Forestry*. Washington, D.C., U.S. Department of Agriculture, 1950.
Portland. Portland, Me., Greater Portland Landmarks, Inc., 1972.

341

Powell, Sumner C. *Puritan Village*. Middletown, Conn., Wesleyan University Press, 1963.

Roberts, Kenneth. *Rabble in Arms*. Garden City, N.Y., Doubleday, 1933.

Rowe, William Hutchison. *The Maritime History of Maine*. New York, W. W. Norton, 1948.

Smith, Lincoln. *The Power Policy of Maine*. Berkeley, University of California Press, 1951.

Springer, John S. *Forest Life and Forest Trees*. New York, Harper & Bros., 1851; new ed., Somersworth, N.H., New Hampshire Publishing Co., 1971.

Staples, Arthur G. *Just Talks on Common Themes*. Lewiston, Me., Lewiston Journal, 1919.

Thoreau, Henry David. *The Maine Woods*. Reprint ed., New York, Thomas Y. Crowell, 1961.

Trowbridge, Clifton. *The Crow Island Journal*. New York, Harper & Row, 1970.

Westbrook, Perry D. *Biography of an Island*. New York, Thomas Yoeseloff, 1958.

White, E. B. *The Points of My Compass*. New York, Harper & Row, 1962.

Williamson, William D. *History of the State of Maine*. Glazier, Masters & Co., 1832; facsimile ed., Portland, Me., Cumberland Press, 1972.

Wilson, Charles Morrow. *Aroostook, Our Last Frontier*. Brattleboro, Vt., Stephen Daye Press, 1937.

Wood, Richard G. *A History of Lumbering in Maine, 1820–1861*. Orono, Me., University of Maine Press, 1961.

DOCUMENTS AND REPORTS

An Analysis of the Employment Impact of Constructing a Refinery on Sears Island. José A. Gomez-Ibanez, Ronald T. Luke, Gregory F. Treverton. Cambridge, Mass., John F. Kennedy School of Government, Harvard University, 1971.

An Analysis of Maine Vacation Travel Promotion, Information and Reception Procedure. Augusta, Me., Maine Dept. of Economic Development, 1971.

Deer in Maine. Augusta, Me., Maine Dept. of Inland Fisheries and Game, 1964.

Eastern Maine Harbors: Physical Resources Report. Robert G. Doyle, Augusta, Me., Maine Dept. of Economic Development, 1971.

An Economic Study on the Feasibility of an East-West Development Highway in Northern New England. Boston, New England Regional Commission, 1971.

Employment Opportunities in Maine through Oil Refinery Development, Position Paper. Roderick Forsgren, James Wilson, Kevin Dailey, Harold Price. Orono, Me., University of Maine, 1971.

Energy, Heavy Industry and the Maine Coast. Report of the Governor's Task Force, Augusta, Me., 1972.

The Farmer's Share. Northern Maine Regional Planning Commission, Presque Isle, Me., 1970.

A History of the White-Tailed Deer in Maine. Augusta, Me., Maine Dept. of Inland Fisheries and Game, 1963.

Machias Bay, Environmental Management. Report to Atlantic World Port, Inc. Cambridge, Mass., Arthur D. Little, 1970.

The Maine Coast: Prospects and Perspectives. Center for Resources Studies, Bowdoin College, A Symposium, 1966. Portland, Me., The Antoensen Press, 1967.

Maine Coastal Resources Renewal. Augusta, Me., Maine State Planning Office, 1971.

The Maine Poultry Industry. Orono, Me., University of Maine Cooperative Extension Service, University of Maine, 1970.

Maineland. Background material for land use workshop conducted by The Allagash Group, Bath, Me., 1971.

Man and Nature in the National Parks. Fraser Darling and Noel D. Eichorn. Washington, D.C., Conservation Foundation, 1967.

National Parks for the Future. Washington, D.C., Conservation Foundation, 1972.

The Penobscot Bay Region of Maine, A Review of Its Potential as a Shipbuilding Area. Augusta, Me., Maine Dept. of Economic Development, 1971.

Penobscot River and *Kennebec River*. Separate reports done in 1968 and 1969, respectively, for Maine Dept. of Inland Fisheries and Game, Augusta, Me.

Problems Influencing the Use of Renewable Marine Resources. Robert L. Dow. Reprint from University of Maine Law School/National Science Foundation study, Augusta, Me., Maine Dept. of Sea and Shore Fisheries, 1970.

Progress Reports. North Kennebec Regional Planning Commission. Waterville, Me., 1970, 1971.

Regional and National Demands on the Maine Coastal Zone. Boston, Mass., New England River Basins Commission, 1971.

Regulation of the Coast, Land and Water Uses, University of Maine Law School and National Science Foundation Office of Sea Grant Programs Study, Vol. III. Portland, Me., University of Maine Law School, 1970.

Report on Wildlands Use Regulation to the 104th Legislature. Subcommittee on Wildland Use Regulation, Harrison Richardson, chairman. Maine State Capitol, Augusta, Me., 1969.

State Power and the Passamaquoddy Tribe: A Gross National Hypocrisy. Francis J. O'Toole and Thomas N. Tureen. Portland, Me., Maine Law Review, University of Maine Law School, 1971.

The Tourist Industry in Maine. Bath, Me., Report for the Allagash Group, 1971.

Wildland Planning Issues. James Haskell. Directory of Maine Land Use Regulation Commission, Augusta, Me., 1968.

INDEX

Abenaki Indians, 287
Acadia National Park, 110, 114, 115, 260, 268–273
Agriculture, 16, 204–205; by Indians, 183–184; in Aroostook County, 194–195, 201–202; and nonfarms, 208–209; *see also* Beef raising; Dairy industry; Potato farming; Subsistence farming
Albair, Gilman, and his farm, 195–203
Allagash Wilderness Waterway, 161, 169, 260–261
Aluminum reduction plant, 7
Androscoggin Falls, 75
Androscoggin Valley Regional Planning Commission, 249
Anemone Cave, 270–271
Apollonio, Spencer, 87
Apple growing, 16
Aquaculture, 62, 66, 86–95, 172; definition of, 86; in coastal land use planning, 87; potential of, as an industry, 88, 89, 93–95
Armour Company, 93
Arnold, Benedict, 54
Aroostook County, 66, 194, 201, 202; case study of a farm in, 195–203
Aroostook Federation of Farmers, 201
Aroostook Indian Association, 319
Ashland Petroleum Company, 43
Augusta, 287

Back to the land movement, 14, 18, 228; case studies, 211–221, 229–230
Bait (live) industry, 94
Bangor, 15, 45, 48
Bangor and Aroostook (railroad), 45, 248
Bangor Hydro-Electric Company, 60
Bangor International Airport, 45
Bar Harbor, 257
Bath, 15
Bath Iron Works, 249

Baxter, James Phinney, 236
Baxter, Percival Proctor, 164, 165, 166, 167, 260
Baxter Park Authority, 164, 167
Baxter State Park, 164–167, 168, 260
Beach ownership, 29, 109–110, 116
Beal, Elmer, 115, 115n
Beal, Ossie, 43
Beef raising, 16, 206–207, 208–209
Belgrade Lakes, 286–287
Bellows, George, 256
Beston, Henry, 186–187
Bloodworm industry, 94
Blue Hill, 66
Blue Hill Bay, 113
Boatbuilding industry, 73, 74–85; in Eastport, 54; history of, 54, 74–76; future of, 66, 81, 82; decline of, 76–79
Bobcat, 274–278
Boothbay, 66
Boston and Maine (railroad), 248
Bounty system, 274–277
Bragg, Wendell and Wayne, and their farm, 188–193
Brunswick, 75
Bucksport, 285
Burk, Marshall, 274
Burnt Head, 105–106

Campobello, 60
Campobello Island, 54
Campsites, 161–163
Cape Small, 115
Caribou (animal), 278
Caribou (city), 195, 230, 286
Carson, Rachel, 111
Casco Bay, 66, 235; planned oil depot, 39–41; and supertankers, 68n; oil spill in, 23; islands of, 113
Castine, 54

Land ownership (*continued*)
conservation, 205; by nonfarmers, 208–
209; *see also* Beach ownership; Public
trust, doctrine of; Scenic easement
Land prices, 17, 101, 107; coastal, 34–35,
36, 37; speculative, 37–38; of forest land,
147; of farmland, 204–205
Land trusts (private), 110–113, 115
Land use: of forests, 147, 149, 153; restricted within 250 feet of water, 111–
112; improper, violates public trust, 152;
lack of controls harms Belgrade Lakes
area, 287; as an issue, 325; *see also* Land
use, coastal
Land use, coastal, 25–28, 34, 64–65, 113–
115; summer, 28, 34–36; of public areas,
29; controls for, 29, 36, 37, 65–66, 73, 110,
111–112; policy for, 46, 97; aquaculture
as part of, 87; land trusts and, 110, 111,
112–113, 115; scenic easement and, 113–
115
Land Use Regulation Commission (LURC),
149, 153, 154, 155
Leopold, Aldo, 172
Lily Bay campground, 265
Line trees, 333
Lisbon, 75
Lobster industry, 109; decline, 7; in Penobscot Bay, 43; and aquaculture, 88; catch
statistics, 92; in Muscongus Bay, 108;
on Monhegan Island, 108–109
Longfellow, Henry Wadsworth, 233, 234
Long Island oil controversy, 39–41, 49, 67
Lowell, James Russell, 256
Lubec, 55, 249
Luke, Ronald T., 47
Lumbering: for ship masts, 74–75; traditional, 121; enlightened, 121; machines,
123–128, 135–136; cutting methods, 127,
132–133; diameter limit, 126, 127; uneven growth, 126–127; clear-cut, 129–
130, 131, 134, 136; log drives, 137–146,
149, 285–286; effect of, on forest, 172–
173; *see also* Forest products industry

Machias, 7
Machias Bay, 68n, 113
Machiasport oil refinery (proposed), 7–11,
49; to benefit local economy, 6–7; to
damage environment, 7–11; opposed, 8–
11
Machias River, West Branch, 137–138, 139,
140
McKee, John, 112, 114
McNamara, John J., Jr., 40
Maine: as a refuge, 14, 18–19; as an under-
developed nation, 16; history of, 16–17
Maine Central (railroad), 45, 248

Maine Clean Fuels, 42, 44, 46
Maine coast. *See* Coast of Maine
Maine Coast Authority (proposed), 66, 93,
113
Maine Coast Heritage Trust, 113–114, 115
Maine Industrial Development Corporation,
68n
Maine Industrial Port Authority (pro-
posed), 65–66, 67
"Maine Law," 186
Maine Legislature: passes Site Location
and Conveyance Acts, 10–11, 46; con-
siders land use issues, 11–12; and coastal
oil development, 65–68; passes Public
Law 535, 111–112; and scenic easement,
114; and Indians, 314
Maine Lobstermen's Association, 43, 92
Maine Log Rule, 128
Maine Rivers Authority (proposed), 292
Maine Temperance Union, 186
Maine Times, 12, 66
"Mainetrain," 249
Maine Yankee nuclear power plant, 24, 94,
171
Maliseet Indians, 313n, 319
Mearl Company, 55
Meinel, Aden and Marjorie, 32
Menario, John, 238–239, 240
Meningal worm, 278
Metropolitan Oil Company of New York,
55–56, 57, 58
Micmac Indians, 313n, 319
Millinocket, 139, 147
Mineral resources, 61, 153–154
Monhegan Associates, 106–107, 108, 113
Monhegan Island, 26, 105–109, 116
Monks, Bob, 2
Monsanto Company, 93
Montsweag Bay, 94
Moose, 278
Moosehead Lake, 149, 262; area, 153
Moose Island, 58, 60
Muir, John, 170
Muscongus Bay, 113
Muskie, Edmund, 7, 11, 291–292
Mussels, blue, 89

Nader, Ralph, 148
Nasonville, 315
National Island Trust concept, 115
National parks, 110, 111, 167–168, 170–
171, 172; a new kind of, proposed, 59
National Parks Foundation, 113
Natural Resources Council (Maine), 274,
294
Nature Conservancy, 37, 111, 297
Nearing, Helen and Scott, 211
New England River Basins Commission,
29

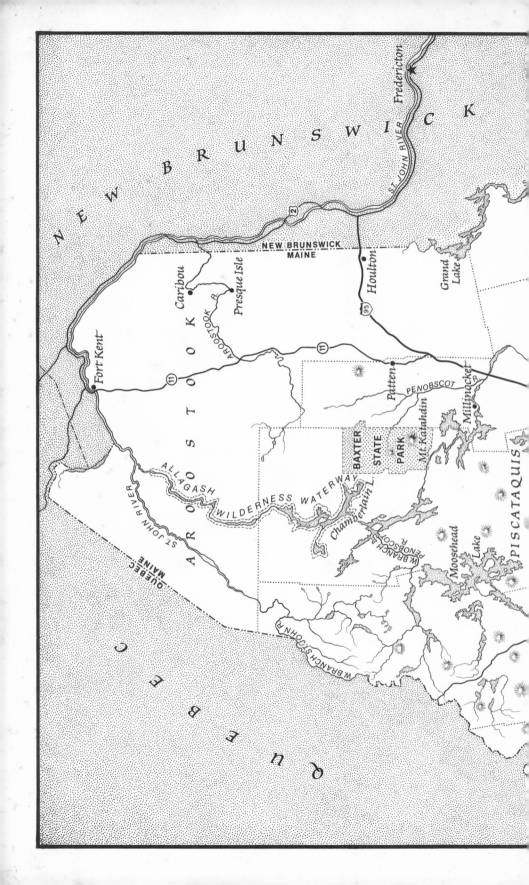